THE ROMANCE OF AN EASTERN CAPITAL

THE ROMANCE OF AN EASTERN CAPITAL

BY

F. B. BRADLEY-BIRT

B.A., I.C.S.

LATE SCHOLAR OF BRASENOSE COLLEGE, OXFORD
FELLOW OF THE ROYAL GEOGRAPHICAL SOCIETY
CORRESPONDING FELLOW OF THE GEOGRAPHICAL SOCIETY OF LISBON
AUTHOR OF
'CHOTA NAGPORE: A LITTLE-KNOWN PROVINCE OF THE EMPIRE' AND 'THE STORY OF AN INDIAN UPLAND'

WITH THIRTY ILLUSTRATIONS
AND A MAP

GYAN

Published by

GYAN

Gyan Publishing House
5, Ansari Road
Daryaganj, New Delhi-110002
Phone: 011-47034999, 9811692060
E-mail: books@gyanbooks.com

Distribution Network
gyanbooks.com
India, USA, Canada, UK, Australia, France

ISBN : 978-81-212-3965-3 (PB)
First Published, 1906

2nd Impression 2020

Printed at: Gyan Press, Delhi.

The Romance of An Eastern Capital
Author: F. B. Bradley-Birt

THE ROMANCE

OF

AN EASTERN CAPITAL

BY

F. B. BRADLEY-BIRT

B.A., I.C.S.

LATE SCHOLAR OF BRASENOSE COLLEGE, OXFORD

FELLOW OF THE ROYAL GEOGRAPHICAL SOCIETY

CORRESPONDING FELLOW OF THE GEOGRAPHICAL SOCIETY OF LISBON

AUTHOR OF

'CHOTA NAGPORE: A LITTLE-KNOWN PROVINCE OF THE EMPIRE'

AND 'THE STORY OF AN INDIAN UPLAND'

WITH THIRTY ILLUSTRATIONS

AND A MAP

LONDON

SMITH, ELDER, & CO., 15 WATERLOO PLACE

1906

Frontispiece. THE LALBAGH FORT AT DACCA. (See page 278.)

PREFACE

EASTERN BENGAL, lying outside the beaten track of the tourist and making no insistent claim to notice, has long failed to attract the attention it deserves. The much-discussed question of the Partition of Bengal, however, has recently brought it prominently before the general public, both in India and at home, and it is hoped that the story of its Capital, which the following pages attempt to relate in popular form, will be of special interest at the present time. The task of setting forth something of its history in a manner calculated to appeal to the general reader has not been without difficulty. Of the record of its earlier years, during Buddhist and Hindu supremacy, little that is authoritative has survived; while so fast did events move, and so rapid were the changes that occurred in later days, that Mussulman annals are apt to degenerate into a confusing medley of unfamiliar names, or a bare recital of the doings of Kings and Governors. Such authorities as these, moreover, are often hard to reconcile with one another, adding to the difficulty of the writer who strives for accuracy. It would have been out of place in a work of this kind to enter at length into controversial points, but, while much has been necessarily omitted, the aim throughout has been to give a connected readable account of the old Mussulman city in the heart of Eastern Bengal, which now, after the lapse of two hundred years, has once more attained the dignity of a Capital.

To Moulvi Sayid Aulad Hasan, who has done much to revive interest in old Dacca, my thanks are due for kindly reading the proofs and for many valuable suggestions. To him I owe the portraits of the Viceroy Shaista Khan, of Guru Nanak, and of the Emperor Farrukh Siyar and his consort. A list of some of the more important authorities consulted is given at the end of the book.

SIMLA: *June 25th*, 1906.

CONTENTS

ILLUSTRATIONS

THE ROMANCE
OF
AN EASTERN CAPITAL

CHAPTER I

A LAND OF RIVER AND PLAIN

FLAT like a map, Eastern Bengal lies spread out vast and limitless, a land of river and plain. The plough of the gods, runs the legend, wielded in swift anger, had in days gone by torn down this way from the Himalayas to the sea, furrowing hill and valley, mountain and plain, to one immense dead level. From the foot of the rocky tree-clad Rajmahal Hills on the west to the banks of the mighty Brahmaputra on the east, from the snow-clad ranges of Sikhim and Nepal on the north to the shores of the Bay of Bengal on the south, it is one great wide-sweeping plain, low-lying and fertile, drained by some of the mightiest rivers of the East as they forge their impetuous way through many and ever-changing channels to the sea. Watered abundantly by nature in generous mood, the trim rice-fields stretch mile on mile, locked close in the embrace of countless streams and rivulets, luxuriant in every exquisite shade of green, like emeralds set in a silver sheen.

In the very heart of this land of river and plain the successive races that have dominated it have built their capital. Time and again, as empires rose and fell, its site has changed. At the whim of kings and conquerors, eager to perpetuate their fame, new cities have arisen with startling rapidity, often but to be deserted in their turn well nigh before the last stones have crowned the minarets and pinnacles of their mosques and palaces. Yet, variable as its site has been, the chief city of Eastern Bengal for over two thousand years has never been far removed from the junction of the great rivers where Megna and Ganges, Brahmaputra and Ishamutti meet at the head of the delta, a hundred miles from the sea. Here, in the days of legend and myth, Vikramadit founded the first capital of which the fame remains. Here to-day, scarce twenty miles away, still stands the time-worn city of Dacca—the once imperial capital of all Bengal, which, so long fallen from its early greatness, now again assumes the proud position of a capital—the capital of the newly formed Province of Eastern Bengal and Assam.

In all India, with its varied interests and its wonderful diversity of character, no province of similar importance has met with less notice and appreciation than Eastern Bengal. Though close within reach of Calcutta, in which, early and late, so much of the interest of the British Empire in India has centred, it yet remains apart, unknown and unappreciated, its vast expanse of river and plain unexplored save by those whom duty takes this way. Even the average official, caught by the glamour of Behar, avoids the eastern districts, and the makers of books have left it for the most part severely alone. Until it sprang into prominence recently in English politics, the very name of Eastern Bengal conjured up in the average Englishman's mind nothing but vague visions of a land of jungle and swamp, and the meeting-place of many rivers. Dacca alone, with the fame of its muslins, was familiar to English ears. The globe-trotter, absorbed in the great spectacular panorama of the beaten track, has passed it by. Treading with unvarying monotony and a strange absence of originality a certain set itinerary, he has gone home, primed with scant knowledge of the real India, to rhapsodise over the great wonders of the East that have been described again and yet again until one well nigh wearies on paper of the beauties of the Taj, the magnificence of Delhi and the memories of Lucknow. Scarce one has turned aside to explore this new field so near at hand. Calcutta seems to have fixed itself as the eastern limit of the tourist's travels in Bengal, and the great Province that lies beyond, making no dramatic bid for the notice of the passer-by, still remains but a name—its story untold and its charm unknown.

Yet it is there, a charm unique among all the wonders of the East. From the dry, sun-baked land of the beaten track, one turns gratefully to rest the eye upon the fair luxuriance of this well-nourished land. Small wonder that ancient chroniclers, revelling in picturesque description, called it 'a land of emerald and silver,' 'a garden fit for kings.' Even in official documents it is styled 'Jannat-ul-bilad,' the Paradise of Countries. Its perennial freshness knows but the lightest touch of autumn. Its wealth of green, in every wonderful shade, from the deepest of olives to the tender green of the earliest rice, covers the earth like a carpet lovingly spread by the gods. Here nature in luxuriant mood has lavishly bestowed the boon most craved by the sun-scorched plains of the East, watering it with the thousand streams that twist and turn like the paths of a maze through all its length and breadth. Almost all the terrible calamities that time and again have fallen upon the Indian people this favoured province has been spared. Plague has not yet forced its way across the network of rivers that stand like a barrier to bar its path. Famine is almost unknown within the memory of man. Yearly the dense population of Eastern Bengal imposes a heavy burden upon the land, but the rich alluvial soil proves equal to the task. In the trim, well-watered rice-fields, men labour with the joy of certain harvest, knowing that bread cast upon the waters, after no long tarrying, will faithfully render up its full return.

It is a scene full of life and interest, as one passes up the great rivers on one of the many steamers that run through the heart of Eastern Bengal, linking the first city of India with the furthermost limits of empire towards the East. There is no easier mode of travelling in all India than this. To the tourist jaded with the noise and rush of the long rail journeys that India entails, and sated with the stir and ceaseless activity of cities, there comes a strange sense of peacefulness and rest. Smoothly the huge steamer glides onward, forging its even way ahead, gallant and determined, buoyant with a sense of joyousness and power. A soft cool breeze blows gratefully. At ease in a long deck-chair, one watches the fascinating life of the river unfolded in brief flashes before one's view like a kaleidoscope, each glimpse a picture in itself more illuminative of the real India than many pages of description. The morning sun comes slowly over the water's edge, bathing the river in exquisite tints of pink and silver and gold. All is still with the wonderful stillness of dawn. Only the river moves ceaselessly, now smooth like glass, mirroring every passing glory of the sky, now murmuring on its way in a thousand laughing ripples, now angry and storm-tossed like a sea in miniature, ever changing, yet fascinating in all its moods. Strange craft glide swiftly by, sails set and bellying proudly in the wind. Tiny fishing-boats curved and narrow, swift *goyna* boats long and pointed fore and aft, larger craft heavy and slow-moving, houseboats snug and neat with mat walls and roof, all pass by, busy, alive, intent, speeding onwards each to its appointed goal. White sails, brown sails, sails in yellow and blue, add exquisite touches of colour as they fall and dip and strain at the mast like things alive with joy in the breeze and the light of the sun. The river throbs with life, yet a life so smooth, so noiseless, that passing it leaves unbroken the exquisite sense of peace that the river has made its own.

Close within hail of the bank the steamer passes, each moment disclosing some new glimpse

IN THE KINGDOM OF VIKRAMPUR.

ON THE BURIGANGA.

of the daily round of Indian life. A group of women, ornaments jingling on wrist and neck and ankle, come gossiping to the water's edge, poising their waterpots upon their heads with the grace that only Eastern women know. A straggling village, mat-walled, thatch-roofed, peeps out among the trees, raised but a foot above the river level. Its inhabitants, slow-moving and deliberate, pursue the daily round seemingly unmindful of the threatened inundation of their homes. A crowd of tiny urchins, innocent of clothing, happy and free in a string of beads, play lazily in the sun. A youth, scarce bigger than they, but with an air, lustily belabours a herd of buffalo, urging them far out into the river until only their great black heads appear as they wallow contentedly in the grateful coolness of the stream. As the sun mounts high in the sky, every bathing ghat along the banks is crowded, picturesque groups of men, women, and children punctiliously performing the daily ablution that their faith enjoins. Then the heat of the day, and life for a space seems lulled to slumber. One by one the bathers quit the banks and every sign of life creeps into the shade. Even the breeze is still, and the sails of the countless craft on the river all lie furled. Only the river itself moves on, ceaseless and untiring. Then a glorious sunset, such as one sees but seldom, save in Eastern Bengal across the face of the waters, that reflect every fleeting shade of brilliance, of amber and red and purple and orange and gold. Then night and a new world of the deep blue vault of the starry sky above and dim shadows beneath, broken only by dazzling flashes from the searchlight as it makes clear the path ahead, throwing upon river and land its ghostly mystic radiance, revealing in brief flashes the secrets of the night as limelight throws a picture on a screen.

In sharp contrast with the peacefulness and quiet charm of Eastern Bengal are the streets and story of its capital. Here there is a charm of another kind, the fascination that a great historic city never fails to cast upon him who treads its streets with the seeing eye, with sympathy and understanding. Mystery, that is as the breath of Eastern cities, baffles one at every turn in Dacca. The crumbling walls of its mosques and palaces rise grim and time-worn, hiding within their ruined turrets and dim walled chambers a thousand unrecorded secrets that no man living knows. Strange things have passed within their ken. They have listened to the whispered mutterings of intrigue, the plotting of foul crimes and dark mysterious deeds, and the softer voices of the fleeting loves and passions of a race swift in love as in war. They have watched the tragic passing of great Viceroys and Princes, and the triumphant entry of those who followed in their wake, to enjoy their brief spell of glory ere their own knell sounded. In rapid flight they have witnessed splendour and decay, triumph and exile, victory and defeat, a very sermon on the vanity of human strivings and desires. But silent, inscrutable, they make no sign, holding fast to their own that no man may wrest it from them. Even the winding alleys and tortuous ways that lead into the heart of the great city seem designed with jealous care to shroud a mystery from the outside gaze. So little is known, so little there is that can now be rescued from the limbo of the past, that one turns aside baffled, foiled in the attempt to wring from the great city the countless mysteries that lie hidden deep within her heart.

Time and man have treated the once imperial city with but scant respect. Many storms and the great humidity of Eastern Bengal have wrought havoc with brick and stone, wearing away at last the wonderful workmanship of a race of great architects and builders. Man, with incredible vandalism, has even outdone Time, pulling down the exquisite structures that he could never rival, to build with the selfsame bricks some hideous modern structure of his own base design. But even in its decay the charm of the city remains. Neither time nor the vandal hand of man can rob it of the wonder and romance of its many vicissitudes, and the great memories that for all time remain its own.

Round all that concerns the early days of Eastern Bengal there is the same impenetrable mystery that has fallen like a veil over so much of the past throughout India. Of the time before the Mussulman invasion well nigh all is legend and myth. The Buddhists and Hindus who then peopled the land were no chroniclers. The compilation of pedigrees seems to have been almost the limit of their literary skill. Of passing events and the strange happenings that befell men in those far-off days they made no note. Life was too strenuous, the struggle for existence too keen, to foster the development of an impersonal interest in the history of the time. In the midst of a life so precarious, of alarms so constant and insistent, there was no time for the chronicling of events. If such was done, the records must have perished with their makers. A few inscriptions, a mass of vague traditions, and brief glimpses of them in the records of their conquerors, are all that remain to tell what manner of men they were, and how life fared with them in the Eastern Bengal of the olden days.

Round Vikrampur, where Dhaleswari and Megna meet, the first traditions cluster. Here for centuries a Buddhist dynasty flourished, yet finally passed away leaving but little trace of its long dominion, and not a single descendant of its faith in all Eastern Bengal. Opposite Vikrampur, across the Ishamutti, in Sonargaon, a long line of Hindu kings held sway, but all that remains to-day in their one-time capital is a single building, once the Royal Treasury. Almost without a struggle the Hindu kingdom in Sonargaon fell before the Mussulman invaders. Bukhtiyar Khiliji, at the head of an Afghan army, speedily drove Lakshman Sen, the last Hindu King of Bengal, from his capital at Lakhnauti, and pressing eastwards, took possession of Sonargaon, founding a great Mussulman viceroyalty under the imperial authority at Delhi.

In pre-Mussulman days there seems to have been no general name for the land now known as Bengal. The Mussulmans themselves first knew their newly conquered province as Lakhnauti, the name of Lakshman Sen's capital, since known as Gaur. The word 'Bengal' first appears in Indian history as 'Banga,' possibly derived from Anga, the East, as in Vangala-Agadha, the Eastern Ocean. It was not till near the end of the thirteenth century that the name apparently reached England. Marco Polo, the famous traveller, is the first European to use it in the form of Bangala, and he gives it as a general name to all the land at the head of the Bay of Bengal—the Vangala-Agadha.

Under Mussulman rule Eastern Bengal suffered many strange vicissitudes. On the furthest frontier of the empire, it was a far cry from the central power at Delhi, and none but the strongest arm could make its power felt as a reality so far afield. The weakness of emperors was the opportunity of ambitious viceroys, and little more than a hundred years after the first Mussulman conquest, Fakiruddin threw off his allegiance to the Imperial Court and proclaimed himself independent king of Bengal.

Then for well nigh two hundred years the kingdom went to the strongest. The mass of the people, still almost entirely Hindu, cared little. The Mussulmans, who had imposed themselves upon Bengal as the ruling race by the sword and by their genius for rule, were still but a small portion of the population. The people, conquered and apathetic, knowing that the oppressor must needs be, stood by indifferent while kings and princes fought out their feuds. It is a terrible record that fills these two hundred years of rebellion and intrigue, of father fighting against son and brother against brother. The strong man arose, sweeping all before him, and while he lived enforced his rule. With his death came anarchy and a fierce struggle for the throne, a reckless riot of plunder, murder, and fratricide. Out of the contest one stronger than the rest at last emerged, ruthlessly forging his way to empire and giving a brief uncertain rest to the exhausted land. With his death—and death came suddenly in those days—anarchy once more reigned. And so the monotonous round goes on. It is a confusing chronicle. Ruler succeeds ruler, only with startling rapidity to meet the fate of his predecessor, and another reigns in his stead, until one grows weary of the oft-repeated tale of treachery and intrigue.

The Afghans were a fighting race, and it was not without a determined struggle that they gave way before the all-conquering Moghul. Once again under their magnificent leader, Sher Shah, they wrested back from the conqueror not only Bengal but the empire itself, and Sher Shah reigned in Humayon's stead. But it was their final effort, and thirty years later the great Akbar's forces destroyed the last hope of the Afghans in Bengal.

These were the days of the greatest prosperity of Sonargaon. The art of weaving, the gift of the Mussulman conqueror, had here attained a perfection wellnigh unrivalled in the East. The fame of the exquisite muslins that its artificers alone could produce had already reached Europe and excited the wonder and admiration even of the most skilled workmen of Italy and France. Travellers dwell in astonishment on the cheapness of provisions, and Ralph Fitch, visiting the district in 1586, speaks of it as 'abounding in rice, cotton, and silk goods.' Not even the wars and alarms of the most turbulent period of Mussulman rule could wholly rob this much favoured land of its prosperity. Even from the repeated attacks of the river pirates, Mughs and Arracanese, aided and abetted by a roving company of Portuguese adventurers, it revived with wonderful vitality, nature rapidly making good the ravages of man.

But with the final triumph of the Moghul in Bengal, and the re-enforcement of imperial authority, the days of Sonargaon drew rapidly to an end. A new ruler, eager to perpetuate his fame and moved thereto by the exigencies of the time, desired a new capital, and the ancient city was left to crumble to decay or forced to yield its very bricks and stones and monuments to grace its rival's triumph. Twenty miles away, on the banks of the Buriganga, rose the new city of Dacca, designed by Islam Khan from its inception to be the capital of all Bengal.

The hundred years that followed were momentous years in the history of the new capital. It was the time of the great viceroys, and distinguished names crowd thick upon its roll of fame.

First the name of Islam Khan its founder, the conqueror of the Afghan, and the trusted minister of Jehangir; then Ibrahim Khan, the victorious in war and patron of the arts and commerce; Shah Jehan, the builder in after-days of the world-famed Taj Mahal, a fitting shrine for the beauty of his queen; Sultan Shuja, foiled in his bid for empire, an exile at its gates, hastening to his ignominious death at the hands of the Arracanese; Mir Jumla, the invader of Assam, whose soaring ambition and consummate ability made even the great Aurungzebe fear; and, greatest of all, Shaista Khan, Lord of the Nobles, brother of the famous Empress Mumtaz Mahal, who has left his mark for all time upon the city he so long ruled.

But this brilliant period in the history of the city came to a sudden end. At the whim of a viceroy it had risen. In like manner it fell. Murshid Kuli Khan, at the beginning of the eighteenth century, transferred his capital to Murshidabad, and Dacca, deserted by the viceroy and all the paraphernalia of courts, was shorn of half its glory. Left to the rule of its Naib Nazims or Deputy-Governors, it sank in dignity and importance, and henceforth its name is heard but seldom in the larger issues that convulsed Bengal. So for fifty years it remained with varying fortunes, prosperous and content under the wise guidance of a Juswant Roy, or harassed and oppressed under the rapacious rule of a Murad Ali. The central power, exhausted by Aurungzebe's life-long struggle, was rapidly falling to decay, and Eastern Bengal, on the outskirts of the empire, was quick to feel when the strong hand had relaxed its hold. Unchecked, the local governors wreaked their will upon the province, and well it was for the people of Eastern Bengal that, in the midst of all the self-seeking violence and oppression that marked the last days of Mussulman rule, there were still from time to time wise administrators and just judges numbered among its rulers.

Then at last, when the Mussulman Empire had reached its lowest ebb, when the Mahrattas were knocking at its gates with no uncertain hand, when imperial rescripts no longer ran, and a despot of the worst type ruled at Murshidabad, there came an unexpected end. A little company of English merchants, bent only upon trade, had made the smallest of beginnings in Bengal some hundred and twenty years before. Battling with true British pluck against innumerable difficulties, they had doggedly pushed their way, checked and harassed at every turn, but insistent, ignorant of defeat, turned aside from their purpose by no let or hindrance. So after many vicissitudes they had won for themselves a place, and the founding of Fort William at the close of the seventeenth century, though they knew it not, was only the first step to far greater things. But a long series of events, culminating in the attack upon Calcutta in 1756, forced the reluctant East India Company, in the protection of its own interests, to assume the functions of government which the ruined and dismembered Moghul Empire was no longer able to perform. To obtain freedom and security of trade it was necessary to enforce law and order, and this the local native authorities had signally failed to do. It was left for the English Company to bring peace and good government to the harassed province. Just over a hundred years after the English factory had been established in Dacca, the first Collector was appointed there to take over the administration of Eastern Bengal.

It was by a strange irony of fate that the commercial prosperity of Dacca should decline with the assumption of power by a Company whose very *raison d'être* was trade and commerce. Such a result, due to a number of causes over which the Company had no control, was as unforeseen as it was unavoidable. But if Dacca suffered through changed conditions in one direction, she gained immeasurably in many another. The days of unrest, when battle, murder, and sudden death stalked everywhere, were past. For the first time in its history Eastern Bengal knew the blessings of a prolonged peace, and, secure in life and property, the long down-trodden people saw the dawn of a new era of prosperity and content. The ryot, assured of the fruit of his labour, and confident that now no longer others would reap where he had sown, rapidly extended his cultivation of the responsive soil, and, deserting Dacca as manufactures declined, sought a new home in the most remote corners of the district, felling the jungle and driving the beasts of prey that once carried off his flocks and herds on the outskirts of the capital itself into the far-distant patches of jungle that still remained.

To-day a new era in its history has dawned for Dacca. After eclipse for just two hundred years, it once more regains the proud position of a capital. Eastern Bengal, withdrawn from its one-time alliance with Bengal Proper, Behar and Orissa, now joins Assam, forming the new Province of Eastern Bengal and Assam, with its own Lieutenant-Governor, and Dacca as its capital. The old Province of Bengal had long been held to be too heavy a burden for one administration ; and Eastern Bengal, being in many directions considerably behind the western portion of the Province, had failed to keep pace with the general progress of the whole, and, from press of interests, to receive the attention on the part of Government that it demanded. The object of the Partition was, therefore, twofold. In the first place it sought to relieve Bengal of a portion of its unduly heavy charge, and in the second place it was hoped, by giving to it its own local government, that the interests of Eastern Bengal would be more jealously safeguarded and its general progress accelerated. The division was carried out as far as possible with due regard to racial distinctions. In the old Province there now remain no fewer than forty-two million Hindus as compared with nine million Mahomedans. On the other hand, in the new Province the Mahomedans predominate to the extent of eighteen millions as against twelve million Hindus. One of the chief objections urged against the Partition was that it severed old ties and split up an ancient Province which long custom had indissolubly made one. Such an argument, however, can have little weight with anyone who is at all familiar with the history of Bengal. Unity and permanence were noticeably absent in Mussulman days. Not only was the capital continually changed by successive viceroys, but the Province as then constituted bore little resemblance to the Bengal of British rule. Behar and Orissa were for the most part provided with their own governors direct from Delhi, Chota Nagpore and the Damon-i-Koh remained practically unconquered, while Bengal itself was continually divided up into deputy governorships under its viceroy. The formation of Bengal into a Lieutenant-Governorship was an entirely modern scheme, that was only carried into effect by the British Government, long after its rule had been firmly established in India, during the first half of the nineteenth century. The Province, as constituted, was therefore considerably less than a century old when the Partition took place on October 16, 1905.

Practically unanimously welcomed by the Mahomedans, it can hardly be doubted that it will immensely promote their welfare in the near future. An extremely backward and ignorant people for the most part in Eastern Bengal, they had shown little of the keenness and adaptability to modern conditions which the Hindus have so strikingly exhibited. The large native press is almost entirely in the hands of the Hindus, and the Mahomedans, without the art of agitating and too ignorant and apathetic to make their grievances known, have inevitably fallen behind in the general advance. Now, included in a splendid Province some one hundred and six thousand square miles in extent, and with great possibilities as yet untried, in which they largely predominate, their interests will meet with the fullest and most sympathetic consideration on the part of their own local government. Already under their first Lieutenant-Governor, Sir Bampfylde Fuller, K.C.S.I., much has been done, and his resignation, which took effect on August 20 last, was deeply deplored by the Mahomedan community. Under the Honourable Mr. Hare, however, who has succeeded him, the progress begun will doubtless continue and justify beyond dispute in the near future the creation of the new Province.

To Dacca itself the Partition has brought a wonderful revival. Already there is an unwonted stir of life and interest in the old imperial city. The sense of awakening is in the air. New buildings are rapidly rising to accommodate the army of officials, and all the following that Government necessarily carries in its train. The pulse of the city, so long weak and listless, throbs with renewed vigour. Once more it is the centre of affairs where great issues are fought out, and important decisions arrived at, affecting no fewer than thirty millions of people. The long sleep of the city is past. It may even be that, with the present movement to resuscitate native arts and commerce, the weaving of muslins may be revived in Dacca, and its workmanship once more excite the wonder and admiration of the West. The art is not yet lost, and the encouragement that it has so long lacked may even now revive it. The crumbling walls of its mosques and palaces, also, it is not too much to hope, may be at last arrested in their decay and carefully preserved among the rising evidences of the city's restored prosperity, as perpetual reminders of her great historic past. Dacca, so long folded in the fatal sleep that falls upon all Eastern cities once their greatness has departed, has at length awakened, and standing at the parting of the ways, midway between the memories of her past and the possibilities of the future, looks hopefully along the vista of the coming years, and awaits with confidence the fulfilment of their promise.

CHAPTER II

THE KINGDOM OF VIKRAMPUR

ENCIRCLED in a network of rivers where Ganges and Buriganga, Megna, Ishamutti and Brahmaputra meet, lies the ancient kingdom of Vikrampur. At the very centre of the great watercourses of Eastern Bengal, it occupied a position unrivalled in the days when roads were few and jungle covered the land. On every side stretched broad highways, ever open, offering the swiftest means of communication with the world beyond. On land, innumerable perils beset the wayfarer. Dense forests covered Eastern Bengal from end to end. It needed an army with a train of elephants to force a passage through, and beasts of prey lay in wait for him who passed by alone. The storms that caught the traveller on the great rivers were indeed to be feared, and annually they claimed a heavy toll in human life, but they were as nothing to the unknown dangers that awaited him who passed through the forest tracks on foot.

Everywhere the influence of the great rivers

has made itself felt in the story of Vikrampur. Silted up by them in days gone by, when the world was young, it is practically an island set in their midst. Having brought it into being, they made of it their special care. Raised but little above their level, it almost disappears beneath them in the rains, its rich alluvial rice-fields drawing new sustenance from this bountiful supply of moisture, annually renewed. But not only did the rivers give the land new life, they proved for it a never-failing bulwark of defence. For almost half the year the waters covered the land, and the enemy incautious enough to stay was driven out by the floods. It was impossible to fight for a kingdom where there was no dry land, and time and again the invader was driven back baffled, from this land that the great rivers encircled and defended with such protecting care.

It was here, says the Hindu legend, that the famous Raja Vikramadit made his home. Feeling the desire for rest after his many journeyings to and fro, he sought for a place where he might spend the remainder of his days in peace. Coming upon this fertile island in the midst of many waters, restful in its garment of luxuriant green, it pleased him more than all the lands that he had visited, and here he set up his kingdom. But the annals of his rule are a sealed book, and even tradition is content with the bald record that he ruled with justice and wisdom, and that the fame of his piety and learning spread far and wide. There the first brief chronicle of Vikrampur ends, and only the name of its capital still survives to give some point to the vague uncertain legend.

Of the years that follow there is still less told. How Brahminism lost its early vigour in Vikrampur, and well nigh died out, it is impossible to say. The coming of the Buddhist Rajas of the Pal dynasty, and the manner in which they, a comparatively small company of men, imposed themselves upon the mass of the population and ruled for a thousand years, is equally shrouded in oblivion. But that they came, carried on the crest of the wave of the mighty influence that suddenly stirred the India of that day, there can be little doubt. The fourth century before Christ had seen the rise of one of the most wonderful forces that ever stirred the world to its depths. Gautama the Buddha, after much searching of heart, had at last found the Truth and given to his disciples a new religion —that marvellous faith, simple, yet hard to attain, which taught that duty was better than sacrifice, and self-respect than many prayers, and that the path of purity of thought and word and deed alone led to the great and perfect peace that weary and suffering humanity had so long sought in vain.

It was a strange gospel to men who had sought that same end by much mortifying of the flesh, by the repetition of long prayers, by the washing of cups and platters, and by the purifying of the outer man. Yet so great was the veneration Gautama the Buddha inspired by his life and teaching that men, in those days of the youth of the world, were found to forsake all and follow him into the unknown paths of this new teaching, which led them by such stern and searching ways.

With the early history of the rise of this new religion the name of Asoka the Great is closely associated. Extending his empire until it stretched from Kabul to Bengal, he established Buddhism as the State religion. It is a strange and unexpected picture of early India, this enforcement, not of creeds and tenets that man loves to propagate, but of purity and integrity, of the faithful fulfilment of the daily round of man's duty towards his fellow-man and the whole wide world of nature. Religious toleration was complete. Persecution of creeds and faiths was a thing unknown. All that Asoka and Buddhism required were that men should obey the dictates of morality and live in quietness and amity one with another.

It was with the high ideals of this great religion that the Pal kings came to Vikrampur. Strong with the enthusiasm of a young faith, they easily imposed themselves upon the followers of Brahminism whose first fervour had long since waned. But from first to last Buddhism remained only the religion of the ruling race, affecting not at all the vast mass of the population, which still clung to the lifeless forms of Hinduism though its spirit was long since dead. Buddhist monasteries flourished side by side with Hindu temples, both content to strive, though by far different ways, for the attainment of the same great end. But between them there was a great gulf fixed. Centuries of existence in close proximity failed to draw them together, and, with the rigid exclusiveness of Eastern creeds, each remained untouched in spite of long contact with the other. A State religion, Buddhism perished with the State. With the passing of the Pal dynasty, it disappeared as completely from Vikrampur as if it had never been.

Of the decline of Buddhism in Vikrampur and the revival of Hinduism, typified by the rise of the Sen dynasty, history and tradition relate but little. It may be that Buddhism, after more than a thousand years, had fallen from its first nobility of purpose, and that its representatives, the ruling race, sated with long exercise of power, had fallen a prey to that apathy and effeteness which has overtaken almost every conquering race in India in turn. Or it may be that King Adisur, the first of a famous line of Sen Rajas in Eastern Bengal, at last awoke the great mass of the Hindu population to a sense of its own strength and power, and by right of might displaced the Buddhist kings and founded a new Hindu kingdom of his own in Vikrampur.

Slowly the mists of antiquity begin to lift, and the memory of King Adisur stands out clear and distinct against the uncertain background of his time. To the Hindu his name has been handed down as worthy of all respect, for to him is ascribed the restoration of Brahminism in Eastern Bengal. So far had the Hindu religion fallen during the long centuries of Buddhist rule that King Adisur, it is said, found no Brahmin in all his kingdom who could faithfully perform the ceremonies and ritual of his faith. If Brahminism was to be restored, help must come from without, from some source that had not suffered under the long supremacy of an alien faith. King Adisur, sending out emissaries far and wide, found that the purest form of Brahminism had been preserved in the city of Kanouj. Thither he despatched a minister of his court with a letter setting forth the deplorable state of Hinduism that existed in his kingdom, and praying that a company of learned Brahmins might be sent there to restore the faith among their co-religionists who had so far fallen from its teaching. So there came, in response to King Adisur's request, from the famous city of Kanouj five Brahmins learned in all that appertained to their religion. Welcoming them with fitting respect, the king established them in his capital of Rampal, and there they flourished, they and their descendants, restoring for a time by their teaching and example the great doctrines of the Hindu faith.

After Adisur reigned Ballal Sen, the most famous of the Sen kings in Vikrampur, round whose name gather almost all the traditions that still linger in Rampal. So great was his repute that many things, of which in later days the origin was unknown, seem to have been attributed to him on the universal principle of 'to him that hath shall be given.' Such confusion has this wrought that events centuries apart are placed by tradition as happening within his reign. While one story makes him the son of King Adisur, the founder of the Sen dynasty in Rampal, another places him at the end of a long line of kings with whose death the kingdom fell into the hands of the Mussulman invaders. It seems evident that there must have been two Ballal Sens, one the son of Adisur, and the other the last of the Sen Kings, but such is the maze of rumour and tradition that surrounds their names, that to disentangle their life stories is well nigh impossible at the present day.

The object of so much veneration, it is not strange that a miraculous birth should be ascribed to the first Ballal Sen, or that the miracle should be attributed to the great river, the Brahmaputra, which has so indelibly impressed its influence for all time upon this land and people. Desiring to clothe its hero with every conceivable honour, Hindu legend has given him for parentage the great river itself, materialised in the form of a god. His mother was the favourite among King Adisur's wives, and the king, discovering her infidelity and unwitting of the intention of the gods, banished her in anger from his court. An outcast, in despair, she threw herself into the Brahmaputra. But the sacred river, folding her in its embrace, carried her swiftly and safely to the opposite shore, placing her under the care of the goddess Durga, whose home was on the banks of the Buriganga, close at hand. There, in the jungle beside the river, her son was born, and grew up under the protection of the goddess, proficient in all manly exercises and endowed with the wisdom that became one of such illustrious birth and such high destiny. One day, while still a youth and roaming in the forest, he

THE DHAKESWARI TEMPLE OF TO-DAY

found, hidden in the jungle, the image of Durga, his protectress, and on this spot, in her honour, he raised the temple of Dhaka Iswari, the concealed goddess, from which tradition says the city of Dacca took its name in after-days. So, favoured of the gods, Ballal Sen grew to manhood, and his father, hearing at last of his kingly qualities, desired to see him, and when the young man was brought into his presence he conceived for him so great an affection that he made him the heir of all his kingdom.

Such is the tradition of the birth and up-bringing of Ballal Sen, obviously an invention to surround with yet greater glamour a famous name. Another story, less ambitious and more probable, makes him the son of Bijoy Sen, a great warrior who had invaded the adjoining kingdom of Kamrup, and places his accession to the throne in the historic year when William the Conqueror was wresting the crown of England from the Saxon on the field of Senlac. Almost all that remains to this day in his capital of Rampal is associated with his name. Ballal Sen was a great builder and maker of roads and tanks. The outlines of his palace, still visible, show on how large a scale it was planned, though no architectural remains survive to show what manner of building it was. Covering an area of something like three thousand square feet, it was surrounded on every side by a moat two to three hundred feet wide, a pathway on the eastern side providing the only means of access to it. Nothing but scattered mounds of earth now survive where the palace within the moat once stood, and to-day the cultivator peacefully tills the very soil whereon kings and princes once held their courts and great armies pitched their camps. Many of the bricks that once graced the royal palace were used to build the modern houses of Rampal, some of them having been carried across the river to Dacca when that city was built as his capital by Islam Khan. Vague rumours of buried treasure still linger round the long-deserted site, and it is a fact that less than a century ago a ryot, ploughing his field close by, came upon a magnificent diamond worth seventy thousand rupees, which, doubtless, in its day, had shone in the palace of Ballal Sen.

Rampal is full of quaint traditions. Even the roads that Ballal Sen is said to have constructed have their own story. They were broad high-banked roads, planned on the large scale of a bygone age when kings ordered and their subjects hurried to obey. One of the finest ran from Rampal to the Padma river, and its name has furnished material round which to weave a legend. The astrologers had predicted that Ballal Sen would die from the effect of fishbones sticking in his throat. Alarmed by this prediction, the king resolved to banish fish from the royal table. But in the Padma river there was a fish known as Kachki, which is boneless, and in order that he might readily obtain a supply of it from the river he constructed the road, which has ever since been known in consequence as the Kachki Darwaja.

The great Rampal Dighi, a huge artificial lake near Ballal Sen's bari, has likewise a legend of its own. A mile long by some five hundred yards wide, it was in its day a fine example of the magnificent scale on which the old Hindu kings planned their works. Like all else in Rampal, it has suffered from neglect, and much of it has now become filled up, remaining dry for a great part of the year, while the cultivator has seized upon it as a fertile land wherein to grow his paddy. It was undertaken, runs the legend, by Ballal Sen as a work of charity in gratitude for some favour of the gods. To determine its size he fixed upon a quaint device. Its length should be as far as his mother could walk at one stretch without stopping to rest, and he vowed that he would excavate the whole of it during the following night. His mother doubtless had done but little walking in the whole of her life, and her son imagined that the length of the tank would not exceed reasonable limits. But it was soon evident, to his dismay, that he had greatly underestimated his mother's pedestrian capabilities. Closely veiled and attended by the whole of her court, she set out from the palace. Starting off towards the south, she walked with unexpected sprightliness and showed no sign of weariness as time went on. Ballal Sen, in alarm, soon saw that if she proceeded much further he would be unable to keep his vow and excavate so large a tank in a single night. Yet to break his vow would be a sin unpardonable. The King grew desperate as his mother still marched on. Knowing that the extent of the work of charity which would so greatly benefit the people depended upon her powers of endurance, she plodded on, seemingly miraculously endowed with new strength. Matters at length became critical, and Ballal Sen was reduced to resorting to an artifice. Ordering his servants surreptitiously to touch his mother's feet with vermilion as she walked, he suddenly gave a great cry that a leech had bitten her, and she, looking down and seeing the red stains upon her feet, imagined that they were of blood and stooped to examine them. The place where she stopped was the southernmost limit of the lake, one mile from the palace. That same night Ballal Sen fulfilled his vow. Collecting a vast army of workmen, the huge tank was excavated before the dawn, of such a length that it was impossible to see from one end to the other. But because Ballal Sen had resorted to stratagem to prevent its size from becoming excessive the gods were angry, and the bed of the lake, in spite of its depth, remained dry. Day after day no water came to fill it, and the king was put to a great shame. At length, however, his chief friend Rampal dreamed a dream. Therein it was revealed to him that he must sacrifice himself in order that the tank might be filled and the full benefit of it accrue to the people. Assembling all the courtiers and people upon the banks of the lake, Rampal told them of his dream. Then, ere they could recover from their astonishment, he rode slowly down into the bed of the lake, and immediately a hundred streams of pure water gushed from beneath and closed rapidly over his head. Suddenly the horror of all those who stood by found vent in one great cry: 'Rampal, Rampal, Rampal!' But already the waters had risen and filled the tank from end to end, and Rampal was no more seen. Then Ballal Sen wept for his friend, and exclaimed, 'Since I, by my sin, am responsible for the death of my friend, let this tank be no more called after me, but after Rampal.' In consequence it is known as the Rampal Dighi to this day.

Not far off is a smaller lake, connected by a curious tradition with the Rampal Dighi. It is said that Ballal Sen, having seen the completion of his great work, ordered all the men who had been engaged upon it to dig one spadeful of earth from a spot close by. So great was the number of men that a large tank, some seven hundred by five hundred cubits, was the result. It still bears the name of the Kodaldhoa Dighi—the spade-washing tank.

A striking feature of the Rampal Dighi is a magnificent *gajariya* tree, rising to a height of a hundred cubits on its northern bank. It has been there long beyond the memory of man, and tradition ascribes it, like all else, to the time of Ballal Sen. Among all the Hindu population it is an object of the greatest veneration, and miraculous powers have been ascribed to it. It is said to be immortal, and every leaf is held sacred. Many are the stories told of its healing and cleansing properties, and none would dare to lay rude hands upon it. The story is told of a fakir who camped beside it, and, needing fuel for his fire to cook his evening meal, lopped off one of its branches, and immediately he vomited blood and expired. The childless have great faith in prayer beside this sacred tree, and the cultivator seeks its protection against the many dangers that beset his crops.

Close by, in its honour, a fair was long held annually on the eighth day of the moon in the month of Chait.

But it is as the founder of Kulinism that Ballal Sen lives chiefly in Hindu legend. Brahminism in Vikrampur had once more fallen into disrepute. King Adisur had for a time revived it by the importation of learned pandits from the great Brahmin city of Kanouj, but in the years that followed society had become disorganised, and Hindu observances had been again neglected and forgotten. Ballal Sen on his accession had found the various grades of Hindu society in a state of great confusion, and he at once set himself the difficult task of reforming them. To prevent the deterioration of the higher castes by their constant intermarriage with those of lower status, he rigidly enforced the caste system. The descendants of the Kanouj Brahmins were first divided into two classes. Those families of acknowledged purity of descent were grouped together in one class and known as Kulins, while those who had intermarried were known as Srotriya. But it appears that these caste distinctions were not always carefully observed, and a further division took place at a later date. Those who stood the new test and were found to be of irreproachably pure descent were known as Mukhya Kulins, or those

Steadfast in Principle; while the remainder, and they were by far the larger number, were made Gauna Kulins, or those who had Deviated from the Right Path. But, strangely enough, a Mukhya Kulin (that is, the purest of the pure) was allowed to marry a girl outside his own caste. Hence the competition in the marriage market for Kulin bridegrooms among those of lower caste with eligible daughters to dispose of became great, and a curious state of things arose. Marriage became a profession. There being no limit to the number of wives a Kulin might have, he found himself in a most fortunate position, any number of men of lesser rank being anxious to marry their daughters to so desirable and high-caste a bridegroom. For the honour of being his first wife a large sum was paid as dowry, but with each succeeding marriage the amount grew less, so that a Kulin's value in the matrimonial market dwindled as the number of his wives mounted up. A case is reported of a Kulin having a hundred wives, while his three sons had no fewer than fifty, thirty-five, and thirty respectively. Fortunately for the peace of society, these huge families made no attempt to live together. A Kulin who made marriage a profession went gaily on his way, leaving his brides behind him. His fathers-in-law, satisfied with the dignity acquired, were content to support their daughters and their families. The only duty incumbent on the Kulin father was to provide for the marriage of his daughters, but as this meant dowries which the gay Lothario of a father was seldom in a position to provide, the result was that the unfortunate maidens but too often went unwed, thus exhibiting one of the rare instances of the existence of old maids in India.

Tradition is as busy with the death of Ballal Sen as with his birth and career. Near Abdullahpur, not far from Rampal itself, it is said, there lived a Mussulman family, one of the first which had penetrated so far east as Vikrampur. But the head of the house was childless, and the denial of the gift of a son for which he had so long prayed had embittered his life. Now it chanced on a day that a Fakir came to his house begging alms. The Mussulman, however, brooding over his own sorrow, roughly bade him begone. 'Since Allah has refused me the blessing that I crave,' he said bitterly, 'I will give no alms in his name.' But the Fakir answered that his prayers were already heard, and that before long a son would be born to him. The Mussulman, overjoyed, gave him alms, and asked what boon he should grant to him when the desire of his heart should be fulfilled. The Fakir asked only that he would sacrifice a bull to the altar of Allah. In due course a son was born, and remembering the Fakir's request the Mussulman at once made preparations for the sacrifice. But the Hindus among whom he lived, holding the bull sacred, rose up and indignantly prevented him. Determined, however, to fulfil his vow, he set out into the jungle and there at a distance performed the sacrifice. Taking with him as much of the flesh of the bull as he and his family could eat, he buried the remainder beneath the ground and returned home. On the way, however, a kite swept down, and, snatching one of the pieces of flesh out of his hand, flew with it towards Vikrampur and let it fall in front of the palace of Ballal Sen. The king, perceiving that it was the flesh of a bull, the sacred animal of his race, sent out men to discover who had committed so great a crime. After much search in the jungle they found jackals tearing up the flesh that the Mussulman had buried, and following the marks of blood that had fallen from the flesh which he had carried in his hand they traced him to his home. The king, hearing the story, ordered that the child on whose account the bull had been killed should be brought before him on the morrow and put to death. It was not meet that one for whom so great a crime had been committed at his birth should live.

The Mussulman, being secretly warned of the king's decree, fled that night with his wife and new-born child, and, escaping out of the kingdom of Ballal Sen, made his way across India to his home in Arabia, whence his family had first come. There, at Mecca, meeting with a Fakir, one Baba Adam by name, he told him the story of his flight. The Fakir, learning that there was a country in which Mussulmans had no liberty to follow the practices of their religion, gathered together as many as seven thousand followers and set out on the long journey to Vikrampur, determined to win for his co-religionists freedom to profess their faith. Arriving there after many adventures by the way, he approached almost within sight of Ballal Sen's capital, and, building a mosque, began to practise openly the rites and ceremonies of his religion. Many bulls and cows were sacrificed, and the Mussulman call to prayer rang out across the plains, and was heard even within the walls of the king's palace. Then Ballal Sen rose up in wrath. He sent messengers hastily to the new-comers demanding that they should leave his kingdom or cease to practise religious ceremonies obnoxious to Hinduism, the faith of himself and his kingdom. But Baba Adam, confident in the support of his numerous followers, sent a haughty reply to the great king. 'There is but one God, and Mahomet is his prophet,' rang out the challenge. He, Baba Adam, would perform the ritual required of his religion, let Ballal Sen the Infidel do what he would. Then the Hindu king, gathering together his forces, set out against Baba Adam. But the fame of the Mussulman victories had already reached Vikrampur, and Ballal Sen, wise in his day, made provision against defeat before he left his capital. Within the walls of his palace he caused to be constructed a great Agnikundi, a pit of fire, wherein, in case he made no return, all the members of his household might commit themselves to the funeral pyre, and so escape the ignominy and dishonour of falling into the conqueror's hands. Lest they of his household might be surprised suddenly by a victorious enemy, the king arranged a signal whereby they might know his fate in case of defeat. As he left the Ballal Bari with his army, he placed in the folds of his robe, at his breast, a carrier pigeon. If the day went ill with him he would release the bird, and its return to the palace should be the signal for the lighting of the funeral pyre and the immolation of all that he held most dear.

On the site where the mosque of Baba Adam now stands the two armies met, and a long and fierce battle was waged between this first advanced guard of the Mohammedan onset and the last great Hindu king of Vikrampur. For long the issue was uncertain, but at length the tide of victory set steadily in favour of Ballal Sen. The Mussulmans were finally defeated with great slaughter, and in the end Ballal Sen came face to face with Baba Adam. It was the hour of sunset, and the Fakir knelt with his face towards Mecca, praying the time-honoured prayers of his faith, unmindful of the fate that drew near. Even while he was still at prayer, Ballal Sen rode up to him and smote him with his sword. But the blow was miraculously of no effect, and Baba Adam rose up from his knees and stood before Ballal Sen—the representative of Islam over against the chief of Brahminism. 'Why hast thou come to disturb me at my prayers?' asked Baba Adam at length. 'I have come to slay him who has slain and dishonoured what I and my race hold sacred,' answered Ballal Sen, and again he smote the Fakir with his sword. But the Fakir's body might have been of iron, for the sharp steel fell upon it again with no effect. Then Baba Adam, looking upon his dead followers who lay scattered over the plain, cried out, 'It is the will of Allah that I should die at thy hands. Yet not by the sword of the Infidel. Take my sword and destroy me, for no other sword than mine can do me hurt. And upon thee may the curse of Allah fall speedily.' So, taking his sword, Ballal Sen smote the Fakir and killed him at one blow, cutting his body into two parts, one of which was miraculously transported to Chittagong, where a mosque dedicated to his memory still stands.

Ballal Sen, flushed with victory, went down to the river-bank to wash away the stains of battle. But as he stooped over the water the pigeon escaped unperceived from the folds of his robe. So it came to pass that the household of the king, watching eagerly for news from the walls of the palace, saw at last against the evening sky the white wings of the pigeon that flew straight homewards, unconscious of the false message that it bore, and settled with loud-voiced contentment upon the topmost pinnacle of the Ballal Bari. Then there arose within the palace the wailing of women and the sounds of mourning, and hastily lest the conqueror should come and take from them their honour and their pride of caste, which were all that fate had left them, the torch was placed to the funeral pyre in the Agnikundi and the whole of the family of Ballal Sen perished in the flames.

Then, even as the smoke still rose above the ruin of his house, the king returned in hot haste. Having discovered the flight of the bird, he had spurred home furiously, but the curse of the Fakir had fallen speedily and he had arrived too late. Not one of his family remained in Vikrampur, and in his grief and despair he flung himself upon the still-smouldering funeral pyre and perished in its ashes. Thus, the victim of a cruel fate, perished the last great Hindu king of Vikrampur. To this day he is remembered as the Pora-Raja—the Burnt King.

On the site where Baba Adam met his death a mosque was erected after many days by the Mussulman conquerors when they had finally established their supremacy in Eastern Bengal. It was built, as the inscription states, 'in the middle of the month of Rajab, in the year 888 A.H., during the reign of Jalaluddin Fateh Shah' (1483 A.D.). It is sadly fallen from its first estate. Yet, half in ruins as it now stands, it gives full evidence of what it must once have been. Highly ornamented, with the thin bricks of the Mussulman period, polished and carved, its six domes, three only of which remain intact, are supported by two stone pillars in the centre of the hall, huge monoliths of white stone which tradition calls the *godas* or clubs of Ballal Sen. Moisture oozes out from these pillars in the rainy season, and this sweating has caused them to be regarded with superstitious awe. The Hindu women who enter the mosque to pray before them and mark them with *sindur* are but another instance of the strange mingling of Hinduism and Mohammedanism that occurs so often in Eastern Bengal. Not far from Baba Adam's mosque is another mosque, plainer and less famous in the neighbourhood, but curious on account of the stone idols of Hindu gods and goddesses preserved in the verandah, doubtless as the spoils of a conquered race, which the Hindus of the neighbourhood still worship beneath this dome raised by an alien faith.

After the death of Ballal Sen, Vikrampur seems for a time to have fallen back under the rule of the Pal dynasty. The Mussulman had not yet arrived in full strength to take possession, and in the brief interval the Buddhist Rajas enjoyed their last brief spell of power before their final disappearance from the land. Lakshman Sen, the son of Ballal Sen, had built a capital for himself which he had named Lakhnauti, but the last years of his long reign were spent at Nadia, whence, at the venerable age of eighty, he was forced to flee before the advancing Mussulman host of Bukhtiyar Khiliji. One tradition relates that he and his son Bisvarupa returned to Vikrampur, and there his family reigned for over a hundred years more before the final overthrow of the Hindu power in Eastern Bengal. With him fled many of the most learned Brahmins from Nadia, the seat of learning, and, settling in Vikrampur, they made that place the centre of Brahminism in Eastern Bengal. Vikrampur, for many centuries, was famous for its learning, and clerks trained in its schools went out to earn their livelihood in other parts of Bengal in such large numbers that it became a saying in Vikrampur that a boy who was good for nothing at home might yet make a living as a clerk elsewhere.

The story of the kingdom of Vikrampur is almost done. Two miles from the ancient capital stands Munshigunj, the present headquarters of the subdivision of that name, now part of the Dacca district. Rampal, through all the centuries that have passed since the days of Ballal Sen, has found no place in history. Under the Mussulmans it was but one of the many outposts on the outskirts of empire. Sonargaon, on the opposite bank of the Ishamutti, became the capital of Eastern Bengal, and the ancient kingdom of Vikrampur, placed under a Kazi, a subordinate government officer, sank into insignificance, with only the memory of its former greatness and its many traditions to distinguish it. The centre of interest passes across the river to Sonargaon.

CHAPTER III

SONARGAON

It is hard to realise that this was once the capital of kings. At first glance, with its trim rice-fields and patches of jungle growth, it might have been in the beginning as it is now, peaceful, thriving, and content, undisturbed by the noise and clamour of passing events in the world beyond. Strangely little of all that is past has survived. To-day the ancient kingdom of Sonargaon is but a collection of insignificant villages. Scattered here and there over the land, they still cling faithfully round some battered and time-worn memory of the past. Gone are the retainers of kings and princes, the marts of merchants, and the camps of armies: gone the stir of great events and the busy hum of life. Generation after generation has passed away to whom its stirring history has been but as a tale that is told, and the humble cultivator to-day lives and dies on the very scene of its former greatness, careless and ignorant of its long-forgotten past.

From the banks of the Lakhiya, the Megna and the Ishamutti on the east and south and west, the kingdom of Sonargaon stretched seventy miles away to the north, where the Brahmaputra, fickle in its course, then flowed from west to east. Enclosed thus like an island in the midst of the great rivers, it was admirably fitted for defence. But it was in the south, in the angle formed by the Megna and the old bed of the Brahmaputra, that the chief centre of interest lay. Here, in what are now the villages of Aminpur, Pannam, Goaldi, and Moghrapara, the ruler of the day placed his headquarters. Sonargaon was apparently the name given to the whole district, and also particularly to the place where for the time being the king held court. Further afield all over the district there are the remains of a past civilisation. Huge tanks and mounds and mosques survive, and the ruins of many forts, thrown up to defend the frontiers from attack, which in their day played their part in the history of Sonargaon.

It was to this land, well fitted for defence, that the descendants of the last Hindu kings of Bengal fled before the advance of the victorious Mussulman armies. Here, undisturbed, they continued to rule for well nigh a hundred years after the Mussulmans had conquered Central Bengal. Bukhtiyar Khiliji lived but three years to enjoy his triumph, and throughout that time he was fully occupied with his ambitious schemes for the conquest of Tibet. The Sen Kings made no attempt to repel the Mussulman invader and regain their lost position. Without a struggle they gave way before a stronger than themselves. Living peacefully in Sonargaon they constituted no political danger, and the earliest Mussulman rulers attempted to impose upon them but the slightest form of control. Busy with their own schemes far away in their capital of Gaur, they asked nothing more from them than a payment of tribute and a formal acknowledgment of their dependence. Dispossessed of all political authority, they soon sank to the position of mere zemindars and local magnates, and their final disappearance from the stage which they had so long occupied was not long delayed. With Danuj Roy, grandson of Lakshman Sen, the end came. It was in the days of the Viceroy Tughril Khan, who, from a Tartar slave of the Emperor Balin, had by his wonderful ability and address risen to be Governor of Bengal. But success and advancement had so inflamed his ambition that neither gratitude nor prudence restrained him from open rebellion against his master. Fresh from his latest triumph in Tipperah, whence he had returned laden with immense treasure borne by a train of a hundred captive elephants, he gave

A FERRY BOAT ON THE DULLASERY.

AN EARTHENWARE VESSEL USED AS A BOAT ON THE BRAHMAPUTRA.

CROSSING THE MEGNA NEAR SONARGAON.

out that the Emperor was dead, and, assuming all the insignia of royalty, proclaimed himself independent King of Bengal. But the Emperor, enraged at this treachery of his former slave, raised an army and set out against him with all despatch. Panic seems to have seized Tughril Khan as his master approached, and, collecting all the wealth on which he could lay hands, he fled with a huge train of elephants and a picked company of troops towards the east, intending to take refuge in the last resort in Tipperah, where he had recently achieved so great a triumph. Following in his wake, the Emperor Balin reached Sonargaon. It had been a long and difficult march across the hot bare plains of Upper India, through Behar and the Teliagharia Pass, and down the great rivers of Bengal—an undertaking not to be lightly entered upon. It was an historic occasion for Eastern Bengal. Never before had an Emperor of Delhi visited this eastern frontier of the empire, and Danuj Roy, trembling at his approach, pursued the traditional policy of his race and offered no resistance. Setting out from Pannam, where he had placed his capital, he met the Emperor as he entered Sonargaon, and, giving in his allegiance, offered his help against the rebel Viceroy. Shortly afterwards the imperial troops came up with those of Tughril Khan and won a great victory on the banks of the Megna. There is a tradition that Tughril Khan himself, attempting to escape across the river into Tipperah, was taken captive and spent the remainder of his days in prison in Sonargaon.

The shadow of imperial affairs had at length fallen across the ancient Hindu kingdom of Sonargaon, and from this time onwards, during the next three centuries, it became the headquarters of Mussulman rule in Eastern Bengal. The Sen Rajas quietly disappear from its annals, making a tame and spiritless exit after their long centuries of kingship. Almost every trace of their rule was speedily obliterated by the new Mussulman governors, who everywhere lost no time in transforming the Hindu capitals well nigh out of recognition and imparting to them a new character of their own. Hindu temples were ruthlessly pulled down that the stones might be used to build mosques wherein the faithful might worship, and on the site of the forts and palaces of the Hindu kings rose the far grander and more imposing buildings of the Mussulman conquerors. The Sen and Pal kings had proved themselves great builders of temples and palaces, as there is sufficient evidence elsewhere to show, yet so completely has the Mussulman obliterated the traces of their rule in Sonargaon that only one

Hindu building survives. Under the shadow of the official residence of the Imperial Karori, the Mussulman tax-gatherer, whose descendants still live close by, it stands, a building of no architectural distinction, and interesting only as the solitary survival of centuries of Hindu rule. Known as the Jhikoti, it is formed of concrete with elongated dome-shaped roof, its walls pierced with numerous openings. Until recently it was used as a meeting-place for worship by the Hindus of the surrounding villages, but now it stands deserted and neglected, moss-grown and falling to decay, yet having survived to see the passing of the Mussulman empire in Sonargaon and the strange revenges that time takes.

The last year of the thirteenth century marks the opening of a new era in the history of Sonargaon. In that year the Emperor Alla Uddin divided the government of Bengal into two parts, and appointed Bahadur Khan to be governor of the eastern portion, with his capital at Sonargaon. For the next three hundred years it remained, with varying fortunes, the seat of the Mussulman government in Eastern Bengal. It was a troublous period that was opening for the newly formed province. Events succeeded one another with startling rapidity. Situated on the easternmost limits of the empire, it had all the advantages and disadvantages of a frontier province. Free from immediate control, Viceroy after Viceroy was tempted to throw off his allegiance and proclaim his independence. Time and again the empire, beset on every side, was forced to relax its hold. To the people these things mattered not at all. They were content to sit by, unmoved spectators of the drama, yet perhaps not without a touch of humour, as they watched their rulers fall out and war continually among themselves. Still, though these contests interested them but little, in other directions the mass of the people felt to the full the advantage and disadvantage of their position on the frontier of the empire. On the one hand Eastern Bengal enjoyed an immunity from strife and bloodshed unknown in the lands that lay nearer the heart of the empire, where great issues were constantly at stake, and vast armies for ever passed to and fro, leaving ruin and desolation in their wake. Though the lot of the cultivator in Eastern Bengal was by no means a secure one, yet he suffered comparatively little from these human locusts. It was no easy country for the transport of troops, and the armies that came this way to subdue some rebellious Viceroy, or to attempt the conquest of Assam, wandered little afield from certain well-defined highways, keeping always close to the great rivers. Delhi was far off, and the journey down through Oude, Behar, and Bengal, was beset with difficulties and a matter of many days. Sonargaon, set in a circle of great rivers, was inaccessible by road for a great part of the year, and well fitted by nature to defy attack. It was a foolhardy general who lingered in Eastern Bengal as the cold weather drew to an end. Annually the rivers rose and swept the invader out of the land, or, cutting off his retreat, left him at the mercy of the enemy. But, on the other hand, Sonargaon suffered to the full the disadvantages of a frontier province. Beyond, away to the east, lived the Mughs and Arracanese, and the unknown tribes of further Kamrup and of the jungle lands at the foot of the Himalayas to the north. Its eastern boundaries ill-defined, the province suffered terrible things at the hands of these wild tribes, freebooters and marauders by natural instinct. To the peaceful inhabitants of Eastern Bengal the Mughs close at hand were a constant source of terror. Sailing up the rivers, they robbed and plundered and laid waste whole villages along the banks. Allied in later days with the Portuguese, who taught them better seamanship, they became so great a menace that a new capital of Bengal was founded nearer the easternmost limits of the empire to protect the province from their depredations.

The first governor of Eastern Bengal under the new *régime* was not slow to take advantage of the opportunity his position on the outskirts of the empire offered. The Emperor Balin's march from Delhi to Sonargaon was still fresh in men's minds, but it had been a marvellous feat, and Bahadur Khan might well regard it as an event beyond the common that would not soon occur again. The death of the Emperor Alla Uddin and the accession of the dissolute Prince Mubarik Shah occasioned a great weakening of imperial authority, and in the years that followed Bahadur Shah gradually threw off his allegiance and at last boldly proclaimed his independence. Assuming the white umbrella and all the insignia of royalty that an Eastern monarch loves, he ordered the coin to be stamped with his name, and for over a quarter of a century ruled undisturbed in his kingdom of Sonargaon. Of the passing of those years, with all the varied incidents that must have filled them, history and legend have little to relate. They must remain for ever a book that fate has closed.

But again a turn in the wheel of fate, and a strong hand was once more at the helm of imperial affairs. The Emperor Tughlag, hearing complaints from Sonargaon that 'the Emirs and magistrates were exercising great cruelties and injustice towards the inhabitants,' set out to visit the Eastern Province and call Bahadur Khan at last to account for his insubordination and misdeeds. Again an Emperor of Delhi entered Sonargaon, and again the governor went out to meet him and offer his submission. For Bahadur Khan, during his long rule, had not succeeded in winning the fidelity of his army or the devotion of his courtiers, and, deserted by all in the hour of need, he cast himself upon the mercy of the Emperor. He was finally pardoned, but only on resigning all his wealth and offices and attending the Emperor to grace his triumphal return to Delhi. To this humiliation came the first Mussulman Viceroy in Sonargaon who strove for independence.

In his place the Emperor appointed Bhiram Khan, and for fourteen years he ruled, it is said, with singular wisdom and equity. But again the book of the chronicles of the Kings of Bengal is silent. Nothing is recorded of his reign. On his death, in 1338, the first of a long series of palace revolutions disturbed the peace of Sonargaon. It was a scramble for the throne, and the prize went to the strongest. Fakiruddin, who had been armour-bearer to Bhiram Khan, finally triumphed, and not only succeeded in seizing the governorship of the province, but with consummate effrontery declared himself independent of imperial authority, assuming the exalted title of Sultan Sikunder. The usurper, however, was not left long in undisturbed possession. Events moved fast, and it was an exciting drama that was played out in Sonargaon during the two-and-a-half years of Fakiruddin's brief reign. The Emperor, hearing of the violence and disorder that had followed the death of Bhiram Khan, sent orders to Khudder Khan, the Viceroy of Gaur, to proceed with all haste to Sonargaon and bring the usurper to swift justice. In the battle that ensued Fakiruddin was defeated, but refusing to despair he escaped from the field, fleeing into the jungle with a few devoted followers, there to await the turn of events. His chance was not long in coming. Khudder Khan, having taken possession of Sonargaon, at once loyally prepared to send to Delhi the large amount of treasure that he had discovered there. Fakiruddin, fully informed of all that was taking place, learned with dismay of the proposed dispersal of the treasure which he had himself accumulated. With this treasure would depart his last hope of regaining the province, and he conceived a bold design to obtain possession of it. Sending emissaries secretly to Khudder Khan's own troops, he made them promises that if they would kill their leader and assist in restoring to him his kingdom he would distribute the whole of the treasure among them. The soldiers, mercenaries willing to fight for the highest bidder, grew wild with cupidity at this chance of sudden wealth, and having on a fixed day assassinated Khudder Khan they marched to join their new leader, who lay in hiding close by. Fakiruddin at once made a triumphal entry into his capital, and, being still dependent on the troops who had so recently become his allies, he was forced to keep his promise, and all the treasure was distributed among them.

For the moment the triumph of Fakiruddin was complete. Khudder Khan, the Viceroy of Gaur, having been slain, he proudly proclaimed himself king of all Bengal, and, ordering the coin to be stamped with his name, threw defiance at the Emperor's wrath. But his triumph was short-lived. Not content with the kingdom of Sonargaon, his soaring ambition led him to dream of yet greater conquests. But Fakiruddin was no general. He had won his way solely by intrigue and his ready wit. On the field he showed neither generalship nor the power to inspire con-dence in others, and, realising this, he sent his favourite slave, Mukless Khan, in charge of the great expedition that he fitted out to take possession of Gaur. But though Mukless Khan had made a reputation as a leader, his troops proved no match for the army which Ali Mubarik, the new Viceroy of Gaur, led out against him, and he suffered a crushing defeat, himself being slain in the battle. Ali Mubarik, at the Emperor's orders, followed up this success by invading Sonargaon, and Fakiruddin, again defeated, was captured as he fled from the field. In his capital, which had witnessed the many dramatic events of his brief reign, the final curtain was rung down on his meteoric career. He met with a brutal death at the hands of his conqueror, and his body was flung contemptuously out of the gate of the city which he had entered in triumph so short a time before. His career was typical of the rapid turns of the wheel of fate in Mussulman days in Bengal. Starting from the lowest rung in the ladder, he attained, by the most unscrupulous means, to wealth and power. A brief period of prosperity, then another more powerful than he arose, and his place knew him no more.

But Ali Mubarik, the latest conqueror of Sonargaon, enjoyed even a briefer spell of power than Fakiruddin. After a reign of only a year and five months he was assassinated by his own foster-brother, Ilyas Khaji, who immediately took possession of the kingdom. It is strange to read in the old Mussulman chronicles that the perpetrator of this treacherous act was of a mild and generous disposition, 'a man much respected and beloved by the people.' So constantly had fratricide, intrigue, and murder paved the way to empire that they had come to be but lightly regarded as the natural accompaniment of each new king's accession, and thus the memory of Ilyas Khaji, whose reign was inaugurated by the treacherous murder of his foster-brother, remains as that of one of the most just and honourable kings who ever reigned in Sonargaon. Assuming the high title of Shamsuddin, he ruled the whole of Bengal for ten years, undisturbed by any interference from the imperial authority at Delhi. Then again the strong hand gathered together the reins of empire, and strove to bring the outlying provinces back to their obedience.

The Emperor Ferose Shah was not the man to brook lightly the insubordination of rebellious Viceroys. The unchecked ambition of a Viceroy had proved too often the ruin of an empire, and the reports that reached Delhi of the wealth and strength of Shamsuddin roused deep suspicion in the mind of Ferose Shah. Resolving to be first in the field, he set out with a large army to reduce the Eastern Province to submission. On his approach Shamsuddin fell back upon Ekdala on the Banar river, which he deemed the strongest fortress in all Sonargaon. Built by the Pal kings in days gone by, it had been neglected since their disappearance after the Mussulman invasion, but Shamsuddin, recognising that its situation would be well nigh impregnable against attack, hastily restored it and staked his kingdom upon its strength. The ruins of the fort that can still be traced show how admirably it was designed for defence. The river, three hundred yards wide and in some places forty feet deep, itself affords sufficient protection along its front. Here the banks, unlike those of most rivers in India, rise abruptly out of the stream, showing, when the river is low, like a solid wall of masonry that it was well nigh impossible to scale. Like a crescent on the river's bank runs the outer wall of the fort, some two miles in circuit, with a broad moat surrounding it on the further side. Within this outer circle can still be traced the lines of a second defence, the citadel, with walls and bastions. Beyond, the country rises in hilly ridges, intersected by innumerable small ravines, and covered with low shrub jungle. The imperial army soon discovered to its cost the strength of the enemy's position. For twenty-two days the Emperor Ferose Shah invested it without success. Even the small triumph that followed was due to accident. Determining to change his plan of attack, he withdrew his troops to reform his en-

AT ANCHOR FOR THE NIGHT NEAR SONARGAON.

campment at another point. Had the movement been designed as a stratagem to draw the enemy from his entrenchment, it could have met with no greater success. Shamsuddin, mistaking it for a retreat, hastily sallied out to the attack. But the Emperor, though baffled in his attempts to take the fort, was by no means vanquished, and he met the sortie with such vigour that Shamsuddin was forced to seek shelter again ignominiously within the fort, leaving in the hands of his enemies no fewer than forty-four elephants, his umbrella, and all the insignia of royalty.

Re-forming his troops, the Emperor continued the siege. Little is recorded of the days that followed. Only one legend lifts the veil as the armies face one another across the ramparts of the fort, uncertain as yet of the result. In the neighbourhood, it is said, there lived a saint named Raja Biyabani, to whom Shamsuddin was much attached. During the siege the saint died, and Shamsuddin, anxious to pay the last tribute of respect to his friend, disguised himself as a fakir and attended the funeral ceremonies outside the fort. Then, seized with the whim as he returned, he passed on into the enemy's camp and solemnly made his obeisance to the Emperor himself, returning to his fort unrecognised and unmolested.

For many days the imperial troops lay before

the walls of Ekdala, unable to break down its magnificent defence. Already the rivers were rising and the rains were at hand. Soon retreat would be well nigh impossible, and the Emperor had no desire to be caught so far from the imperial city and forced to wait the abating of the rains in the enemy's country. Rather than this he finally acknowledged himself beaten, and, accepting the vague promise of an annual tribute from Shamsuddin, he raised the siege and returned to Delhi. Three years later the Emperor Ferose Shah, distracted by other cares, was reduced to granting to Shamsuddin a definite treaty formally acknowledging the independence of Bengal.

Full of honours, and after a uniformly successful reign of sixteen years, Shamsuddin died in 1358. No sooner did the Emperor Ferose Shah hear of his old enemy's death than he made preparations to restore the imperial authority in Bengal. But in Sekunder Shah, the son of Shamsuddin, he found an enemy no less determined and adroit, and the fort of Ekdala as impregnable as before. Sekunder Shah, on the approach of the imperial forces, following his father's prudent example, shut himself up in this safe retreat, and though Ferose Shah invested it again with a greater army than before, he was forced, after a long and fruitless siege, once more to acknowledge his defeat. Thus twice had the fort of Ekdala baffled and defied the power of the empire. For the second time Ferose Shah withdrew, taking with him a present of forty-eight elephants and a sum of money with which Sekunder Shah regarded the independence of his kingdom as cheaply bought.

Then for a few brief years there was peace. Sekunder Shah, busy with his schemes for rebuilding Pandua, where he had fixed his capital, was content with the independence he had won. But, successful abroad, his last years were clouded by domestic strife. It was the old story of intrigue to secure the succession, of plot and counterplot among the courtiers and the women of the palace. Sekunder Shah had married two wives, by the first of whom he had seventeen children, by the second only one son, Ghyasuddin. But this one son was loved by his father more than all the children of his first wife. The latter, in consequence, regarded Ghyasuddin with hatred and suspicion as the rival of her own sons for the succession. Having obtained the king's ear, she endeavoured to set him against his favourite son, saying that he was plotting not only against her sons, but against his own father's life, and advising the king to avert the mischief he intended, 'either by sending him to prison, or, by depriving the pupils of his eyes of their visual powers, rendering him incapable of effecting his flagitious schemes.' Although Sekunder Shah indignantly rejected this horrible suggestion, Ghyasuddin, afraid of his stepmother's influence, fled to Sonargaon and, collecting an army, openly defied his father. Sekunder Shah, enraged at this ungrateful conduct of his favourite son, set out against him, and the armies came face to face at Goalpara. Ghyasuddin had given strict orders to his troops before the battle that not a hair of his father's head was to be injured, but in the midst of the fight news came to him that Sekunder Shah had been mortally wounded. Hastening to his side, Ghyasuddin wept bitter tears of repentance and implored his father's forgiveness. The dying monarch, raising his hand in blessing, let it fall upon his son's head, murmuring 'My kingdom has passed. May thine arise and live for ever.'

Scarcely had the breath left his father's body when Ghyasuddin, relinquishing the last offices of the dead to others, hastened to Pandua to secure the throne. Arrived there, he perpetrated one of the most revolting deeds that has ever stained the accession even of a king of Bengal. Partly out of revenge for the hostility of his stepmother, partly to rid himself of rivals for the throne, he ordered the eyes of all his stepbrothers to be torn out and sent on a salver to their mother. Yet this same Ghyasuddin, it is recorded, was a mild and just ruler, and legends survive of him that make him a very Solomon for wisdom and judgment. The character of an Oriental is full of contradictions and surprises, yet it is strange to find such a story as the following told of one who could be guilty of such cruelty and injustice towards his own flesh and blood. It is related that one day while practising with the bow he accidentally wounded a boy, the only son of his mother, who was a widow. The woman, ignorant of the king's identity, went and complained to the Kazi, demanding justice. The Kazi, perceiving who it was who had wounded her son, was torn between his desire to do justice and his fear of the king. But, fearing God more than the king, he finally sent a messenger to summon Ghyasuddin to his court. The latter, on receiving the summons, immediately arose and, concealing a short sword beneath his cloak, repaired to the court of the Kazi. There, showing him no especial respect, the Kazi ordered him to compensate the woman for the injury done to her. The king complied, and, giving her a large sum of money, sent her away content. Then, the case being disposed of, the Kazi descended from his seat and prostrated himself at the king's feet. But Ghyasuddin, raising him up, showed him the sword which he carried beneath his cloak, and said: 'Kazi, in obedience to your commands as the expounder of the sacred law, I came instantly at your summons to your tribunal, but if I had found that you deviated in the smallest degree from its ordinances, I swear that with this sword I would have taken off your head.' Then the Kazi, laying his hand upon the scourge which hung in the court, replied: 'I also swear by the Almighty God that if you had not complied with the injunctions of the law, this scourge should have been laid upon your back as upon that of any other criminal.' The king, pleased to find justice so impartially administered in his kingdom, handsomely rewarded the Kazi, and raised him to great honour.

Ghyasuddin was a man of a gay and convivial disposition. He it was who invited the poet Hafiz to visit him at Sonargaon, sending him as a gift some of the exquisite muslins for which his capital was famous; but the poet, although he wrote an ode which is to be found in the 'Diwan,' was not sufficiently tempted to undertake the long journey to Eastern Bengal, far removed from the pleasant delights of Shiraz. Ghyasuddin's favourite wives were poetically named by him the Cypress, the Tulip, and the Rose. Once being near to death, he ordered that, in case of his demise, none but these three should wash his body and prepare it for the last funeral rites. But the king recovered, and the other ladies of the harem had their revenge upon the Cypress, the Tulip, and the Rose for the favour shown them by nicknaming them Ghossalehs, or Washers of the Dead.

The tomb of Ghyasuddin is still to be seen in Sonargaon. On the outskirts of the village of Pannam, it lies sadly ruined and neglected. Yet even in decay it is a striking testimony to Mussulman skill. Of dark grey basalt stone, it is elaborately carved, and the intricate arabesque tracery on the sides and corners of the slabs is as perfect to-day as when it was first executed over five hundred and thirty years ago. The stones lie prone and scattered, the sport of many a storm of wind and rain. Half buried in the earth at their head lies a sandstone pillar, doubtless used as a *cheraghdan*, where a light was kept burning in the days ere yet the memory of this one-time great and famous king of Bengal had faded into the forgotten things of the past.

For almost a century after the death of Ghyasuddin, Sonargaon figures but little in imperial affairs, and of local history there is little that has survived. Deserted as a capital for the more famous cities of Gaur and Pandua, the eastern province passed on its uneventful way under the control of local Mussulman officials. From this comparatively peaceful period dates the oldest inscription in Sonargaon. Facing a modern mosque in the village of Moghrapara is a small graveyard of nameless graves enclosed within plain brick walls. Let into one of the walls is a large black stone, round which for centuries a curious superstition has lingered even down to the present day. Over the stone was placed a thick coating of lime, and if any theft occurred in the neighbourhood all the villagers were summoned before it and, placing their hands upon it, swore their innocence. The belief held that the hand of the thief would stick so tightly to the lime that he would be unable to remove it without great difficulty. The stone is still completely covered with a thick coating of lime, and it was only recently discovered that beneath it is an inscription bearing the name of Jalaluddin Fateh Shah, A.H. 889 (A.D. 1484). There is only one older inscription than this in Eastern Bengal—the inscription, dated one year earlier, in the mosque of Baba Adam near Rampal.

It is not until 1489, a hundred and sixteen years after Ghyasuddin had been laid to rest in Sonargaon, that the chief interest in Bengal once more turns eastwards. Attracted by the fame of the fortress of Ekdala, which had twice so stoutly resisted the attack of the imperial forces, Hossain Shah, on his appointment as Viceroy, fixed his headquarters there. Hossain Shah's career was typical of the possibilities that awaited the adventurer on the outskirts of empire in early Mussulman days. Quitting the deserts of Arabia to seek his fortunes in Hindustan, he was forced at first to accept a subordinate post at the Viceregal Court in Bengal, but being of good birth though an adventurer, he won the daughter of the Kazi of Chandpur in marriage, and by his conspicuous ability rapidly made his way to the front rank. So wisely did he rule as King of Bengal that it is recorded that no insurrection or public disturbance occurred throughout his long reign of twenty-four years. Of Eastern Bengal in his day a brief glimpse is obtained from the pen of a European writer. It was in 1503 that Lewis Vertomannus, a gentleman of Rome, visited Hossain Shah's kingdom when that monarch was waging war against Orissa. The traveller is astonished at the extent of his dominions and the size of his army, which he declares to have consisted of no less than two hundred thousand footmen and cavalry.

Like all Mussulman rulers, Hossain Shah was a great builder. In Sonargaon a mosque still preserves his name. Even amid many things that are old, this mosque is known among the villagers of Goaldi as the Purana Musjid, the Old Mosque. It was a fine building in its day. Sixteen and a half feet square, the four walls as they ascend give place to the eight walls of an octagon. As usual, there are three arched recesses or *mihrabs*, the centre one formed of dark basaltic stone well cut and ornamented with arabesque work, the two side ones of brick, clear cut and cunningly laid. The sandstone pillars are evidently the plunder of some Hindu shrine, forced from their resting-place to grace the triumph of another faith. Until recent years the call to prayer still rang out from this Purana Musjid of Hossain Shah, but time has told at last even upon its massive structure, and its worshippers, after nearly four hundred years, have deserted it for the modern mosque of Abdul Hamid, a hundred yards away, whence at morning and evening the same call to prayer is heard across the plain.

Away in Hindustan great events were pending at the time of Hossain Shah's death. The empire was passing away from the Afghans, who had held it for so many generations, falling beneath the yoke of the all-conquering Moghuls and their great chief Babar. But Babar's career as Emperor was short, and his death in 1531 was the signal for a brief revival of the Afghans. Once more with lightning rapidity the much-tried province changed hands. Sher Shah, the famous Afghan adventurer, defeating the son of Hossain Shah, secured possession of Bengal, and finally, after a nine years' struggle, overcame the Emperor Humayon and established himself upon the throne of Delhi.

Sher Shah, triumphant, was careful to avoid the dangers which had been the ruin of so many of his predecessors. As an independent king in Bengal, he himself had proved a menace to the empire, and his first care was to see that no subject of his acquired sufficient power to follow in his footsteps. Partitioning the whole province of Bengal into minor governorships, he arranged that none should be of such importance as to render an attempt at independence possible. So admirably did this plan succeed that in his day there was peace throughout Bengal, so strange and perfect that it was known as the Peace of Sher Shah. Men slept on the highway at night without fear, wrote the chroniclers of the day, such was the terror that Sher Shah had inspired in evildoers. From Sonargaon he built a road as far as the Indus. a distance of three thousand miles, erecting serais at distances of every twenty miles, and digging a well at the end of every *kos* (two miles). Also along this great highway he erected many mosques, so that those who travelled by it might never be far from the sound of the call to prayer. For the welfare of travellers he planted trees on either side of the road, to give shelter to those that needs must travel in the heat of the day, and fruit-trees to provide them with refreshment by the way. To communicate quickly with all parts of his dominion, horse-posts were established at intervals along the road, so that news might be carried to him quickly, and all rebellion and disturbance quelled at the outset. It was much to accomplish in five short years. 'It was the will of God,' he said in his last days, pathetically fingering his white beard, 'that I should only obtain the empire towards evening. Therefore it behoves me,' he added, rousing himself from vain regrets, 'that I be up and doing before night falls.'

It is during this brief revival of Afghan rule that we get a fresh glimpse of Eastern Bengal from the writings of another European traveller. Cæsar Frederick, a Venetian merchant, touring in this part of India in 1565, mentions with astonishment the cheapness of provisions. In Sundeep he notes that he purchased 'two salted kine for a larine (2*s.* 6*d.*), four hogs for the same price, a fat hen for a penny, and other commodities at a like price.' And yet he naïvely adds that his men said that he paid twice their worth. This abundance and cheapness of provisions seems to have long been characteristic of Eastern Bengal. 'All ages have spoken of Egypt as the best and fruitfullest part of the world,' writes Bernier a hundred years later, 'but as far as I can see by the two voyages I have made to the kingdom of Bengal, I am of opinion that that advantage belongs rather to it than to Egypt.' Hamilton, speaking of Bengal from personal observation at the end of the seventeenth century, writes that 'the plenty and cheapness of provisions are here incredible.' It was a wonderful land, whose richness and abundance neither war, pestilence, nor oppression could destroy.

But, the strong hand of Sher Shah removed, Bengal speedily fell back into the old paths of turbulence and disorder. Sher Shah's successor once more appointed a governor for the whole of Bengal with fatal results. He and his successors quickly proclaimed their independence, and it was not until the days of the great Akbar, in the reign of Daud Khan, that they were finally reduced. With the death of Daud Khan, in 1576, the long line of Afghan rulers in Bengal comes to an end, nearly four hundred years after Bukhtiyar Khiliji had led the first Mahomedan army to the conquest of the province.

The Afghans, however, were not the men tamely to accept defeat. Ousted from Central Bengal, they long continued the struggle for independence in the outlying provinces. Sonargaon, in the furthest east, where imperial authority was proverbially weak, offered them a secure retreat, and there, led by the famous Isha Khan, they long made a determined stand. This chief was the grandson of Kalidas Gozdani, a Hindu, who, it is said, delighted in religious controversies, and having been worsted in argument by a learned Mussulman, acknowledged his defeat and embraced the faith of Islam.

From the outset Isha Khan's career had been full of adventure. In his young days, hearing of the fame of the beauty of Sona Bibi, the widowed daughter of Chand Roy, Zemindar of Vikrampur, he determined in spite of all difficulties to win her for his wife. Besides the difference of religion there was the fact that she was a widow, and remarriage for such was contrary to the tenets of her faith. But Isha Khan, not to be denied, carried her off by force, and, pursued by Chand Roy and her indignant relatives, he held her against all odds in the fort of Kalagachhia, where Lakhiya and Megna meet. Sona Bibi, won by the courage and address of her captor, soon ceased to repine at her lot, and renouncing Hinduism, she embraced her husband's faith, remaining throughout his life a devoted helpmate, and defending his kingdom against his enemies, her own kith and kin, even after his decease.

On the death of Daud Khan, Isha Khan fled

to Chittagong and thence to Jungalbari, near Haibatnugger, in Mymensingh. So large a body of troops had he gathered together that the Raja of Cooch Behar fled at his approach, and Isha Khan fixed his headquarters there, far removed from the seat of the new Moghul government in Bengal. Thence he gradually extended his kingdom, building forts at Dewanbag, Hajigunj, Egarasindu, Sherpur, and Rangamatti, drawing a ring fence round his capital to protect himself on all sides from attack. So powerful did he become that Akbar finally sent his famous Rajput general Man Singh against him. The story of the meeting of Man Singh and Isha Khan reads like a romance. Advancing to the banks of the Lakhiya, Man Singh encamped at Demra, where a large tank named Gangasagar still marks the site of his halting-place, and marching along the river bank drew near Egarasindu fort, strongly situated on the Brahmaputra, where the forces of Isha Khan lay. Outside its walls a great battle took place. All day the armies strove in deadly combat, and when at last it grew towards evening neither side could claim the victory. Then as night fell, to save further bloodshed on the morrow, Isha Khan sent a messenger to call Man Singh to single combat at dawn to decide the issue. The Rajput general accepted the challenge, but when the moment came, he sent his son-in-law in his stead, and Isha Khan, ignorant of the trick that had been played upon him, fought with him and slew him. Then, finding that he had been deceived, he challenged Man Singh again to combat, and this time the Rajput general himself came to do battle with the Afghan. On horseback the combat took place, and after a long struggle the victory lay with Isha Khan. Thereupon, according to the legend, there ensued a dramatic scene. The Afghan, dismounting, hastened to raise the fallen general from the ground, and each silently clasped the other's hand in unspoken admiration of his prowess. Suddenly like a whirlwind from the door of her tent, where she had watched the combat, came the wife of Man Singh. Regardless of convention, she flung herself in the abandonment of her grief at the feet of Isha Khan. If her husband returned defeated, she cried, his head would pay the forfeit, for Akbar knew no mercy to the unsuccessful. Was it the wish of Isha Khan to see her widowed and her children fatherless? With a torrent of words she implored the mercy of the conqueror, and Isha Khan, struck with her beauty and moved by her distress, chivalrously consented to accompany Man Singh to Delhi and throw himself upon the Emperor's clemency. Akbar, knowing him at first only as a rebellious Afghan chief, threw him into prison, but afterwards learning the full story of his courage and generosity, he released him and promoted him to great honour. Giving him the titles of Dewân and Musnad Ali, he appointed him commander-in-chief in Bengal, and gave him twenty-two parganas in the neighbourhood of his old capital. He returned to Jungalbari and, appointing twelve ministers, he assigned them to different portions of the province to carry on the government in his name. Great prosperity is associated with his reign. In his day, it is said, rice sold at four maunds to the rupee, and trade and commerce flourished. His was the strong hand, and during his life the land had rest. After a wise and just rule of many years he died, and was buried at Bukhtarapur, not far from the famous fort at Egarasindu.

His wife, Sona Bibi, survived him, and heroically carried on his great traditions, furnishing almost the sole instance in the history of Sonargaon of a woman publicly taking an active part in political affairs. Isha Khan's death was the signal for his enemies to sweep down upon his kingdom and wreak the vengeance which they had so often before attempted in vain. Kedar Rai, the Raja of Chandpur, with the Raja of Tipperah, sailed up the Megna with a great fleet, confident of success now that the great Afghan chief was gone. But they were soon to find that, though Isha Khan was dead, a valiant defender remained to guard his memory and protect his kingdom. Their own kinswoman, the Afghan's widow, was as vigorous and determined a foe as Isha Khan himself. Entrenched in the fort of Sonakunda on the Lakhiya, she held out stubbornly for many weeks, defying all the forces of her enemies, and at length, when the end drew near, determined that her dead lord's fort should never surrender to his foes, she ordered it to be burned to the ground, and, perishing in its ashes, made of it her funeral pyre. To this day the memory of Sona Bibi is held in honour on the banks of the Lakhiya.

Once again a glimpse is obtained of Sonargaon from without. It was during the time of Isha Khan that Ralph Fitch, an envoy of Queen Elizabeth to the Emperor of China, visited Eastern Bengal. 'The chiefe king of all these countries,' he writes, 'is called Isacan, and he is the chiefe of all the other kings, and is a great friend to all Christians.' The country he describes as extraordinarily fertile, rice and cotton and silk goods being the chief articles of trade. The inhabitants were rich and prosperous. 'The women weare great store of silver hoopes about their neckes and armes, and their legs are ringed with silver, copper, and rings made of elephant's teeth.' Of Sonargaon itself he gives a general description. 'Sinnergan,' he writes, 'is a towne sixe leagues from Serrepore, where there is the best and finest cloth made of cotton in all India. The houses here, as they be in the most part of India, are very litle and covered with strawe, and have a fewe mats round about the walls and the doore to keepe out the Tygers and the Foxes. Many of the people are very rich. Here they will eate no flesh, nor kill no beast: They live of Rice, milke, and fruits. They goe with a little cloth before them, and all the rest of their bodies is naked. Great store of Cotton cloth goeth from hence, and much rice, wherewith they serve all India, Ceylon, Pegu, Malacca, Sumatra, and many other places.'

The fall of Sonakunda was one of the closing scenes in the history of Sonargaon. The Rajas of Chandpur and Tipperah plundered and ravaged far and wide over the whole country to the south, and in their wake came the Mughs, a wild race of pirates and freebooters, whose name soon struck terror among the peaceful cultivators along the banks of all the great rivers of Eastern Bengal. The ancient kingdom of Sonargaon was falling on evil days, and the end drew near. Disorganised and without a leader, the last vestige of unity had vanished, and the land lay an easy prey to the enemies who had so long hovered round its gates. When the Mughs were reinforced by bands of roving Portuguese, expert seamen, who taught their new allies new methods of navigation and attack, they became a menace which the new Moghul government in Bengal could not long overlook, and Islam Khan, quitting Rajmahal, resolved to remove his capital further eastwards, where he might hold them more firmly in check. But Sonargaon, already falling to decay and exposed to the attacks of the Mughs, offered no desirable site, and Islam Khan founded a new capital, more securely situated, across the Lakhiya. On the banks of the Buriganga the great city of Dacca sprang rapidly into being as the capital of all Bengal, and from this time onwards Sonargaon passes out of history almost as completely as if it had never been.

Scattered over the land, hidden in thick patches of jungle or stranded like things forgotten in the open rice-fields, lie the few memorials of the past that still survive. Great tanks and earthworks alone preserve the memory of the Buddhist kings. The outlines of their forts, wherein the ploughshare has long since replaced the sword, and the cultivator tills the fertile soil, mark where the Afghan fought his last fight for independence, while countless mosques and the tombs of holy men witness to

A CARGO BOAT LADEN WITH JUTE LEAVING SONARGAON

ON THE BRAHMAPUTRA NEAR THE TOMB OF THE FIVE PIRS.

the strength of a great and inspiring faith. Everywhere are to be found the rough mounds of earth or *gadis* that mark the resting-places of saints and worthies of a bygone race. In the last days of its greatness, Sonargaon, it is said, swarmed with Pirs and fakirs, religious mendicants, who gathered here from all quarters of India. Of all those whose memory remains, the greatest were the Five Pirs. Who they were, and when they lived and died, has long since been forgotten. That they came from the west is the one vague tradition preserved among those who still worship at their shrines. Only the memory of their sanctity still survives. Unprotected from the storms that sweep the rivers, they lie beneath five mounds of earth raised parallel, a small mosque beside them keeping guard, and rapidly itself falling into decay. Once the Brahmaputra flowed close by them ; but the river, ever fickle in its course, has long since changed its bed, and the sacred water no longer washes by their feet. So sacred are these tombs of the Five Pirs still deemed, that even Hindus make reverence as they pass, while Mahomedans come from great distances to worship at their shrine. Only to two other shrines in Eastern Bengal do Mahomedans make pilgrimages—to the tomb of Shah Ali Sahib at Mirpur, a few miles north-west of Dacca, and to the *durga* of Pir Buda Auliya at Chittagong, the patron saint of all Hindu and Mahomedan boatmen on the great rivers.

In the small market village of Moghrapara, where once the kings of Sonargaon had their capital, is the tomb of Munna Shah Darwesh. At its foot a lamp is still lighted as darkness closes in, and every Mahomedan stops to mutter a prayer as he passes by. Close by is the *durga* of Sheik Muhammad Yasuf, a still more famous Pir. It contains the tombs of himself, his wife and his son, and consists of two elongated dome-roofed buildings, each surmounted by two pinnacles, said to have been once covered with gold, of which all trace has long disappeared. Even the Hindus pay homage at the shrine of Sheik Muhammad Yasuf. If the ryot is in fear for his crop, he brings a handful of rice. If his child is ill, or his cattle a prey to disease, he lays some small propitiatory offering on the tomb. If the harvest has been plenteous, he gives a bundle of rice straight from the field as a thank-offering. In joy or in sorrow the tomb of the Saint plays its appointed part in the inner life of the people.

Close by is a ruined gateway called the Naubat Khana, where in the days of its prosperity musicians played to announce to fakir and traveller that a place of rest was at hand. The music has long since ceased, but until recently the majestic words of the Koran were still heard in the time-worn building near by, where the old men taught the youth of their race the elements of their religion, repeating in unison the resounding phrases of a great faith.

Many other quaint traditions linger in Sonargaon. Suddenly, in the midst of the jungle, grass-grown and neglected, with the water rapidly rising round it, one comes upon the tomb of another Pir. The story is told that Ponkai Diwanah, as he was popularly known, desiring to live a life of righteousness, retired into the forest, where he sat for twelve years absorbed in meditation and unconscious of the lapse of time. When at last he was found by his *Chelas*, who had long sought for him, he had to be dug out of the mound which the white ants had raised all round him as he sat and which covered him up to his neck. This legend must have sprung up in comparatively recent years, since men still living say that they knew the son of this famous Pir. Father and son lie buried side by side, and at the head of the former is placed the stone lattice on which he spent his twelve years of meditation.

A short distance away, across the fields, there lies the tomb of Pagla Saheb (Madman), so much venerated by both Hindus and Mahomedans that parents offer at it the 'choti' or queue of their children when dangerously ill. Why Pagla Saheb was deemed mad one asks in vain. Some say that he went mad from the fervour and intensity of his devotions. Another tradition has it that he vowed vengeance on all thieves, and catching all whom he could, he nailed them to a wall and himself cut off their heads. Then, stringing the heads together like a necklace, he threw them into an adjoining *khal*, which has ever since been known as Munda Mala—the Necklace of Heads.

Little else, save legends such as these, has survived the passing of the years in Sonargaon. Its records are few and scanty and its long and varied history, mostly unrecorded, was soon forgotten as the centre of interest passed westwards to the new city rising on the banks of the Buriganga. Deserted and forgotten, it passed out of the realm of history, and none cared to record the annals of a kingdom whose day was done. So Sonargaon slept unminded, and itself unmindful of its past.

CHAPTER IV

THE RISE OF DACCA

'He had grown up with me from youth and was one year my junior,' wrote the Emperor Jehangir of Islam Khan. 'He was a brave man, of most excellent disposition, and in every respect distinguished above his tribe and family. Up to this day he has never tasted any stimulants, and his fidelity to me was such that I honoured him with the title of Farzand (*son*).' Such in his master's eyes was the Founder of Dacca, the new Capital of all Bengal.

It was no easy task that awaited Islam Khan on his appointment to the Viceroyalty of Bengal in 1608. The province, torn by the long struggle between Afghan and Moghul, lay exhausted and disorganised. Such cohesion as it had known under its independent kings was gone. Petty chiefs, freed from immediate control, gave full vent to their inherent love of lawlessness and independence. The Afghans, defeated again and again, yet clung stubbornly to their last footing on the outskirts of the province. Established in Orissa and the furthest limits of Eastern Bengal they were a constant menace to the empire. Not even the strategy of Raja Todermal or the brilliant generalship of Man Singh had altogether succeeded in completing the conquest that had been so brilliantly begun. Only the timely death of the great Afghan chief Kutlu Khan in Orissa had at length freed the recently established Moghul power from a danger that at one time threatened its extinction in Bengal. But Osman Khan, the son of the great chief, still lived, a source of much anxiety to Islam Khan in after days. Petty Afghan chiefs, driven back on Eastern Bengal, still held the forts of Gonakpara, Gauripara, and Dumroy on the Bunsi river, finding in the Bhowal jungles a secure and safe retreat. The whole of the ancient kingdom of Sonargaon lay practically at their mercy, Moghul authority never as yet having been fully imposed upon it. Islam Khan, seeing on his accession that Central Bengal had settled down peacefully under the new rule, resolved to take up his headquarters in the midst of Eastern Bengal, which so urgently required the grip of a strong hand.

But there was yet another and more urgent reason that induced Islam Khan to move his capital eastwards. A new danger had arisen in Eastern Bengal, threatening to lay waste its fertile rice-fields and drive its peaceful inhabitants in terror from their lands. Taking advantage of the general confusion and the weakness of the central government, consequent on the struggle between Afghan and Moghul, the Mughs had boldly sailed up the great rivers and robbed and plundered in every direction unchecked. A wild, turbulent people, pirates and adventurers by nature and profession, they swarmed up from their homes in Chittagong and Arracan as news spread of the plunder to be obtained from this rich and unprotected land. Along the river-banks they swept like locusts, leaving desolation in their wake. Of mercy and honour they knew nothing, and every form of cruelty and oppression was practised upon the unfortunate inhabitants of Eastern Bengal who fell within their reach. Buddhists by religion, they had fallen far from the high ideals of that great faith. A chronicler of the time quaintly records the Emperor Jehangir's impression of them when some prisoners of their race were produced before him. Their customs, it seems, appeared to his Majesty 'very reprehensible,' as he was informed 'that they ate animals of every kind, married their half-sisters, and that their religion was of the greatest idolatry.'

Torn by dissensions from within and ravaged by the Mughs from without, Eastern Bengal presented a happy hunting-ground to yet other adventurers who had lately appeared upon the scene. The century that had just closed had seen the Portuguese at the height of their fame. Bold seamen and skilful navigators, they had eagerly pressed forward at the head of the nations of the West in the search for new lands beyond the sea. As early as 1517 a little company of four ships, flying the Portuguese flag, had sailed up the Bay of Bengal and entered the Ganges, first in the field here, as in the new world in the West. Twenty years later the unfortunate Mahomed Shah, pressed by the Afghan in his capital of Gaur, had sent an urgent appeal for help to Nuno de Cuna, the Governor-General of the Portuguese settlements in India. In response a squadron of nine ships had set sail from Goa, but the journey was long, and they arrived only after the surrender of the city. The Portuguese, however, had made the first armed entry of a European force into Bengal, and they were not the men to let slip an advantage that offered them so much. Here was a land of promise, rich and unexplored. A people of the sea, the great rivers of Eastern Bengal made to them special appeal, giving as they did full scope to their love of navigation and all that appertained to ships and shipping. Many of them had already settled in Chittagong and Arracan, and a small company sailing up the Megna established themselves at Serripore, only twenty miles south of Sonargaon itself.

They were a strange crew, from all accounts, these first Portuguese adventurers in Bengal. François Bernier, the celebrated French traveller, writing of them in the seventeenth century, speaks of them as men who had been forced to flee from the older and more law-abiding Portuguese settlements to the south. 'They were such as had abandoned their monasteries, men that had been twice or thrice married, murtherers.' They were a desperate, buccaneering crew, ready for any adventure, and rivalling in recklessness and daring the wildest heroes of romance. 'Such as had deserved the rope were most welcome and most esteemed there.' It needs no great stretch of imagination to believe that the life they led, unchecked by any of the restraints of civilisation, was 'very detestable and altogether unworthy of Christians, insomuch that they impunely butchered and poisoned one another, and assassinated their own priests, who sometimes were not better than themselves.' Bernier's description of them is delightfully graphic and realistic. 'Their ordinary trade was robbery and piracy,' he continues. 'With some small and light gallies they did nothing but coast about the sea, and entering into all rivers thereabout, and often penetrating even so far as forty or fifty leagues up country, surprised and carried away whole towns, assemblies, markets, feasts, and weddings of the poor Gentiles, and others of that country, making women slaves, great and small, with strange cruelty; and burning all they could not carry away. This great number of slaves, which thus they took from all quarters, behold what use they made of. They had boldness and impudence enough to come and sell to that very country the old people which they knew not what to do with; where it so fell out, that those who had escaped the danger by flight and by hiding themselves in the woods, laboured to redeem to-day their fathers and mothers that had been taken yesterday.'

It was not surprising that the King of Arracan at first looked upon these turbulent adventurers with suspicion and distrust. In fact, so great a source of danger had they become that at the beginning of the seventeenth century he determined to extirpate them from his dominions. But his plans miscarried, and many of them, escaping from Chittagong, made their home on the islands at the mouth of the Ganges, where they continued their acts of piracy undisturbed. The year before Islam Khan was appointed Viceroy, Futteh Khan, the local Moghul governor of that country, had at length attempted to suppress them; but, miscalculating their strength, he had suffered a complete defeat, he himself, with the greater part of his troops, having been killed, and his fleet annihilated.

Such was the position of affairs that confronted Islam Khan on his appointment as Viceroy in 1608. In order to cope with the danger that beset Eastern Bengal, he at once resolved to take up his headquarters there, at the very centre of the scene of disturbance. Quitting his capital of Rajmahal, with all his court, he set sail for the eastern province, and the Afghans evacuating their fort of Gonakpara, on the Bunsi, at his approach, he halted there with the intention, it is said, of making it his capital. But finding the land too low-lying, and the Bunsi river prone to overflow its banks, he quitted it and moved on down the Dullasery and Buriganga, in search of a more convenient site. Arriving opposite the spot where Dacca now stands, Islam Khan was struck with its strategical position and the facilities offered by the wide stretch of high ground that lay beyond it, and at once determined to build his capital there.

What Islam Khan found on the site of his future capital at his first arrival is a matter of considerable uncertainty. So shrouded in doubt is its previous history that it is almost impossible to state with any definiteness whether a town of considerable importance or merely a collection of insignificant villages was formerly in existence there. Several attempts have been made to identify this site with the city mentioned by European travellers and in Mussulman chronicles as Bengalla. Tradition says that in pre-Moghul days there existed here fifty-two bazaars and fifty-three streets, and the town, from this circumstance, acquired the somewhat unwieldy name of 'Bauno Bazaar and Teppun Gulli.' One of these fifty-two bazaars, known as Bengalla, is said to have been the most important of them all, and its fame as a centre of trade was well known throughout the neighbouring district. It is possible that, from the importance of this bazaar, its name was accepted by travellers in place of the more cumbrous one of 'Bauno Bazaar and Teppun Gulli.' The identification of Bengalla with Dacca is strengthened by the fact that no traveller or chronicler ever mentions them both. The traveller Methold, in the sixteenth century, speaks of Rajmahal and Bengalla as fine cities, making no mention of Dacca. Mandelslo, who visited Bengal about the same time, mentions Dacca, Rajmahal, and Satgaon in his book, but in his map he has written Bengalla making no mention of Dacca. If Bengalla is not to be identified with Dacca, its site remains a mystery. Had it met the fate of Serripore, and completely disappeared from sight, washed away by the river, it would assuredly have left some tradition in the neighbourhood where it once stood. But none such remains.

How Dacca acquired its name is almost as great a mystery, and the endeavour to explain it has been fertile in many inventions. One story is that it derives its name from ancient pre-Mussulman times, when Ballal Sen, having found the image of the goddess Durga concealed in the jungle, raised a temple to the 'Hidden Goddess,' the Dhaka Iswari, by which name the city that gradually sprang up round it came to be known. Another story is that the town takes its name from the dhak tree (*Butea frondosa*), which is said in ancient times to have covered the whole of the river-bank where the town now stands. Yet another tradition associates the name with 'dhak,' the Bengali term for a drum. The story runs that when Islam Khan first landed to inspect the site which he had chosen for his new capital, he found a party of Hindus performing one of their ceremonies to the accompaniment of drums and music. Struck by the noise of the drums, a whim seized him, and he ordered the musicians to stand on the river-bank and beat their loudest. Then, sending out three of his attendants, he ordered them to proceed two in either direction along the river-bank, and one inland as far as they could within sound of the drums. Where the sound ceased, they were ordered to place flagstaffs, and here Islam Khan erected boundary pillars, and fixed the limits of his capital.

It seems probable, however, that the name Dacca was in use before the time of Islam Khan, as that of one of the numerous local bazaars that went to form the town. In tracing the history of Indian towns it is repeatedly found that, owing their origin to a collection of small villages which gradually expanded and united, they eventually took their name from the largest of these villages, or from some famous shrine or temple in their midst. The villages themselves often retain their own individual names long after they have become known collectively under a common appellation. Dacca itself to-day is a striking example of this retention of local names still used to distinguish the different quarters of the town. It is probable that the fame of the Dhakeswari temple, or the fact that Islam Khan first resided in that quarter, accounts for its having given its name to the new capital. Islam Khan, in compliment to the Emperor, gave the city the official name of Jehangirnagar, by which name it is generally known in Mussulman annals.

Established in his new capital, Islam Khan at once set himself to check the incursions of the

Mughs and Portuguese. A new and entirely unexpected change had recently taken place in the relations of these two peoples, threatening a still greater danger to Eastern Bengal. From the deadliest of enemies they had suddenly become allies, intent on driving the Moghul out of his newly acquired province. Elated with their victory over the local Moghul governor, the Portuguese had elected a chief from among themselves, a common sailor named Sebastian Gonzalez, and under his leadership they seized the island of Sundeep, with the intention of making it the headquarters of a permanent settlement in Bengal. The adventures of Sebastian Gonzalez read like a mediæval romance. A bold adventurer, of limitless ambition, unscrupulous, roistering, always spoiling for a fight, he yet possessed many of the qualities of a born leader of men. Putting a thousand Mahomedans to the sword, he established himself in Sundeep, wringing a servile recognition from the terrified Hindu population. Thither, drawn by the fame of his exploits, came adventurers of every sort from all directions, until Gonzalez numbered among his adherents no less than a thousand Portuguese, two thousand Indian soldiers, two hundred cavalry, and eighty sail, well mounted with cannon.

It was towards this force that the Raja of

Arracan turned envious eyes. Always closely watching the fortunes of the Mussulman Empire, which had for so long loomed, a powerful and dangerous neighbour, on the border of his kingdom, he saw in the accession of the Moghul conquerors, and the removal of the capital of Bengal to the easternmost limits of the province, a new menace to his independence. Desiring to strike while the new capital was still in its infancy, and while Islam Khan was engaged in a last struggle with the Afghan in Orissa, the Raja of Arracan looked upon the Portuguese in a new light. With their skill as seamen they would be the most desirable of allies against the Moghul, and the Raja, sending messengers to Sundeep, quickly concluded a peace with Gonzalez and solicited his help. The terms of an alliance being agreed upon, it was arranged that the Portuguese should sail up the river while the Arracanese marched by land, and, forming a junction below Dacca, should make a combined attack upon the capital. Victorious, they would proceed to divide Bengal between them. But they had to reckon with Islam Khan. Learning their plans, he sent out a large body of cavalry, which caught the Mughs before their junction with the Portuguese and defeated them with great slaughter. Gonzalez, having no desire to measure forces with the Moghul viceroy unaided, withdrew to Sundeep. Mutual recriminations ensued between the allies, and for a time Eastern Bengal had rest from their designs.

After a rule of only five years, Islam Khan died at Dacca in 1613. But before his death he had had the satisfaction of seeing his labours everywhere crowned with success. By his efforts the invasion of the Mughs and Portuguese had been repelled, and his armies had robbed the Afghans of their last semblance of power in Bengal and Orissa. The year before his death he had seen his victorious general, Shujat Khan, make the first triumphant entry into his new capital, bearing in his train the son and brother of Osman Khan, the Afghan, with a crowd of elephants and a howdah full of jewels as the spoils of war. So, in peace and honour, passed Islam Khan, the first Viceroy of Dacca.

As a mark of the esteem in which he held Islam Khan, the Emperor appointed his brother, Cassim Khan, to succeed him as Governor of Bengal. But the new Viceroy had little of his brother's ability, and after five years, during which the chief interest centred in the renewed activity of the Mughs and Portuguese, he was recalled from office. Between the Raja of Arracan and Sebastian Gonzalez a bitter feud had soon succeeded their brief alliance, and during the whole of Cassim Khan's reign they had made common cause only in their hostility to the constituted Moghul authority in Bengal. After many years of extraordinary success, Gonzalez's adventurous career at last came to an end. Failing in an attack on Chittagong, he was forced to fall back on the island of Sundeep, and being pursued there by the Arracanese, he was overwhelmed by numbers, and finally defeated and slain. The Mughs, once more victorious, established themselves in Sundeep, and again had leisure to renew their incursions into Eastern Bengal.

In the third Viceroy, Ibrahim Khan, the strong hand was once more apparent in Dacca. Though he owed his position at Court to the fact that he was the brother-in-law of the Empress Nur Jehan, he had already earned for himself the title of Victorious in War. For four years, under the strong rule of Ibrahim Khan, Eastern Bengal had rest. Trade and commerce revived, and agriculture, encouraged by the cessation of war, was greatly extended. The weaving of muslins, for which this part of the country had long been famous, now, under imperial patronage, received fresh stimulus. At the Moghul court the Empress, Nur Jehan, intent on enhancing her loveliness in Jehangir's eyes, was introducing many new fashions in adornment, and all the finest products of the weavers were bespoken in Dacca and despatched to Delhi. It was the dawn of the brief period of Dacca's greatest industrial and commercial prosperity and success.

But the years of peace were few, and again the shadow of imperial affairs fell darkly upon the Province of Bengal. Nur Jehan, who bore no son to Jehangir, was intriguing to secure the throne for Shariar, the Emperor's fourth son, whom she had married to her own daughter by her first husband, Sher Afgan. But Shah Jehan, the Emperor's third son, seeing his father's health decline, determined to make sure his own succession, and, openly taking up arms, marched with his army upon Delhi. Jehangir, however, ill though he was, would brook no rival while he lived. Rising from his sick bed in anger at his son's unfilial conduct, he advanced to meet him at the head of all his troops. Defeated, Shah Jehan fell back upon the Deccan, and there resolved to seize the government of Bengal, considering it the most favourable province whence he might later make good his claim upon the Empire. The Viceroy Ibrahim Khan, loyal to his master, hastened from Dacca to meet his master's rebellious son, but he was defeated and slain in the famous Teliagharia Pass, the Gateway of Bengal. Shah Jehan rapidly pursued the advantage he had gained, and made good his hold on Bengal. Collecting all the boats that were available in the neighbourhood, he hastened down the river, with all the pomp and circumstance that he could muster, towards Dacca. Arrived there, he found the gates thrown open to receive him. Ibrahim Khan's nephew, who had been left in charge of the city, finding himself powerless to oppose his entry, came out to meet him, and delivered to him all the elephants and state property of his late uncle, together with forty lacs of treasure from the Government treasury.

From the first, Shah Jehan looked upon Dacca and Bengal only as stepping-stones to greater things, and his stay in the eastern capital was brief. Again the gates of the city were thrown wide, and a splendid cavalcade rode forth as Shah Jehan set out on his way to make his second bid for empire. Darab, son of Khani Khanan, Chief of the Nobility, his favourite courtier, was left as governor of Bengal, but Shah Jehan had learned to trust not even his dearest friend, and he carried Darab's son with him in his train, half honoured guest, half hostage. Shah Jehan's march, begun with so much pomp, continued for a time in triumph. The governor of Patna fled at his approach and the city opened its gates. Daunted by his success, the governor of Rhotas gave up to him the keys of that magnificent fortress. But defeat soon followed at the hands of the imperial army, and Shah Jehan barely escaped with his life back to Rhotas, where he had left his family in safe retreat. Thence he sent urgent messages to Darab Khan in Dacca to advance to his help with what force he could. Darab Khan, however, proved a broken reed. In spite of the fact that his son was in the hands of Shah Jehan, he treacherously betrayed his master when his fortunes seemed to be on the wane, and falsely sent word that the zemindars and people all round Dacca had risen in arms, and prevented him leaving the city. His son paid the penalty of his father's perfidy in Rhotas when the news came. But vengeance speedily overtook Darab Khan, and when he surrendered to the victorious army of the Emperor, expecting to be met with honour, he met instead the fate that he deserved, and his head was sent to Delhi, that all men might see the end of traitors.

On Shah Jehan's flight from Bengal, his father, Jehangir, appointed Khanazad Khan to be governor. But his rule was short, and nothing noteworthy is recorded of him, save the fact that he remitted to Delhi no less than twenty-two lacs of rupees in specie, being the surplus revenue of the province. That it was possible for such a sum to be remitted when Dacca had recently been occupied by a rebel army speaks much for the wealth of Bengal. Then followed Mukurrum Khan, who ruled for only six months. His reign, though brief, was one of great magnificence and splendour. Never before had such pageants been seen upon the river as those arranged by Mukurrum Khan. He is reported to have been passionately devoted to aquatic sports and pageants of every kind, and the city by night, illuminated along the bank and on the river, with hundreds of boats of every description, made a veritable fairy scene. It was an ill fate that this man, who so loved the river, should perish by it. He had been Viceroy for scarce six months when, hearing that a firman conferring fresh favours upon him was on its way from the Emperor, he organised a great procession of boats upon the river to go out to meet it with every token of honour and respect. All day they sailed up the river, the state barges a gorgeous sight in gala dress, and the white sails of the escort fleet gleaming in the sun. It grew to evening, and the messenger tarried on the way. At the hour of prayer, when the muezzin's voice rang out across the stillness of the water, the Viceroy gave orders for the fleet to put ashore. The state boat that he had chosen for himself was long and narrow, a swift-going boat usually propelled by oars, but upon which a sail had been hoisted. A strong current was running, and in endeavouring to turn towards the bank the boat capsized in a sudden squall of wind, and the Viceroy and several of his courtiers who were in the state-room, unable to escape, perished miserably in sight of the whole fleet.

Then for a year Fedai Khan ruled as Viceroy, but on the Emperor Jehangir's death, Shah Jehan, who some time before had made his peace with his father, appointed Kassim Khan, a favourite of his own, to the coveted viceroyalty. Kassim Khan was a zealous Mussulman, and the worship of the Christians seems to have excited the same repugnance in him that it had in Mumtaz Mahal, the beautiful wife of Shah Jehan, when a few years previously she had lived in Bengal. Evil days were at hand for the Portuguese, who, since their first settlement at Hooghly in the Bay in 1575, had flourished there and prospered. Here were the better class of traders, having but little in common with the pirates of their name and race who, in alliance with the Mughs, had so harassed the Moghul governors. At Hooghly they had established themselves with every hope of permanence, building a church and a ring of forts that might place them in a strong position of defence. But Kassim Khan viewed their increasing strength with suspicion and alarm. He complained, with some justification, that they had arrogated to themselves sovereign rights and levied tolls from all the boats that passed down the river, administering their own rough justice upon the neighbouring people, and committing many acts of violence upon the Emperor's subjects. They had already drawn all trade away from the royal port of Satgaon. Dark stories, besides, were whispered of their doings. It was said they had kidnapped Mussulman children and sent them away to Goa to be educated in the Christian faith, and daily within the handsome church that they had raised in their midst the mystic service of the Catholic Church created wonder and alarm. The images that decorated the interior seemed, to zealous Mussulmans like Mumtaz Mahal and Kassim Khan, sure signs of the idolatry of the worshippers.

When the report of their doings reached the imperial court, the Portuguese could expect little sympathy from Shah Jehan. A few years before, when his fortunes were at their lowest, he had appealed to Michael Rodriguez, the Portuguese governor of Hooghly, for help, and it had been denied him in no courteous terms. Shah Jehan, remembering these things, and with his empress at his side urging him to exterminate the idolaters, sent an order to Dacca that the Portuguese should be driven from Bengal.

Accordingly, in 1631, a great expedition set sail from Dacca to carry out the Emperor's commands. Kassim Khan planned the campaign with consummate skill. Three armies concentrated upon the doomed city, closing it in on every side, and for three and a half months Hooghly knew all the horrors of a siege. Day after day the defenders held out, hoping for the help from Goa that never reached them. Finally, the besiegers blew up the largest bastion of the fort, and the end came. A thousand of the Portuguese were killed, and over four thousand taken prisoners, many of whom were sent in chains to Agra. So complete was their defeat that out of sixty-four large vessels, fifty-seven 'grabs,' and two hundred sloops which had been anchored opposite the town, only one 'grab' and two sloops escaped. The church and all the symbols of their religion were ruthlessly destroyed. Kassim Khan rapidly rebuilt the fort and city, establishing it as the royal Fort of Bengal. But it was only a few months that he survived his triumph. That same year he died in Dacca, his death foretold, as the superstitious remembered, by a Portuguese priest who was slain at the altar of his church in the sack of Hooghly.

It was by a strange turn of events that only two years later, while Azim Khan ruled at Dacca, the English received their first permission to trade in Bengal. The firman granted by Shah Jehan is dated February 2, 1634; but as the Moghul Government had seen the unwisdom of allowing foreign traders to sail up the Ganges and establish themselves on its banks as the Portuguese had done, the English vessels were only allowed to enter the port of Pipli in Balasore, and it was there that they established their first factory in Bengal. It was perhaps as much due to Azim Khan's indifferent and negligent disposition as to any other cause that the English obtained their first firman. Azim Khan, content with the pleasures of life at Dacca, felt no call to military glory or to fame as a ruler, and so lax was his rule that the Mughs and Assamese, quickly aware of the governor's weakness, once more sailed up the rivers and resumed their old piratic depredations.

Azim Khan was soon recalled; but the fact that his daughter, destined in after days to meet with so tragic a fate, was married to Prince Shuja, the Emperor's son, caused his weakness to be overlooked, and he was soon afterwards appointed to the less onerous post of governor of Allahabad.

Islam Khan, his successor, was a man of different stamp. An old and experienced statesman and soldier, he was eminently fitted to cope with the difficulties that beset the easternmost province of the empire. Scarcely had he made his state entry into Dacca than there sailed up the river a fleet of Mugh ships, the first that ever came this way on a voyage of peace. Makat Rai, the governor of Chittagong, having quarrelled with the King of Arracan, came to seek the protection of the Moghul governor. He was received in audience by Islam Khan in his palace by the river at Dacca, and there acknowledged himself a vassal of the empire. The name of Chittagong, out of compliment to the Viceroy, was changed to Islamabad. But Islam Khan was too much occupied elsewhere to press his advantage in this direction, and it was not till twenty-eight years later, under the greatest of Viceroys, Shaista Khan, that the sovereignty of the Moghul became more than a name.

This same year there came another fleet almost within sight of Dacca—this time on no peaceful errand intent. The Assamese, ever ready to take advantage of weakness at the Moghul court, and encouraged by the supineness of the late governor, had collected a huge fleet of five hundred boats to plunder and lay waste the fertile fields of Bengal, and make a dash for the eastern capital. For miles on either side of the Brahmaputra, as they advanced, they burned and looted the towns and villages, and the inhabitants, deserting their homes, fled in terror into the jungles to escape this new foe. But Islam Khan, hastily setting out from

Dacca, turned his cannon upon them from the river-bank, and wrought havoc in the Assamese fleet. Many of their ships were set on fire, and the crews, forced to seek the shore, were mowed down by the Moghul cavalry. The wild, untrained levies of the 'barbarian' were no match for the disciplined troops of the Moghul empire. Pursuing the ships that escaped into Assam, Islam Khan subdued the whole of Cooch Behar, and took possession of many of the frontier forts; but, baffled as all the previous invaders of Assam had been by lack of provisions and the difficulty of transport, he was forced on the approach of the rains to return to Dacca. There he found an order summoning him to court, to take up the office of vizier, and the Emperor's second son, the ill-fated Sultan Shuja, was appointed to the viceroyalty of Bengal in his place.

For some reason not recorded, Sultan Shuja transferred the capital from Dacca to Rajmahal, where he built for himself a magnificent palace, and lived in luxury such as Eastern Bengal had not previously beheld.

But Dacca, deserted for a time, was a few years later to prove an asylum to the very man who had deserted it. The Emperor Shah Jehan was growing old, and once more a struggle for the throne was about to disturb the peace of the empire from end to end. Shah Jehan in his day had rebelled against his father; it was but the nemesis of fate that his sons should rebel against him in after-days. Sultan Shuja, relying on his possession of Bengal, was the first to take the field, but his younger brother, Aurungzebe, had already forestalled him at Delhi. Seizing his father's person and proclaiming himself Emperor, he advanced at the head of the imperial forces against Sultan Shuja as against a rebel, and inflicted upon him an overwhelming defeat. Shah Shuja was no fit match for Aurungzebe in generalship, and he was forced to fall back upon Tondah, the fortifications of which he hastily repaired. Defeated a second time, he made his escape, accompanied by his family, on swift rowing-boats, setting out on the long journey for the city which he had at first disdained as his capital. It was a humiliating entry into Dacca, such as no Viceroy had yet made. There were no signs of welcome. Even the honours due to a prince of the empire were omitted, for the city had no warning of the fugitives' coming, and as Shah Shuja and his few faithful friends landed from their country-boats at the river ghat, only a great crowd of people, hastily gathering, watched them silent and open-mouthed. Defeat was stamped plain upon the faces of Sultan Shuja and all his party.

Among the small band of faithful courtiers who followed the drooping fortunes of Shah Shuja was Mahomed, Aurungzebe's son. This youth had become Sultan Shuja's son-in-law under the most romantic circumstances, while the war raged round Tondah. Before Shah Shuja and Aurungzebe took the field as rivals for their father's throne, the latter's son, Mahomed, had been betrothed to Shah Shuja's daughter, the fame of whose beauty was said to rival even that of her grandmother, the famous Mumtaz Mahal. In the heat of the contest all talk of the marriage had naturally ceased, and Mahomed, at his father's order, had accompanied the army which he despatched under Mir Jumla against Shah Shuja. At Tondah, while the armies lay encamped over against each other waiting until the rainy season had passed to resume hostilities, the daughter of Sultan Shuja, moved by her father's misfortunes, wrote a touching appeal with her own hand to the man to whom she had once been betrothed, and who now, by a turn in the wheel of fate, had become her father's enemy. She lamented this state of things in such pathetic terms that Mahomed, touched by the appeal, chivalrously resolved to relinquish all that his position as his father's son might promise in order to go to her assistance. Secretly by night he crossed the river that lay between the two camps, hoping that a large portion of his army would follow at dawn. On the bank Shah Shuja, warned of his coming, received him with open arms, but the advantage that he hoped to gain from his accession to his ranks was not fulfilled. Through Mir Jumla's prompt action, Mahomed's troops did not follow him into the hostile camp. Yet, in spite of this, Aurungzebe's son, even though he came alone, was no mean ally, and in Tondah the rejoicings were great, the marriage being celebrated with all the splendour that the besieged city could afford.

Fleeing with Shah Shuja after his defeat, the newly married couple took up their abode with him in Dacca. But Aurungzebe, furious at the conduct of his son, was not above resorting to artifice to withdraw so powerful an adherent from Shuja's camp. Writing a letter addressed to his son, he sent it by a trusty messenger with instructions that he should allow himself, as if by accident, to fall into the hands of Shuja's spies, and permit the letter, after a show of resistance, to be taken from him. The letter ran as follows:—

'To our beloved son Mahomed, whose happiness and safety are joined with our life. It was with regret and sorrow that we parted with our son when his valour became necessary to carry on the war against Shuja. We hoped, from the love we bear to our firstborn, to be gratified soon with his return, and that he would have brought the enemy captive to our presence in the space of a month to relieve our mind from anxiety and fear. But seven months passed away without the completion of the wishes of Aurungzebe. Instead of adhering to your duty, Mahomed, you betrayed your father and threw a blot on your own fame. The smiles of a woman have overcome filial piety. Honour is forgotten in the brightness of her beauty, and he who was destined to rule the empire of the Moghuls has himself become a slave. But as Mahomed seems to repent of his folly, we forget his crimes. He has invoked the name of God to vouch for his sincerity, and our parental affection returns; he has already our forgiveness, but the execution of what he proposes is the only means to regain our favour.'

This letter, falling into the hands of Shuja as Aurungzebe had designed, was not calculated to increase the confidence between the prince and his son-in-law. Privately, Shuja sent for Mahomed and showed him the letter, but all Mahomed's protestations failed to eradicate the suspicion that it had aroused in his father-in-law's mind. Shuja, attracted at the outset by Mahomed's chivalrous conduct, had since come to love him as his own son, and the very possibility of his treachery grieved him to the heart. Finally, calling together his council in the hall of audience in his palace by the river, he told Mahomed that it was impossible that the same love and trust could ever again exist between them, and with singular magnanimity in that age of violence he asked him to depart with his wife, and all the wealth and jewels that he had bestowed upon them. 'The treasures of Shuja are open,' he said, generous even in his grief and the mistrust that he could not conquer; 'take therefrom what pleases thee. Go, lest him whom I have regarded as a son I must perforce count henceforward among my enemies.'

Bursting into tears and protesting his innocence, Mahomed cried out that he was willing to swear even by the holy temple of Mecca. But Sultan Shuja was firm, and Mahomed and his wife set out from Dacca in one of the Viceroy's state boats, Sultan Shuja himself accompanying them to the landing-stage and bidding them farewell with every mark of honour. There were few princes of that day who would have allowed thus honourably to depart from their court one on whom the suspicion of treachery had fallen. It was this nobility and generosity of disposition that secured for Sultan Shuja his many friends, a faithful little company of whom followed him even to the end of his chequered and unfortunate career.

It was not long before Mir Jumla, having settled affairs in Western Bengal, set out in pursuit of Sultan Shuja to Dacca. The latter, hearing of the great army that accompanied the imperial general, recognised that he could not hope to hold out against it. He had withdrawn the troops and the greater part of the fleet from Dacca when he placed his capital at Rajmahal, and the city was ill calculated to stand a siege. With all the members of his family, and the wealth that still remained to him, mounted on elephants and escorted by a small body of cavalry, he left Dacca by the eastern gate, a fugitive as he had entered but a few months before. Crossing the river, he plunged into the wild hill country of Tipperah, hastening on towards the miserable fate that, after many adventures, awaited him at the hands of the Arracanese.

The English Company, which had begun its struggle for existence in Orissa six years before his accession, met with little opposition from Sultan Shuja. In 1633 a small band of Englishmen, sailing up the Bay, had established factories at Hariharpur and Balasore, and eighteen years later, by the favour of the Viceroy, they were allowed to settle at Hooghly, pushing their out-factories as far inland as Patna, Cossimbazaar, and Rajmahal. To account for the unusual favour shown to the English by Sultan Shuja, a story is told of a ship's doctor and a princess quite in the typical style of Indian romance. Jahan Ara, the sister of Sultan Shuja, and the eldest and best-beloved daughter of Shah Jehan and the beautiful Empress Mumtaz Mahal, while passing closely veiled along one of the corridors of the palace, by accident brushed against a lamp which stood there. Her light silken sari at once caught fire, but as 'her modesty, being within hearing of men, would not permit her to call for assistance,' she fled to her own apartments, and thus fanning the flames, was so severely burned that her life was despaired of. The Emperor, distracted at the misfortune which had befallen his favourite daughter, sent an urgent message to Surat, asking the English Company to send a surgeon to attend her. The Council at Surat, in reply, despatched Mr. Gabriel Broughton, a ship's doctor, who was fortunate enough to cure the princess of her hurt. In consequence of this, Mr. Broughton was naturally in high favour at the imperial court, and a certain measure of the favour with which he was regarded fell upon his fellow-countrymen. For some time Mr. Broughton stayed with Sultan Shah Shuja in his capital of Rajmahal, and it may have been partly due to his influence that the English Company obtained its first authoritative *nishan* about the year 1651. The original of this grant is lost, but a copy has been preserved in the diary of Streynsham Master, who played so prominent a part in the affairs of the Company in the days that followed. The letters patent of the 'great Emperor, whose words no man dare presume to reverse,' decreed that 'the factory of the English Company be no more troubled with demands of custom for goods imported or exported either by land or by water.' After-events show with what 'special care' these commands of the 'great Emperor, whose words no man dare presume to reverse,' were obeyed.

Mir Jumla, the victorious general who had driven Sultan Shuja from Bengal, was appointed as his successor in the viceroyalty. He was a native of Persia, and, like many of his fellow-countrymen before him, he had come east in search of fortune. Recognising Aurungzebe as by far the most able of the four sons of Shah Jehan, he had early attached himself to his fortunes. By Aurungzebe's influence he had been appointed Vizier, with the command of 6,000 horse, and his military abilities meeting with quick recognition, he was shortly afterwards appointed generalissimo of the imperial army, with the high-sounding title of Khan-i-Khanan, the Chief among the Nobles. His success and loyalty to Aurungzebe in the war against Shah Shuja met with their due reward in the Viceroyalty of Bengal. Being at Dacca when the news of that appointment reached him, he resolved to restore the city again as the capital of the province, and from this time dates the second brief period of its greatest prosperity.

Mir Jumla's short rule of three years in Dacca was almost wholly taken up with his wars in Cooch Behar and Assam. A soldier by profession, he was never so happy as when in the field at the head of his troops, and the desire for military glory was the guiding influence of his career. Cooch Behar, though often overrun and forced to pay tribute, had never been a part of the Moghul Empire except in name, and Raja Bim Narain, taking advantage of the struggle between Shah Shuja and Aurungzebe in Bengal, had seized upon the imperial district of Kamrup. Mir Jumla, once secure in Dacca, had an excuse immediately at hand to set out on a fresh campaign. Round his standard gathered one of the largest armies that Dacca had yet seen. For miles the vast encampment stretched outside the northern gate of the city, while the river was crowded with a great fleet in the making. Embarking all his artillery and stores on board the boats, specially designed as the easiest mode of transport, Mir Jumla marched his army along the right bank of the Brahmaputra. By this route there was no made road, and it was often necessary to cut a way through the dense jungle that covered both banks of the river. It was a three months' journey, and so great were the difficulties that, to encourage his men, Mir Jumla himself worked among them axe in hand. The proud Moghul cavalry, inspired by his example, followed suit, and, with the help of the three hundred elephants that formed his advance guard, the long journey was at length accomplished. The Raja Bim Narain, not expecting the enemy in this quarter, which he considered sufficiently protected by the impenetrable jungle, was taken by surprise and fled from his capital as the enemy approached. Mir Jumla entered Behar in triumph, and in compliment to the Emperor, renamed it Alumgirnugger. It was a dramatic scene that was enacted on his entry. Mir Jumla was a zealous Mussulman, and the conquered province was one of the outskirts of empire where Hinduism still reigned supreme. In the chief temple in the centre of the city stood the celebrated image of Narain, the tutelary deity of the Raja and the people. Halting in his triumphal entry opposite the temple, Mir Jumla waited while the whole army formed up within view. Then, amidst a breathless pause, he entered, and, carrying out the idol, destroyed it with his own hands in the sight of all. Then, it being the hour of prayer, he ascended to the roof of the temple and himself acted as muezzin. For the first time in its history the Mussulman call to prayer rang out from the chief temple in the city of the Rajas of Cooch Behar.

Nothing could well have appealed to the victorious Mussulman army more than this dramatic triumph of their religion. In spite of the hardships they had already undergone, they were willing to follow Mir Jumla onwards to the conquest of Assam, to bring yet other lands within the Fold of the Faith. Save for his suppression of the Hindu religion, Mir Jumla suffered no other hardship to fall upon the conquered people of Cooch Behar. It was not until he had made provision for the good government of the conquered province that he set out, leaving fourteen hundred horse and seven thousand musketeers to guard what he had won. The revenues of Cooch Behar he fixed at ten lacs of rupees.

Mir Jumla's march into Assam was destined to meet with the same disastrous results that had attended so many previous attempts on the part of Mussulman governors to subdue that country. It was a wild, untamed land of immense extent, with no roads and a scattered population, with nothing to oppose to the huge invading army, yet fertile in resource to harass it on the march. The difficulties of the way would have appeared insurmountable to anyone but a general burning with the desire for military glory. Mir Jumla worked like the meanest among his soldiers, and they, ashamed, could not but follow where such a leader led. Yet often they progressed no further than a mile a day. Determined not to lose touch with the artillery and stores which he had placed in the safe keeping of the fleet, he marched close beside the river bank, which often entailed the cutting of a road through dense jungle. In Semyle the full strength of the Raja's army awaited him, but before his cannon the fortress was unable to hold out, and Mir Jumla entered it in triumph, naming it Atta Allah, the Gift of God. The dry season of the year, however, was at an end, and he was forced to settle his troops in a huge encampment that stretched for seven miles along the river-bank to await the termination of the rains.

It was from here that, misled by his first triumph, he sent his famous despatch to the Emperor. He had opened, he proudly asserted, the road to China, and the next campaign, he foretold, would see the Moghul standards meeting those of the Tartar relatives of the Emperor, the descendants of Jengriez Khan, who had long since founded their kingdom in the farthest East. The Moghul Empire united should stretch from sea to sea. But Mir Jumla's triumph was brief. He little knew the force of the rains in the upper reaches of the great rivers, and that year they exceeded all bounds. The country lay beneath a vast expanse of water, and food and fodder were almost impossible to obtain. The Raja, reappearing with a new force, harassed them on every side, and such dire sickness attacked the camp that scarce one man in ten was left untouched. Mir Jumla himself fell a prey to disease, and with the clearing of the rains the inevitable retreat began. Again the bright hopes that lay towards the East were relinquished, and the army, unconquered by the enemy, was yet forced to set its face towards the setting sun. At Gauhati fresh ill-news awaited it. The Raja of Cooch Behar had returned from Bhutan, whither he had fled at Mir Jumla's first approach, and, the whole country rallying round him, had driven out the imperial troops. Baffled, robbed of his dreams of military glory, and worn out with disease, Mir Jumla hurried on towards Dacca, whence three years before he had set out with such high hopes. But he was destined never to see the city again. At Khijerpore, on the 2nd of Ramzan, 1663, he died, to the great grief of the whole army, which, even in the evil days that had befallen it, never faltered in devotion to the general who had so often led it to victory in the days gone by.

So influential and powerful a Viceroy was Mir Jumla deemed at the Moghul Court that the saying went that only on the day of his death did Aurungzebe become King of Bengal. The Emperor himself is said to have watched his exploits and his growing authority with jealous eyes. 'You have lost a father,' he said, turning to Mir Jumla's son when they brought to him the news of the Viceroy's death, 'and I the greatest and most dangerous friend I had.'

CHAPTER V

SHAISTA KHAN

No other name in Mussulman annals, not even the name of Islam Khan, its founder, is so closely connected with Dacca as that of Shaista Khan. At a time when Eastern Bengal, on the outskirts of the empire, had become the sport of princes, a stepping-stone to greater things, and all was change, confusion, and disorder, this greatest of Eastern Viceroys, strong in the enormous influence he wielded at the Court of Delhi, ruled undisturbed for well nigh a quarter of a century. In the midst of the chequered careers of his contemporaries his own stands out with singular force, his authority undiminished until the end, enabling him to retire full of dignity and honours at the advanced age of eighty-one.

Proud, high-born, the Amir-ul-Umara Nawab Shaista Khan started life with all the advantages that even in those days of royal favouritism and interest could have been desired. Yet, born in the purple as he was, the fortunes of his family had only begun two generations before. Among all the romances of the East there are few more fascinating than the romance of the family to which Shaista Khan belonged. No women of the East are better remembered in history and legend than Jehangir's beautiful Empress Nur Jehan, the Light of the World, and the Empress Mumtaz Mahal, whose fame will live for ever in the wonderful Taj at Agra which Shah Jehan's love raised as an everlasting memorial of her beauty and his grief. Shaista Khan was the nephew of the Empress Nur Jehan and the brother of the lady who sleeps within the Taj.

The rapid rise to wealth and dignity of this once obscure Tartar family is typical of Mussulman annals. A native of Western Tartary, of a noble but impoverished family, Shaista Khan's grandfather Khaja Ghayas, with no prospects in his own land, turned his thoughts to Hindustan, that Eldorado of the needy Tartars of the north, determined to follow that road to fortune which so many of his countrymen had taken with such eminent success. The legend of his setting out is a tale of poverty and distress. With a young wife, frail and delicate, and one sorry steed as their only means of transport, their progress was slow, and, their small stock of money exhausted, they came nigh to perishing in the inhospitable

DESCENT AND CONNECTIONS OF SHAISTA KHAN

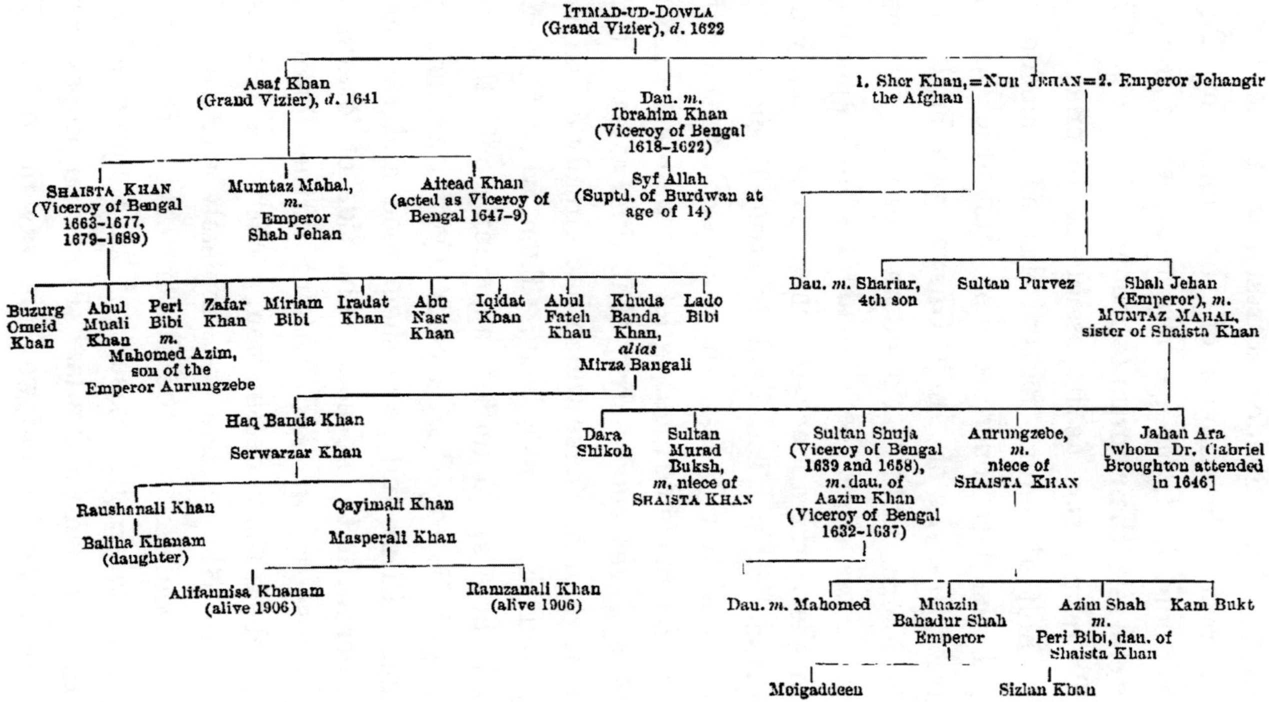

wastes that divided Tartary from the furthest limits of the empire of the house of Timur. Without food, on a lonely road where travellers were few, their fortunes reached their lowest ebb. To return was as impossible as to proceed, and no hint of coming fortune cheered them on. To put the last touch to their difficulties and distress, the wife of Khaja Ghayas gave birth to her first-born child. No infant destined for future greatness could have made its first appearance in the world under circumstances apparently more inauspicious. Too weak to struggle on with the child at her breast, the mother left the infant by the roadside; but, grief overtaking her, Khaja Ghayas returned only just in time to save it from a huge black snake which had already coiled itself round the infant's body. Then, when they were all three again united, apparently only that they might die together, a company of travellers came upon them and gave them food and the means wherewith to proceed. The tide of fortune had at last set in, and without further harm they reached their destination. Within a few years Khaja Ghayas had so completely won the favour and confidence of the Emperor Akbar that he was appointed High Treasurer of the Empire under the title Itimad-ud-Dowla. From an impoverished adventurer he had won his way in an incredibly short space of time, with all the determination of his race, to one of the highest and most coveted positions in the empire. Now, surrounded by many of the members of his family, he sleeps his last sleep in the magnificent mausoleum at Agra, across the Jumna, not far from the wonder of the Taj.

But it was the child born in poverty and abandoned in the desert who was destined to raise her family to the highest pitch of greatness. Named Mehr-un-Nissa, the Sun among Women, she justified the lofty title and grew up more beautiful than all the women of the East. The ambitious adventurer was careful that no extraneous advantage that might enhance his daughter's beauty should be wanting. In music, in dancing, in poetry, in painting, we are told, she had no equal among her sex. Her disposition was volatile, her wit lively and satirical, her spirit lofty and uncontrolled. Betrothed young, she was a fit mate for the famous Sher Afgan, the Conqueror of the Lion, but Mehr-un-Nissa, Sun among Women, aimed higher than an adventurous Turkoman noble. The Emperor Jehangir, having once seen her, desired her for his wife above all women; and, shut up in Burdwan as the wife of Sher Afgan, she waited while her royal lover devised scheme after scheme to rid him of the obstacle that stood in his path. It is the story of David and Uriah the Hittite retold. The evil designs of Jehangir and the prowess of Sher Afgan, who time and again defeated them, have become part of the legends of the race, and live in the memory when much else has been forgotten. But at last Sher Afgan was destroyed and Mehr-un-Nissa, the Sun among Women, became the Empress Nur Jehan, the Light of the World.

The woman whose ambition led her to defy the traditions of her race and marry her husband's murderer on the plea that that husband had urged her to do so, since he feared that his exploits would be forgotten unless they were associated with the fact that he had given an Empress to Hindustan, was not likely to neglect the advancement of her family. Her influence with Jehangir was supreme. Jointly with him she ruled the empire. 'By order of the Emperor Jehangir,' runs the inscription on a coin of the period; 'Gold acquires a hundred times additional value by the name of the Empress Nur Jehan.'

Itimad-ud-Dowlah died in 1622, six years before his son-in-law the Emperor, leaving his daughter Nur Jehan scheming for the accession of her own son-in-law, Jehangir's son, who had married her daughter by Sher Afgan. Her brother, Asaf Khan, succeeded his father as Grand Vizier to

Jehangir, and retained that post under his successor, Shah Jehan, over whom his influence was still more complete as the father of his wife, the beautiful Mumtaz Mahal. Asaf Khan died in 1641, and his son, Shaista Khan, succeeded to his honours. A man of thirty-three, Shaista Khan had already, during his father's lifetime, enjoyed a distinguished career. Governor of Behar, Grand Vizier to the Emperor, Viceroy of Guzrat, and Generalissimo of the Golconda war and Viceroy of the Deccan, he had played many parts and occupied many posts before finally becoming Viceroy of Bengal, the dignity he so long held.

Thus, closely connected with the Imperial Court, Shaista Khan occupied a secure position vouchsafed to few of his contemporaries. Brother-in-law of one emperor and uncle of another, yet with no claim or aspiration to the imperial throne, he had already won the life-long gratitude of Aurungzebe, having done much to secure for him the throne against his eldest brother Dara Shikoh, who at one time threatened to forestall him in the race for empire. In the very year, 1663, that he was appointed Nawab Nazim of Bengal, he was suffering from the wounds he had received from the assassins of the Mahratta chief Sivajee while fighting Aurungzebe's battles in the Deccan. It was not until the following year that he arrived in

Dacca and assumed the viceroyalty. His tenure of office falls into two parts, the first from 1663 to 1677, and the second, after an interval of less than two years, from 1679 until his final retirement ten years later.

The first great difficulty with which the new Viceroy had to contend lay in combating the incursions of the Mughs and their allies, the Portuguese pirates, who still troubled Eastern Bengal. No vengeance having been inflicted upon the King of Arracan for his shameful treatment of Sultan Shah Shuja, the late Viceroy and son of the Emperor himself, the Mughs had resumed their piracy with increased vigour, harrying unchecked even within sight of Dacca itself, which Mir Jumla four years before had restored as the capital of Bengal. But Mir Jumla's brief reign had been fully occupied by his war with Cooch Behar and his ambitious undertakings in Assam. It was reserved for Shaista Khan to bring the long struggle with the Mughs and the Portuguese to an end, and by so doing confer an unintentional benefit on the struggling English factory laboriously making firm its footing on the low-lying lands at the head of the Bay.

Recognising how greatly the English factories at the mouth of the Hooghly would benefit by the extermination of the pirates, it is said that Shaista

Khan made the not unreasonable request that they should aid him with a company of European gunners from their factories. But the English, still strong in their resolve to abstain from all interference in native politics, and particularly in warfare of any kind, refused, and Shaista Khan, incensed at their refusal, doubtless was not unmindful of it when in later days the Company was bent upon obtaining new concessions. Failing with the English, Shaista Khan endeavoured to enlist the support of the Dutch, and sent ambassadors to Batavia asking them to join in exterminating the pirates and subduing the kingdom of Arracan. The general of the Dutch Company, anxious to break the power of the Portuguese, readily consented, and despatched two men-of-war to join the Moghul fleet in the Bay. But Shaista Khan meanwhile, by threats and promises, had secured the submission of the Portuguese in Sundeep. The two Dutch men-of-war arrived later, but Shaista Khan, freed for the moment from fear of the Portuguese, now saw his way clear without the embarrassment of outside help, and, politely thanking them for their goodwill, gently hinted that he had no further use for them. 'I saw these ships in Bengal,' writes Bernier, 'and their commanders, who were but little contented with such thanks and liberalities of Shaista Khan.'

It was an imposing expedition that Shaista Khan fitted out at Dacca. The Buriganga was alive with craft as the three hundred boats of the fleet were hastily equipped and manned. Of the army of forty-three thousand men, three thousand were placed on board the ships, and, under the command of Hossain Beg, sent on ahead of the main army to clear the rivers of the pirates. The troops under the command of his own son, Buzurg Omeid Khan, were ordered to proceed by land, and in conjunction with the fleet, after driving the Mughs from the islands of which they had taken possession in the delta of the Ganges, pursue them to their own land and once for all rid Eastern Bengal of their presence.

Sailing from Dacca after the rains were over, Hossain Beg led his fleet down the Megna and driving the Arracanese before him from the forts of Jugdea and Alumgirnugger which they had wrested from the Moghuls, he sailed on towards the island of Sundeep, which had so long been the headquarters of the Portuguese adventurers. But it was no light task to drive them from the island which for fifty years they had fortified and strengthened. They were adepts in the art of fortification and defence, and it was only after a determined resistance that they were finally expelled.

Hearing of this first hard-won victory, Shaista

Khan sought to lessen the difficulty of the conquest of Chittagong by detaching the Portuguese adventurers who still adhered to the King of Arracan from his service. Offering them all the advantages and more than they were obtaining from the Mughs, including a grant of lands near his own capital with freedom of trade, and threatening to exterminate them if they persisted in their attachment to the Mughs, he won them to his side. They recognised in Shaista Khan the strong ruler that Eastern Bengal had so long awaited, and they realised that their days of piracy and freebooting unrestrained were over. Consequently, escaping by stealth from the territories of the Raja of Arracan, they set sail for the island of Sundeep, where they were welcomed by Hossain Beg. The most useful of them he retained in his service to assist his forces against their late allies, sending their wives and families, with the less adventurous spirits, to the lands on the Ishamutti which Shaista Khan had promised them. At Feringhi Bazaar, not far from the ancient capital of Vikrampur, they settled down into peaceful ways and long continued in the neighbourhood, many of them becoming officers in the cavalry of Shaista Khan, while others established a factory for trade in Dacca itself. They lived in the city in the vicinity of the Dullaye Creek, where they built an Augustinian monastery and a church, which Tavernier admired, on his visit to Dacca, for the beauty of its architecture. Another church of theirs still survives four miles away at Tezgaon, beyond which the city in its heyday once far extended, but from which it has long since shrunk away.

Meanwhile the land army, under Shaista Khan's own son, had by forced marches reached the river Feni, the boundary of the Arracanese territory. Here Omied Khan found the Arracanese waiting to receive him, but it was the first time that they had ever been confronted by the Moghul cavalry, that splendid force before which far finer troops than they had been forced to give way. These rude, unskilled adventurers fled in terror before their onslaught, and the entry into the kingdom of Arracan was easily won.

Hossain Beg, hearing of the arrival of the land forces, endeavoured to effect a junction with them, and set sail from Sundeep. But the Arracanese were on the watch, and sailing out from Chittagong, hurried to intercept him. Taught by the Portuguese, with whom they had been so long associated, they were no mean seamen, and their fleet of three hundred ships was no unworthy match for the Moghul navy. But Hossain Beg had the best of the Portuguese seamen in his fleet, and they did much to turn the tide in favour of their new master. The arrival on the bank of Omeid Khan and the main body of the army, who turned the guns upon the attacking fleet, completed their discomfiture, and they were forced to retreat. The way was open to Chittagong, and it was here that the Mughs made their last stand. It was well fortified, and its walls well manned, but the garrison, looking out anxiously to see the victory of its fleet, saw only its irretrievable defeat, and grew disheartened ere the fight began. Beset by land and sea, the Mughs gave up the struggle and sought to escape to their own country in the dead of night. But the dreaded Moghul cavalry pursued them in the morning, and as many as two thousand of the luckless survivors were caught and sold as slaves. Chittagong, however, proved a source of untold disappointment to the victors. On so extensive a scale had been the piracy of the Mughs that the Moghul troops expected to find great stores of treasure in the fallen city. But beyond an extraordinary collection of pieces of cannon, numbering, it is said, twelve hundred and twenty-three, there was little found. Shaista Khan changed the name of the conquered city to Islamabad, the City of the Faithful. Chittagong was thus for the first time conquered by the Moghuls, and permanently annexed to the Kingdom of Bengal.

Beyond this single expedition, the whole course of Shaista Khan's rule in Bengal was of a strangely peaceful nature. After the continual wars and invasions of the Mughs and Portuguese from which Eastern Bengal had so long suffered, these years came as an inestimable boon to the much-harassed land and people. It was a time of prosperity in Dacca hitherto unknown. The number and variety of things exported at this period are sufficient evidence of its flourishing condition. To almost every country in the world Dacca sent her produce. With the discovery of the Cape route to India, Surat on the western coast had quickly become the chief emporium for the goods of India and Europe. Through this busy mart Dacca carried on a great trade in cloth, and although chanks and tortoiseshell were taken in exchange, the balance of trade lay so greatly in her favour that it was necessary to import specie direct, which accounts for the appearance of the Arcot rupee in Eastern Bengal. Tavernier, visiting the city in 1666, found 'cossas muslin, silk, and cotton stuffs, and flowered or embroidered fabrics' being exported in large quantities to Provence, Italy, and Languedoc. To Bhutan, Assam, and Siam went coral, amber, and tortoise-shell; to Nepal, large quantities of cloth, otter skins, and shell bracelets; to the Coromandel coast, rice, which sold in Dacca at the extraordinary rate of 640 lbs. to the rupee. But in spite of the great export of cloth, all the best and finest kinds were reserved for the imperial and viceregal courts. Manufacturers were forbidden by imperial rescript to sell cloth exceeding a certain value to any native or foreign merchant. To supervise the carrying out of this order a special agent was appointed to reside on the spot to see that none of the finest muslins went astray. He had full authority over the weavers and brokers, and jealously watched their output, that none but his masters might obtain the best and finest of the produce. All the cloth and muslin, however, that was not required for the royal household might be disposed of as the producers pleased, and much of it, in addition to that sent abroad, was despatched all over Hindustan and overland as far as Persia and the Arabian seaports.

Of the exquisite fineness of the Dacca muslins much has been written. 'In this same country,' runs one of the earliest accounts of them, 'they make cotton garments in so extraordinary a manner that nowhere else are the like to be seen. These garments are for the most part round, and wove to that degree of fineness that they may be drawn through a ring of middling size.' Tavernier relates that a turban sixty cubits in length, 'of a muslin so fine that you would scarcely know what it was that you had in your hand,' was contained in a cocoanut about the size of an ostrich's egg. There were many different kinds of muslins manufactured, and some of them were given figurative names indicative of their exquisite texture. The Ab-i-rawan or Running Water, and the Shabnam or Evening Dew, were some of the most highly prized, while no less beautiful were the Jamdani, flowered muslin, and the Malmal Khas, the King's muslin. For transparency, fineness, and delicacy of workmanship, these fabrics have never been equalled, and not all the improvements in the art of manufacture in modern times have been able to approach them. Yet the implements used by the weavers at their work were primitive in the extreme. They consisted only of pieces of bamboo or reeds roughly tied together with thread, and so laborious was the process of manufacture that it is said that one hundred and twenty instruments were necessary to convert the raw material into the finest fabrics, such as the Ab-i-rawan. Infinite care and skill were demanded, and the strain on the eyesight was so great that it was only between the ages of sixteen and thirty that weavers could be employed on the finest work. The excellence of their muslins was largely attributed by the Dacca weavers to the peculiar dampness of the climate, and they were careful not to work in the middle of the day lest the heat of the sun might affect them. A story is told illustrative of the delicacy of the texture of the muslins and the value placed upon them. One of the weavers spread the piece he had just finished on the grass to dry in the cool of the evening, and, carelessly leaving it unguarded, let it be eaten up by a cow which was grazing near at hand. So great was the indignation against him that he was ignominiously turned out of the city and allowed to weave no more.

It is during the viceroyalty of Shaista Khan that we get another of those brief illuminating glimpses of Eastern Bengal from the pen of a European traveller writing at first hand. François Bernier, visiting Bengal in 1666, cannot say enough in praise of its wonderful fertility and abundance. 'You may there have almost for nothing three or four kinds of legumes,' he writes, 'which together with rice and butter are the most usual food of the meaner people; and for a Roupy, which is about half a crown, you may have twenty good pullets and more: geese and ducks in proportion. There is also plenty of many kinds of fish, both fresh and salt; and, in a word, Bengale is a country abounding in all things.' Apparently there was a proverb in those days among the Portuguese, English, and Dutch, to the effect that there were a hundred open gates to enter into the kingdom of Bengal, and not one to come away again. 'As to the commodities of great value, and which draw the commerce of strangers thither, I know not,' continues Bernier, 'whether there be a country in the world that affords more and greater variety: for besides the sugar I have spoken of, which may be numbered among the commodities of value, there is such store of cottons and silks, that it may be said, that Bengale is as 'twere the general magazine thereof, not only for Indostan or the empire of the Great Mogol, but also for all the circumjacent kingdoms, and for Europe itself. I have sometimes stood amazed at the vast quantity of cotton-cloth of all sorts, fine and others, tinged and white, which the Hollanders alone draw from thence and transport into many places, especially into Japan and Europe; not to mention what the English, Portingal and Indian merchants carry away from those ports. The like may be said of the silks and silk-stuffs of all sorts: one would not imagine the quantity that is hence transported every year.'

Though Bernier never made his way as far east as Dacca, the waterways along which he travelled at the head of the Bay are typical of those of Eastern Bengal. He speaks of the country as of 'incomparable beauty,' very fertile, 'filled with fruit-bearing trees and all sorts of verdure, and interlaced with a thousand little channels which you cannot see the end of, as if they were so many water-mails all covered with trees.' Though here and there the banks were well cultivated, for miles dense jungle covered the lands on either side, with 'no other inhabitants but tigers, and gazelles, and hoggs, and poultry grown wild.' Tigers then, as for many years afterwards, constituted a continual source of danger to travellers in Eastern Bengal. 'For there are now and then men surprised,' writes Bernier, 'and I have heard it said that tigers have been so bold as to come into the boats and to carry away men that were asleep, choosing the biggest and fattest of them, if one may believe the watermen of the country.' In spite of many dangers by the way, Bernier could 'not be satisfied with beholding such beautiful countries,' even although he writes that 'in the meantime my trunk and all my baggage was wet, my pullets dead, my fish spoiled, and all my biscuit drunk with water.'

Of the climate, however, Bernier does not speak so favourably. 'It cannot be denied that the air, in regard to strangers,' he writes in his own delightfully quaint, inimitable style, 'is not so healthy there, especially near the sea: and when the

English and Hollanders first came to settle there many of them dyed. Yet since the time that they have taken care and made orders that their people shall not drink so much *Bouleponges*, nor go so often to visit the seller of *arac* and tobacco; and since they have found that a little wine of Bourdeaux, Canary or Chiras is a marvellous antidote against the ill air, there is not so much sickness amongst them, nor do they lose so many men. *Bouleponge* is a certain beverage made of *arac*, that is of strong water, black sugar, with the juice of limon water, and a little muscadine upon it; which is pleasant enough to the taste, but a plague to the body and to health.'

Another French traveller actually visited Dacca itself about this time, and he has left on record a brief account of his visit. Jean Baptiste Tavernier, travelling a portion of the way across India with Bernier, with whom he parted company at Patna, arrived in Dacca on January 13, 1666. He had met Shaista Khan before at Ahmadabad, when the latter was Governor of Gujarat, and he gives elsewhere an amusing account of a pecuniary transaction between them, which he ends with the sad reflection that 'this Prince who is otherwise magnificent and generous, shows himself a stern economist in matters of purchase.' In Dacca, however, things went more smoothly. He speaks of Shaista Khan as 'the uncle of King Aurungzebe, and the cleverest man in all his kingdom,' and proceeds to relate his dealings with him.

'The day following my arrival in Dacca,' he writes, 'I went to salute the Nawab, and presented him with a mantle of gold brocade with a grand golden lace of "point d'Espagne" round it, and a fine scarf of gold and silver of the same "point," and a jewel consisting of a very beautiful emerald. During the evening, after I had returned to the Dutch with whom I lodged, the Nawab sent me pomegranates, China oranges, two Persian melons and three kinds of apples.' By which exchange of presents it appears that the astute Nawab distinctly scored. Yet so valuable did the merchant-traveller consider his custom that on the following day he presented still more valuable gifts. 'On the 15th,' he writes, 'I showed him my goods and presented to the Prince, his son, a watch having a case of enamelled gold, a pair of pistols inlaid with silver, and a telescope. All this which I gave, both to the father and to the young lord of about ten years of age, cost me more than 5,000 livres.' The secret of Tavernier's apparent generosity is probably to be found in his entry of the following day. 'On the 16th I agreed with him as to the price of my goods,' he writes, 'and afterwards I went to the Vizir to receive my bill of exchange,' which was doubtless sufficiently large to make good the value of the presents.

Though the English did not formally establish their factory in Dacca until two years later, they already had agents there at the time of Tavernier's visit. 'On the 22nd,' he writes, 'I went to visit the English, who had for chief or president Mr. Prat,' and he also mentions their house in his brief description of the city itself. 'The residence of the Governor is an enclosure of high walls, in the middle of which is a poor house merely built of wood. He ordinarily resides under tents which he pitches in a large court in this enclosure. The Dutch, finding that their goods were not sufficiently safe in the common houses of Dacca, have built a very fine house, and the English have also got one which is fairly good. The church of the Rev. Augustin Fathers is all of brick, and the workmanship of it is rather beautiful.' From the 23rd to the 29th Tavernier was busy making purchases to the value of 11,000 rupees, the nature of the purchases not being divulged but probably consisting of the famous Dacca muslins. 'On the 29th, in the evening, I parted from Dacca,' he concludes the narrative of his story in the Eastern capital, 'and all the Dutch accompanied me for two leagues with their small armed boats, and the Spanish wine was not spared on this occasion.'

The viceroyalty of Shaista Khan is the period of great advance among the European companies in Bengal. The Portuguese had settled at Hooghly as early as 1575, only to be expelled thence by Shah Shuja in 1632. The Dutch had probably arrived at the close of the first quarter of the seventeenth century. The English, setting out from Fort St. George, had established factories at Hariharpur and Balasore in Orissa in 1633. Eighteen years later, twelve years before Shaista Khan became governor of Bengal, Stephens and Bridgeman had established a factory at Hooghly, which they made their headquarters station in the Bay. It was later, during the viceroyalty of Shaista Khan himself, that the Dutch finally established themselves at Chinsura, the French at Chandernagore, and the Danes at Serampore. Further, it was in 1668, the year of the establishment of the Bengal pilot service, when the first English ship sailed up the Hooghly, that the English opened their new factory at Dacca itself, Shaista Khan's own capital. Thus, though Shaista Khan is vilified as the enemy of the Europeans, it cannot be denied that his reign synchronises with a great advance in their position throughout Bengal.

Affairs were in a critical condition for the struggling English Company in the Bay when

Shaista Khan succeeded in 1663. They had already, by the high-handed capture of a native boat, incurred the wrath of Mir Jumla, and it was only because he was fully occupied with his expedition to Cooch Behar and Assam that they had escaped condign punishment. Shaista Khan at his accession viewed the interlopers with all the distrust with which they had inspired the Moghul on their first arrival in the East. Yet during the first half of his viceroyalty the relations between him and the Company appear not to have been openly hostile. If the imperial rescripts which the English Company obtained are any criterion, its position was rapidly improving. Aurungzebe himself issued letters patent in their favour in 1667. Five years later Shaista Khan confirmed the English privileges in the kingdom of Bengal. He followed the practice of his predecessor, Mir Jumla, in exacting an annual tribute of three thousand rupees from the Company, but his *perwana* sternly forbade his officers to impose illegal exactions upon them on their own account.

Apart from their relations with their Moghul neighbours, these were stormy days for the English Company. The established and privileged corporation was engaged in a fierce struggle with the free traders—'interlopers' and 'pirates,' as the Court angrily dubbed them. The long rivalry between the Old and the New Company was just beginning, dividing the small English community in Bengal into hostile camps, and weakening its front against their common enemy, the Moghul Viceroy at Dacca, and their Mussulman neighbours close at hand. Interlopers sailed up the Hooghly, openly defying the Company on its own ground. Most notorious of all the intruders was Thomas Pitt, discoverer of the most famous diamond in the world, and the ancestor of two of the most celebrated among the statesmen whose names are inscribed for all time upon the roll of England's fame. Later, in more reputable days, Governor of Madras and the honoured servant of the Company, he was long the most notorious of its rivals, and contemptuously termed in official correspondence the 'Pirate Pitt.' Married to the niece of Matthias Vincent, Chief of the English factories in Bengal, he had friends at court in high places, and Vincent soon fell under the suspicion of aiding and abetting piratical trade in the person of his nephew—the most heinous crime in the Company's eyes that its servants could commit. The Bengal factories were still under the Governor of Fort St. George, Madras, and twice Streynsham Master, deputed by the Court at home, had visited them to correct abuses, issuing a number of regulations for 'advancing the glory of God, upholding the honour of the English nation, and preventing of disorders.'

Shaista Khan may well have looked on content while these disorders and disputes divided the English traders against themselves. In 1668, he had allowed the English to set up a factory at Dacca, thus bringing them into closer touch with the central Moghul power in Bengal. At first it was only an out-station of small beginnings, but within a few years, in 1677, the sales of Dacca goods, principally muslins, for which the city had long been famous, turned out so profitably that the Court raised the stock of the Company from 85,000*l*. to 100,000*l*. Four years later the Court determined to set the factories in Bengal upon an independent footing. With this purpose they superseded Vincent, whose 'odious infidelity in countenancing interlopers' had long enraged the Directors, and on Nov. 14, 1681, appointed William Hedges, with special powers, to be their Agent and Governor in the Bay of Bengal, assisted by the famous Job Charnock as second in command, and a Council of five others who were already engaged in the English factories in the Bay.

Then ensued one of those comedies that enliven the pages of the annals of the English in Bengal. On January 28, 1682, Mr. William Hedges, the

Company's Governor, set sail in state from England with a guard of a corporal and twenty soldiers, on board the 'Defence' commanded by Captain William Heath. Three weeks later came the news that 'Pirate Pitt' was also setting sail for Bengal in the 'Crown,' attended by three or four other vessels in his pay. The Court of Directors was frantic. Every means in its power was employed to stop the 'pirate' and 'interloper' from starting, but in vain. Failing this the Court consoled itself with the fact that Governor Hedges, with his three weeks' start, would have already ousted Vincent and be prepared to give Pitt the reception he deserved. In fact they became quite hopeful of the 'total wreck of the interloper,' which they trusted would 'have such an effect upon all men's minds as to convince the deluded world of the vanity and folly of these persons.' But the Court counted without Thomas Pitt.

It was a race between the 'Defence' and the 'Crown.' In a six months' voyage a three weeks' start, though considerable, was not impossible to overcome, and Thomas Pitt had chosen an admirable vessel for speed in the 'Crown.' Within two months she sighted the 'Defence,' pursuing her dignified way with legitimate authority on board, unconscious of the danger in her wake. The 'Crown' easily outdistanced the larger and heavier vessel, and on July 8 Pitt landed at Balasore, eleven days before the 'Defence' was sighted. Every day was of value to the 'interloper,' and he was not slow to make use of the advantage he had gained. Giving out that a new Company had been founded, of which he was the authorised agent, and attended by a company of Portuguese and native soldiers and trumpeters, he sailed up the river to Hooghly in three ships, with all the state due to the Governor of the English Factories in the Bay. Vincent, knowing that his credit with the Court was small and that it was only a question of time before he was superseded, joined his adventurous nephew, and together they treated with the native governor of Hooghly, obtaining commercial privileges and a *perwana* to build a factory in the name of the New Company.

It was in the midst of this confusion that William Hedges arrived, the first independent Governor of the English Factories in the Bay. Shaista Khan may well have smiled at the situation, content to play a waiting game. To him Hedges appealed, but negotiations dragged on interminably. The astute Moghul governor was not ill-pleased that such dissensions should continue among the English. The Interlopers, anxious for his favour, willingly paid the dues that he demanded from them, and though at length the

Governor obtained an order from him to Balchandra Das, the Customs officer, and to the native governor of Hooghly to arrest Pitt and his associates, a further bribe easily secured their immunity. Shaista Khan had no intention of advancing the interests of the English Company by removing the Interlopers from its path.

In the following year the Interlopers reached what the Directors considered the 'height of impudence.' One Captain Alley openly sailed up the Hooghly in great state, 'habited in scarlet richly laced, while ten Englishmen in blue caps and coats edged with red, all armed with blunderbusses, went before his palanquin, eighty peons before them and four *musmins* playing on the waits, with two flags before him like an Agent.' In this state he had the impertinence to call upon the Governor, and Hedges bitterly complains that every considerable person in the factory except himself returned his visits. He openly negotiated with Balchandra Das, the Viceroy's Customs officer, agreeing to pay three-and-a-half per cent. on all goods imported and exported, upon which, says Hedges, 'they parted good friends.' Hedges at last succeeded in getting an order from Shaista Khan to the governor of Hooghly directing him to arrest the interloping captains and send them to Dacca. But they had proved themselves too valuable to Balchandra Das to be allowed to slip so easily out of his hands. He sent urgent representations to Shaista Khan, pointing out that the Interlopers were no enemies of his. It was all the fault of the Old Company, which wanted the monopoly of trade. The Interlopers were traders too, and they were willing to pay even five per cent. duty. Why should he drive such useful and profitable subjects from his realm? Shaista Khan was not slow to see the wisdom of the reasoning of his astute Customs officer, and in spite of his *perwana* to the Old Company the Interlopers met with little interference at his hands. Hedges had only been installed a few months in the factory on the banks of the Hooghly when the Council found trade in such a disorganised condition that it was 'agreed and concluded in consultation that the only expedient now left was for the Agent to go himself in person to the Nawab and Dewan at Dacca as well to make some settled adjustment concerning the customs as to endeavour the preventing Interlopers trading in these parts for ye future.' To go with the Agent, Mr. Richard Trenchfield and Mr. William Johnson were appointed, and it was thought convenient to go by way of Cossimbazaar in order to consult with Mr. Job Charnock, second in Council and high in favour with the Directors at home.

Governor Hedges prepared to set out for Dacca with all the state becoming the Chief of the English Factories in the Bay. Two barges and several small boats for servants were made ready, and on the evening of the 10th of October, 1682, the Governor, with Mr. Trenchfield and Mr. Johnson, escorted by twenty-three English soldiers and fifteen Rajputs, proceeded on the first stage of their journey to the English garden to the north of Hooghly. But the local officials, doubtless guessing that this embassy would be by no means welcome to Shaista Khan in Dacca, took every means in their power to hinder it at the outset. Parmeshar Das, the local Collector of Customs and the creature of Balchandra Das, actually sent out to seize the English boats. Two of them were taken and the English, endeavouring to recover them by force, Parmeshar Das beat and ill-used all the boatmen and footmen on whom he could lay hands, and even succeeded in enticing away many of the Governor's native retainers by means of threats and bribes. The Governor protested in vain. For five days he was kept waiting, unable to start, watched by the minions of Parmeshar Das, who were ready to harass his fleet the moment he set sail. Finally the dignified Governor of the English Factories was forced to run away in the night, under cover of darkness, on the 14th of October. The story is best told in Governor Hedges' own indignant words. 'Resolving now to be abused no more in this manner, I sent all ye laden boats before, with Mr. Johnson to see them make all the haste that might be and not to stop all night. Next to them went the soldiers with ye other budgero. I followed that, and two stout fellows, an Englishman and a Spaniard in a light boat, came last of all. About two hours within night a boat full of armed men came up very near to the Spaniard, who, speaking ye language, demanded who they were and commanded them to stand; but those in the boat returning no answer, nor regarding what he said, he fired his musket in the water, at which they fell astern. About an hour after, when we were got up as far as Trippany, the armed boat came up with ye Spaniard again, who commanded them to keep off, otherwise he would now shoot amongst them, though he shot at random the time before: so the boat fell astern, and perceiving that we resolved not to stay at that place, we saw them no more.'

Such was the commencement of the first voyage undertaken by a Governor of the English Factories in the Bay. It was only a journey of eleven days to Dacca with favourable winds, and Hedges arrived on the 25th of October. The rivers were in flood, the season being just at the end of the rains, and the route lay up the Hooghly and the Jellinghi into the Ganges and thence by many of the numerous streams that intersect all this part of Eastern Bengal. The boats in which they sailed were such that they passed easily up the flooded watercourses, which a month later would be almost completely dried up. It was a pleasant voyage, especially after the heat and discomfort of Calcutta. There is always a breeze on the river in the rains, and the voyagers must have been pleasantly surprised at the coolness and comfort in which the journey was performed. Mr. Hedges fully appreciated the interest and novelty of the voyage. Budgerows, large, flat-bottomed boats, much in the form of an English houseboat, were roomy and comfortable. With a favourable wind, a sail was hoisted and rapid progress made. Venetian windows along each side made the budgerows light and airy, and afforded a full view of the delightful river scenery with its constantly changing interests. Country boats of all sizes and descriptions passed up and down, skimming over the water with their wonderful variety of sails. It was a new experience and constant source of interest to Governor Hedges, who had but recently arrived from home. Here fishermen plied their time-honoured profession, with their huge nets and tiny skiffs that they managed with so much skill: there, majestic and slow sailing, passed a company of sloops, doubtless carrying their own goods down from Dacca to be shipped to England in the Company's vessels that awaited them at Hooghly. At midday the Manjhis rested and took their meal, while the Saheb-log dined beneath the trees on the bank, and stretched their limbs for a while after the somewhat cramped space of the budgerow. In the evening they rowed on again, and at night they were towed from the bank by the boatmen, who chanted their weird songs as they walked, to keep off the wild beasts that infested the river-banks, and to make their labours light.

It was an imposing sight that greeted the embassy as they approached Dacca on the evening of October 25. Facing the river which then flowed beneath its walls rose the towers and turrets of the Lalbagh Fort, begun but a few years before by Prince Mahomed Azim, son of Aurungzebe, during his brief viceroyalty. Not far off, the high imposing front of the Bara Katra, built some forty years before in the time of Shah Shuja, rose the most conspicuous object on the river-bank. Its high central gateway, flanked by smaller entrances and the octagonal tower, faced the river, a magnificent and lofty structure. Beside it stood the Chhota Katra, built by Shaista Khan himself, smaller but scarcely less beautiful, designed in the style of architecture that has come to be popularly known as Shaista Khani, after the great Viceroy himself. Behind lay the Chauk with its handsome mosque, built in the same style of architecture by the same great Viceroy. Further back still rose the Hossaini Delan, constructed during Shah Shuja's time forty years before, and beyond again the Idgah, built about the same time, and then in its first glory; while still higher up on the bank of the river, which has long since receded, stood the beautiful seven-domed mosque just completed by Shaista Khan. Away beyond for fourteen miles the city stretched as far as Tungi, a vast labyrinth of streets and villages, the camps of armies and all that followed in their train. On the river, facing the town, rode at anchor the state barges of the Viceroy and the Nawara, the great fleet of seven hundred war-boats that but a few years before had returned in triumph from the conquest of the Mughs.

The English factory, which has long since disappeared, originally stood where the College now stands, and it was here that Governor Hedges stayed. It was a building of no pretensions, constructed solely with a view to commercial usefulness. The French factory lay a short distance away, on the site now occupied by the palace of the present Nawab of Dacca, while the Dutch factory stood close by on the river-bank, where the Mitford Hospital now stands. Shaista Khan was apparently living in a palace within the Lalbagh Fort, and it was there that Governor Hedges came to interview the great Viceroy and seek better terms for the Company he served. Shaista Khan, with typical diplomacy, was full of fair words and promises. No further countenance should be given to the Interlopers. Mussulman officials should no longer be allowed to oppress the traders, and the Company's servants should be forced to pay nothing beyond what was actually due. The meetings, held with all the Oriental love of stateliness and display, continued with growing satisfaction on Governor Hedges' side. Shaista Khan was gracious, and the English Agent, after a month and a half spent in negotiations in Dacca, departed full of gratification at the result of his embassy. 'My going to Dacca,' he wrote, still pleased and flattered at the fair words of Shaista Khan, 'has in the first place got seven months' time for procuring a Phirmaund; 2ndly, taken off wholly ye pretence of 5 per cent. customs on all treasure imported this and ye three preceding years, besides 1½ per cent. of what was usually paid at ye mint for some years past: 3rdly, procured the general stop to be taken off all our trade, our goods now passing as freely as ever they did formerly: 4thly, got a command to turn Parmeshar Das out of his place, and restore ye money forced from us: 5thly and last, prevailed with ye Nawab to undertake ye procuring a Phirmaund for us from ye King . . . If God gives me life to get this Phirmaund into my possession ye Hon'ble Company shall never more be troubled with Interlopers. I bless God for this great success I have had, beyond all men's expectations, in my voyage to Dacca.'

Fresh from home, Hedges knew little of the tortuous ways of Indian diplomacy. But the glow of satisfaction with which he penned the above words must soon have cooled. Things remained exactly as they had been before. Balchandra Das, the superintendent of customs, and Parmeshar Das, his minion, flourished as of old, unchecked in spite of all the promises of Shaista Khan. Governor Hedges soon learned that his journey to Dacca had been productive of little save promises and fair words. It was small wonder that, smarting under the knowledge that all the high hopes he had built upon his mission to Dacca had come to nought, Hedges angrily wrote of Shaista Khan as the 'old doting Nawab.' But none could have known better than he how fully alive to the situation the 'doting Nawab' really was.

Shaista Khan, meanwhile, doubtless listened with keen enjoyment when the internal affairs of the Company at Hooghly were duly reported to him in Dacca. First came the news, in August 1684, that Governor Hedges had been dismissed by the Company, and John Beard appointed Agent in his place, while the factories in the Bay were once more brought under the control of Fort St. George, Mr. Gifford being appointed President of the Coast of Coromandel and the Bay. But President Gifford soon sailed away from Bengal, and John Beard, weighed down with the anxieties and responsibilities of office, died in the following year.

It was about this time that a momentous change, destined to transform a small trading company into a great political power, first began to make itself felt in the history of the English in Bengal. It was gradually borne in upon those in authority in the English factories that the great Moghul Empire, in whose greatness and authority they had so long believed, was powerless to carry out its obligations. They had all that they could desire in the way of *firmans* from the far-off Imperial Court at Delhi, but these were repeatedly rendered of no effect by the powerful Viceroy at Dacca. The latter, again, seemed equally powerless to check the exactions of his local officers at Hooghly. It was a tremendous change in the political outlook that was only slowly borne in upon the English in the Bay. It left them but two alternatives: either to withdraw from Bengal, where the Moghul Empire was powerless to protect them, or to strengthen themselves until they were able to stand alone in defiance of the local authority if need be. Governor Hedges was among the first to see that the English must look to themselves for their own protection, and he strongly advocated the building of a fort on Saugor Island, at the mouth of the river, whence war might be waged upon Interloper and Moghul alike. President Gifford in 1685 did in fact apply to Shaista Khan for permission to erect such a fort at the mouth of the Ganges to guard their trade against the Interloper and for the general protection of their factories. But Shaista Khan viewed anything in the nature of a military fortification with suspicion, and refused his consent. It was quite clear that what was to be done must be done in spite of the Moghul Governor at Dacca.

But the Company, ever timorous at the outset, deprecated such an extreme measure as falling out once and for all with the Great Moghul, the fame of whose power and authority still lingered in their minds. Yet in the end even they were forced to acknowledge that it was a question of withdrawal or the adoption of a bolder attitude. With their usual caution, however, they contented themselves with half-measures, turning aside from the main point at issue and advocating an attack on Chittagong. Obtaining sanction to retaliate upon Shaista Khan and his minions from James the Second, who was too busy endeavouring to secure his throne to exhibit great interest in so far-off a venture, the Court of Directors despatched the largest force to the Bay that they had yet sent to India. It consisted of ten ships of war, with twelve to seventy guns each, under the command of Vice-Admiral Nicholson, having on board a regiment of six hundred soldiers which was to receive an addition of four hundred men from the Governor of Madras. The avowed object of the expedition was to seize Chittagong and transform it into a place of arms for the English Company on the eastern side of the Bay, as they had already done in the case of Fort St. George on the western shore. It was an attempt to gain a firmer base at a greater distance from Dacca, whence operations might be gradually extended up the Hooghly. No sooner should they be fully established in Chittagong than the expedition had orders to proceed at once to Dacca to dictate terms to Shaista Khan.

It was a strangely ambitious scheme for the timorous Company suddenly to evolve. It assuredly did not err on the side of diffidence. The Directors showed all their usual ignorance of the needs of the moment. Long overawed by the shadow of the Great Moghul, no sooner did they begin to doubt his omnipotence than they flew to the other extreme and talked glibly of sailing up to Dacca and dictating terms to the greatest of Aurungzebe's Viceroys in his own palace. The expedition, born of over-confidence, was dogged by misfortune from the outset. Contrary winds delayed the fleet and storms dispersed it, while the Vice-Admiral, disregarding orders, sailed up the Bay with the few ships that remained to him, the 'Beaufort,' the 'Nathaniel,' and the 'Rochester,' with their attendant frigates, and anchored opposite Hooghly. Here Job Charnock was awaiting them with the four hundred soldiers who had been sent round from Madras, and a company of native Christian infantry, 'very sorry fellows,' as the English termed them. But insignificant as the first British force to enter Bengal was, it was sufficient to alarm Shaista Khan and stir him to action. He at once ordered a large body of troops, three thousand foot and three hundred horse, down to the royal fort at Hooghly to watch events and overawe the English. Thus strengthened, the local Moghul officials adopted a still more overbearing attitude. All trade was stopped, and even the local market was closed to the British soldiers. The English forces were practically placed in a state of siege. It was obvious that only a small incident was necessary to bring about open war, and that incident occurred on October 28. Three English soldiers, entering the bazaar as usual to buy provisions, were not only refused supplies by the native dealers, but when they protested, were set upon by the governor's men and severely handled, being finally carried off as prisoners. The news spread like wildfire within the English factory, and Job Charnock took such active measures that before sunset full vengeance had been exacted, the enemy's battery taken, the guns dismantled, and the governor put to flight. The English soldiers 'firing and battering most part of that night and next day,' and having taken a ship belonging to the Moghul governor, made frequent sallies on shore, burning and plundering all they met with. But Job Charnock, realising the danger, had determined on removing from so dangerous a position and withdrawing to the island of Hijili at the mouth of the Hooghly.

Shaista Khan, on hearing news of this fracas, at once took prompt measures. The Company's agents in the out-stations were seized, and large detachments of horse despatched to reinforce the troops at Hooghly. Mr. Watts, the Company's agent at Dacca, was in no comfortable position, and it speaks much for Shaista Khan that no extreme measures were taken against him. He had a friend at court, however, in one Baramal, a Hindu who had won Shaista Khan's confidence, and who pointed out to his master that the English factory at Dacca was not responsible for the misdoings of the factory at Hooghly, and that Mr. Watts had engaged in nothing but in peaceable trade. So the agent in Dacca escaped, and by the end of December he was on his way down to Hooghly with Baramal, who was sent by Shaista Khan to negotiate terms of peace. Charnock had withdrawn from Hooghly to Sutanati, and thence, through Baramal, submitted his demands to Shaista Khan. The old demand for a fort was again urged, and in addition Charnock asked that all damage done to their factories might be made good, the establishment of a mint permitted, and full freedom of trade allowed. Shaista Khan, as usual, had nothing but fair words when these demands were presented to him. He appointed Baramal and two others to act as commissioners to draw up the terms of peace. At Sutanati, now the northern quarter of Calcutta, the conference took place. Twelve articles, embodying the English demands, were drawn up and signed and sealed by the commissioners. They were then despatched to Shaista Khan for confirmation, with a request from Charnock that they might be ratified by the Emperor himself.

But Job Charnock, with all his thirty years' experience of Indian life, had yet much to learn of the ways of Indian diplomacy. At the sight of his demands definitely formulated on paper, Shaista Khan threw off all pretences. He had previously delayed in order to gain time, but that this small body of men should make these impudent demands upon the great Viceroy of the East aroused the full tide of the old despot's wrath. The English, he declared, should be driven out of Bengal. Orders were sent in every direction that the Company's servants should be seized, the factories closed, and the English at Hooghly driven into the sea. The news of the reception of his terms at Dacca having reached Charnock, he lost no time in doing what damage he could before falling back on the island of Hijili. Burning down the royal offices at Hooghly, he took the Thana forts, 'with the loss only of one man's leg and some wounded.' Then, baffled for the moment, he withdrew to Hijili.

With the withdrawal of all the Company's servants, Shaista Khan seems to have been content. They had chosen the most unhealthy spot in all Bengal, and the most trying months of the year were upon them. News reached him that more than half the European troops had succumbed to malaria, while the remainder were scarce fit for the lightest duties. Shaista Khan may well have deemed them unworthy of further effort, and left them to their fate. Though the local Moghul commander harassed them and drove them to desperate straits, Shaista Khan appears to have taken but half-hearted measures against them. Had he been as bitterly opposed to them as he is popularly supposed to have been, it would have required little energy to have finally driven them out of Bengal. So far from this, he even allowed them, a few months later, to return to the river as far as Ulubaria and continue their interrupted trade. For this unexpected complaisance on the part of Shaista Khan there was probably a double reason. The English on the Bombay side, indignant at their treatment, had withdrawn from Surat and declared open war upon Aurungzebe, and with their superiority at sea had practically annihilated the Moghul maritime trade and interrupted the pilgrimages to Mecca. Aurungzebe was fully occupied, intent on taking Hyderabad, and he was willing to make peace with the English to avoid further contest. They were restored to all their privileges on the Bombay side, and an imperial order was received by Shaista Khan, ordering a similar restoration in Bengal.

The order came but just in time to save Charnock and the remnant that remained to him. Yet Shaista Khan's order, dated Dacca, July 2, was of so grudging a character that Charnock indignantly refused it. A further order, dated August 16, while not granting their demands for compensation, for exemption from taxation, and for the establishment of a mint, gave them permission to return to Hooghly and renew their trade. Job Charnock eventually returned as far as Sutanati, which, after many experiences, he had finally determined upon as the most defensible position on the lower reaches of the Hooghly.

It is not surprising that Shaista Khan should have looked on the small affairs of the English with something of contempt. He was now eighty years of age, and his mind turned to thoughts of peace and well-earned retirement. For nearly a quarter of a century he had ruled Bengal. Though in the annals of the English he figures as a 'tyrant' and as the 'old doting Nawab,' as the ruler of Bengal he appears conspicuous for his wisdom and justice. It was but natural that he should regard the English as interlopers, and their bombastic language and impudent demands enraged one accustomed to excess of deference. But that he had any particular active ill-will towards the English seems improbable. They were entirely in his hands. Had he actively taken sides against them, there can be little doubt that he had the power to sweep them out of Bengal. At the most, even when reinforced by Vice-Admiral Nicholson and his fleet, they were but a handful of men compared with the forces at the disposal of Shaista Khan. The Viceroy who could equip a fleet of seven hundred war-vessels, and had sent an army of one hundred and forty-three thousand men against the Mughs, could have made short work, by sheer force of numbers, of the little company of Englishmen, had he been so minded. Aurungzebe was too busy elsewhere to do aught but call for a map when he heard of these petty disturbances in some obscure island in the Hooghly. All power was in the hands of the Viceroy. That no harm befell even the unprotected servants of the Company at Dacca in his time speaks much for the clemency of Shaista Khan, and the close of his long reign left the English Company in Bengal in a far more flourishing condition than it had been twenty-five years before.

As the Viceroy of a Moghul province, Shaista Khan stands out beyond his contemporaries. Above all things, he gave a distracted country the peace and quietness it so much needed. Not since the Mussulman first came to Bengal had the province enjoyed so long a rest, and the blessings of peace in those days conferred a distinction upon the giver that later days cannot wholly appreciate. His rule was the period of Dacca's greatest prosperity. Noble buildings, designed and executed with all the skill of Mussulman art, rose to beautify the city. The marble tomb and mausoleum that he erected over his favourite daughter Peri Bibi, shorn as it has been of much of its glory, still remains the most beautiful Mussulman monument in all Eastern Bengal. No other viceroy or governor has so impressed his memory upon Dacca. It is truly the city of Shaista Khan. What, one cannot refrain from wondering, would be his feelings could he see it to-day, the new capital of the descendants of that despised little Company whose doings on the far-off island at the mouth of the Hooghly he regarded with so much contemptuous unconcern?

Full of years and honours, Shaista Khan laid down the viceroyalty and quitted the city where he had so long ruled. The manner of his going was full of dignity. Attended by the whole city and all the state due to his rank, he passed out through the western gate. There the great procession halted, and the aged Viceroy took his last farewell of the great city. In his day there had been unparalleled prosperity and rice had sold at

THE MAUSOLEUM OF PERI BIBI, DAUGHTER OF SHAISTA KHAN

the incredible rate of 320 seers to the rupee. His last order was that the western gate through which he had just passed should be closed, and an inscription placed upon it forbidding all future governors to open it until rice should again be sold at the same price. After he had gone they did as he had ordered, and so for forty-seven years the western gate of the city remained closed until in the days of Serferaz Khan, whose wise rule again gave prosperity to the province, the price of rice was reduced to the same rate and the gate of the city once more opened.

Five years after his departure from Dacca, Shaista Khan died at Agra at the age of eighty-six, full of dignity and honours, one of the few examples of a great Moghul prince ending his days in peaceful retirement after a long and uniformly successful career.

CHAPTER VI

THE LAST DAYS OF DACCA AS CAPITAL OF BENGAL

For the moment the English profited little by the departure of Shaista Khan. Aurungzebe, intent upon his wars in the south, had just now turned aside for a moment to wreak vengeance upon the men who had harassed his fleets, fortified Madras and Bombay in spite of prohibitions, and finally entered into an alliance with his life-long enemies, the Mahrattas. In a fit of passion he had issued orders that the English should be extirpated from his dominions. When the order reached Dacca Shaista Khan had already laid down the vice-royalty, and Bahadur Khan, who was acting temporarily in his place, at once proceeded to carry out the Emperor's commands. The Company's agents in Dacca, as well as Messrs. Eyre and Braddyll, two members of Council who had been despatched to Dacca to negotiate peace, were flung into prison, and orders sent to Hooghly to drive the English once and for all from their settlements at the head of the Bay.

But the orders came too late. The English Company, after much deliberation, had finally resolved of its own accord to evacuate Bengal. A few months before, to add to its troubles, had arrived the erratic Captain Heath, a hot-headed swashbuckler, in whom the Court of Directors had unaccountably put their faith to bring about harmony and a final settlement of their troubled affairs in the Bay. Upon Job Charnock and the other servants of the Company, already distracted by dangers and difficulties on every hand, Captain Heath descended like a whirlwind. The days that succeeded his arrival passed in the true manner of comic opera. Arriving at Hooghly on September 20, 1688, in command of a fleet of ten or eleven ships, he at once announced that he had sole authority over the Company's affairs, and that his orders were to convey the whole of the Bengal establishment to Chittagong. Surprised and alarmed by this unexpected news, they were still further distracted by the announcement that they must be ready packed up and all their affairs settled by November 10. Then, hearing that Bahadur Khan at Dacca was fitting out an expedition against the King of Arracan, the irresponsible Heath sent a truculent offer of help, provided that the Viceroy would confirm all the privileges already granted to the Company and further allow them to build a fort, otherwise the

English would shake the dust of Bengal off their feet, refusing to stay there longer to trade 'in fenceless factories.' Finally, however, blustering and impatient, without even waiting for a reply, he set sail two days before the time he had himself appointed, leaving the Company's servants in Dacca to their fate. Thereafter for nearly four months, with the whole Bengal establishment on board, he went 'tripping from port to port' in the Bay, until at last he finally landed Job Charnock and his much-tried Council in Madras on March 4, 1689.

Bengal for the moment appeared lost to the Company as a centre of trade and commerce. Only its agents in Dacca and a few other out-stations, dispossessed and in prison, represented the English in the Province. Meantime Captain Heath swaggered at Madras, full of reasons for his ill-success, while Job Charnock waited with what patience he might, during fifteen weary months, for the coming of the opportunity that his experience of the strange turns of Eastern politics led him to anticipate.

Aurungzebe's sudden burst of anger cooled as swiftly as it came. The main object of his life at that time was the conquest of the Mahrattas, and he was not slow to find that it was better to number the English among his allies than among his foes.

Not only when open war was declared did the English fleet practically clear the Moghul ships off the Malabar coast and stop his merchants' trade with Arabia, and the pilgrims on their way to Mecca, but the pecuniary loss from exactions he had levied upon English trade was by no means inconsiderable. Aurungzebe swiftly inclined to milder measures, and early in 1690 terms of peace were drawn up in his camp at Vijapur in the Deccan between him and the English Commissioner sent from Bombay by Sir John Child.

The result of this peace was a firman from the Emperor to Ibrahim Khan, whom he had recently appointed Viceroy of Bengal. It is dated April 23, 1690, and reads quaintly in the light of other days: 'You must understand that it has been the good fortune of the English to repent them of their irregular proceedings, and that, not being in their former greatness, they have by their vakeels petitioned for their lives, and a pardon for their faults, which, out of my extraordinary favour towards them, I have accordingly granted. Therefore upon receipt hereof, my Phirmaund, you must not create them any further trouble, but let them trade freely in your government as formerly and this order I expect you to see strictly observed.'

Ibrahim Khan at once endeavoured to give effect to Aurungzebe's orders. He was a man of peace, a strange figure, as he sat buried in his books and deciphering his Persian manuscripts, undisturbed in the midst of the stirring events of his time. Utterly unambitious of military glory, he bore no enmity to the English, and was eager to promote the interests of industry and commerce. He at once released the Company's agents in Dacca, restoring to them their factories and all their goods which had been sequestrated in Bengal. Further, he sent letters to Job Charnock at Madras, and after some natural hesitation the veteran representative of the Company returned and once more anchored off Sutanati on August 7, 1690. It was a memorable day in the annals of the English in Bengal. With an escort of only thirty soldiers, the Chief of the English Factories began the difficult task of once more reconstructing from the beginning the whole fabric of the Company's settlement in the Bay. But from the small establishment at Sutanati, which was all that Charnock could at first attempt, was destined to rise in after years the great city of Calcutta. Job Charnock lived only two-and-a-half years after his return, but, though he knew it not, he left behind him the small beginnings which in later days were destined to become the second city in the empire. Under a huge mausoleum in St. John's churchyard the veteran servant of the Company, his thirty-eight years of loyal service done, sleeps his last sleep, not yet forgotten by those who follow in the paths that he made straight.

The strong hand of Shaista Khan once removed, it was not long before disturbances arose in Bengal. In 1696 Sabha Singh, a Hindu zemindar, having a grievance against the Raja of Burdwan, and securing the help of the Afghans in Orissa, who were ever ready for the fray, attacked and killed the Raja and all his family with the exception of one son. This son, Juggut Rai, fled to Dacca and implored the help of the Viceroy. But Ibrahim Khan, immersed in his books, paid little heed, and contented himself with a hasty order to the military governor of Jessore to punish the rebels. It was this supineness of Ibrahim Khan that gave the Company at last the chance it had so long awaited. The rebels, rapidly advancing, took Hooghly, and the English, left to their fate by the local Moghul governor and with no hope of help from the Viceroy at Dacca, were forced, with the rebels at their very gates, to take measures for their own defence. Ibrahim Khan, still unwilling to bestir himself, responded to their call for aid only with vague orders to them to defend themselves. The English at Sutanati, the French at Chandernagore, and the Dutch at Chinsura liberally interpreted these orders and hastily raised fortifications round their factories. Thus for the first time the English undertook military works on Moghul territory. It was a far greater step in advance than they themselves at the time were aware. It was an admission that the Moghul power was no longer able to protect them—that in future they must provide for their own defence. The rise of the ramparts of Fort William was a notable landmark in the history of the English in Bengal.

It is said that Aurungzebe first heard of the rebellion through the newspaper, so careless had Ibrahim Khan been even to report the disturbance to his imperial master. The Emperor, indignant at his Viceroy's neglect of duty, at once appointed his own grandson, Azim Oshan, to the united government of Bengal, Behar, and Orissa. The brief reign of Ibrahim Khan, in striking contrast with that of Shaista Khan, was over. His son, Zubberdust Khan, was left in command until his successor could reach Bengal, and being, unlike his father, a keen soldier and energetic administrator, he undertook a vigorous campaign against the rebels, which he continued with eminent success until the arrival of the new Viceroy.

It was in 1697 that Azim Oshan arrived in Bengal. The first three years of his viceroyalty, during which he made his headquarters at Burdwan, were spent in subduing the western portions of the province. It was not until the year 1700, after having restored peace throughout the kingdom, that he sent for the state boats that Sultan Shuja had built sixty years before, and prepared to make his triumphal entry into Dacca. Once installed there he had leisure to turn to the affairs of the English. The struggle between the two Companies, the Old and the New, was at its height, and Azim Oshan, ever ready to do anything for money, took bribes impartially from both. For 14,000 rupees he was willing to make any number of promises to the New Company, while in July 1698, for 16,000 rupees he had given the English letters patent to purchase from the existing holders the right of renting the three villages of Calcutta, Sutanati, and Govindpur, where they had finally made their headquarters on the Hooghly. The historic ramparts of Fort William, so named in compliment to the reigning monarch, rose rapidly round the English factory in the months that followed. Two years later the final settlement of disputes and the amalgamation of the two Companies enabled the English henceforth to turn a united front to their enemies in Bengal.

Meanwhile the closing scenes in the story of Dacca as the capital of Bengal were taking place. Azim Oshan's chief care was the amassing of wealth, and he looked with envy upon the large amount made annually in trade by the European factories. The idea suddenly dawned upon him that he might become the sole merchant of all European and foreign goods brought into Bengal. He therefore attempted to form a company of his own, despatching agents to all the ports to purchase forcibly the cargoes of all ships that arrived, and afterwards to sell the goods at a profit. This suicidal form of trade he called Sondai Khas and Sondai Aam—special and general traffic. But there were newspapers, it appears, even in those days, that threw a fierce light upon the doings of authority even in these far-off provinces of the empire, and Aurungzebe read of this new form of trade. 'It is not Sondai Khas (special traffic),' he said scornfully, though the originator of it was his own grandson, 'it is Sonda Khas (special madness).' He wrote peremptorily that it must cease, and reduced the military escort of the Prince by five hundred horse to mark his displeasure. Baffled in one source of gain, Azim Oshan turned to another. There were at that time many wealthy Hindus in Dacca, men who, in spite of the oppression and taxation that had fallen heavily upon them through centuries of Mussulman rule, had amassed large fortunes. Desiring to ingratiate himself with these, with his own ends in view, the Viceroy himself took part in the celebration of their holidays. It is related that he even put on yellow and rose-coloured garments, and entered personally into the performance of their festivals. This, too, came to Aurungzebe's ears, and he wrote to his grandson with his own hand a letter of scathing reprimand and contempt. 'A yellow turban and rose-coloured garments,' ran the old Emperor's scornful message, 'suit ill with a beard of forty-six years' growth.'

It was doubtless these follies that induced Aurungzebe to send a man after his own heart to take charge of the Dewani, or revenue administration of Bengal, in the person of Murshid Kuli Khan. The rise to greatness of this prince is another of the many romances of Moghul annals. Born the son of a poor Brahmin, he was purchased by a Persian named Haji Shafi, who took him to Ispahan, where he educated him in the Mahomedan faith. At the merchant's death he received his freedom, and leaving Persia sought his fortunes in the Deccan, where he succeeded in obtaining employment under the Dewan of Berar. Even at that early age he showed his skill in accounts and all matters of finance. His worth once proved, his promotion was rapid, and it was not long before he was brought to the notice of Aurungzebe, who appointed him to the important office of Dewan of Hyderabad. In 1701, dissatisfied with the financial administration of his grandson, Azim Oshan, in

Dacca, he appointed Murshid Kuli Khan Dewan of Bengal. In this province, Aurungzebe's practice had been to keep the military and revenue branches of the government distinct. The Nazim or Viceroy was the representative of the Emperor. His duty was to defend the country from outside attack and to maintain peace and order within. The duties of the Dewan were less prominent, but scarcely less important. His it was to collect the revenue and undertake full financial control of the province. In the days of the great Viceroys the office of Dewan was an entirely subordinate one. The Nazim had the power to send written orders for government expenses to the Dewan, with which the latter was forced to comply. The Dewan, in fact, hitherto had been little more than the collector of taxes and treasury officer of the Viceroy. But with the coming of Murshid Kuli Khan, strong in the Emperor's favour, the office of Dewan grew in dignity and influence. Murshid Kuli Khan soon found that, during the years of peace under Shaista Khan, Eastern Bengal had thriven and developed into a rich agricultural province. But the revenue, carelessly collected, had been dissipated under the weak rule of Ibrahim Khan, and appropriated to his own use by the avaricious Azim Oshan. The new Dewan was a reformer of the most energetic type, and he at once set himself to abolish abuses and restore order. Much of the land had been made over to military *jagirdars* as the reward of past services or in payment of services still rendered, thus withdrawing it from all control of the exchequer. The consequence was that, though the revenue of Bengal should have amounted to a crore (10,000,000) of rupees, it had fallen far short of that amount, and had become insufficient even to pay the expenses of the Viceroy and his administration. Murshid Kuli Khan succeeded in obtaining the cancellation by the Emperor of all the *jagirs* except the stipends of the Nizamut and the Dewani, most of which were transferred to Orissa, where the revenue was still badly collected and the military *jagirdars* might be trusted to restore some semblance of order. Thus the whole of the zemindars of Eastern Bengal were brought under the direct control of the exchequer, and their rents were largely increased, the revenue consequently rising far beyond its recent limits. Within a short time Murshid Kuli Khan was able to despatch royal revenue to Delhi to the amount of one crore and thirty lacs, the greater part in specie, escorted by a guard of three hundred cavalry and five hundred infantry. To the Emperor and the chief ministers he also sent presents—'hill horses, antelopes, hawks, shields made of rhinoceros hide, sword-blades, Sylhet mats, Dacca muslins and

Cossimbazaar silks, filigree work of gold and silver and wrought ivory.' A Dewan who could transmit such a huge accretion of revenue naturally found favour in the sight of his imperial master.

But it was otherwise with Azim Oshan, the Viceroy. Hitherto it had sufficed for him merely to write an order for money required, and the Dewan had submissively provided it. Now, Murshid Kuli Khan claimed control over all pecuniary transactions, and Azim Oshan's power of enriching himself and his unbounded extravagance received a severe check. Even his escort of five thousand cavalry had been abolished by the new Dewan on the plea that cavalry were of no use in a river-locked district like Dacca. The peculations of all the courtiers were also at an end, and Murshid Kuli Khan was soon the most unpopular man in Dacca at the viceregal court. But, strong in the Emperor's favour, he was unassailable. Azim Oshan, enraged beyond measure, finally resorted to violence and intrigue.

It was a dramatic scene that took place in the streets of Dacca in the early days of the year 1702, a scene that led to the final abandonment of the city as the capital of Bengal. Abdul Wahid, the commandant of a corps of horse, known as the Nukedy, devoted to the person of the Viceroy, had willingly listened when Azim Oshan unfolded a plan for ridding himself of his obnoxious Dewan. Murshid Kuli Khan, too wise to flout openly the authority of the Viceroy, was punctilious in attending his court and paying his respects. Azim Oshan held his court in the Pooshtah, a residence now long since decayed, that once stood on the river-bank. Thither Murshid Kuli Khan was accustomed to go in his state palanquin, surrounded by his escort, whenever the Viceroy held court. It was on the way there, in the crowded streets of the bazaar, that Abdul Wahid hoped to catch him at a disadvantage. In a narrow lane not far from the palace he placed his troops to waylay the Dewan. Endeavouring to surround his palanquin as he approached, they clamoured for some arrears of pay which they said were overdue. But Murshid Kuli Khan, well versed in the tortuous ways of Eastern politics, had not failed to arm himself and his escort, and pushing his way through the hostile soldiers reached the palace in safety, surrounded by his guards. There, seeing that the end of all peaceful relations between them had come, he openly accused Azim Oshan of complicity in the design of Abdul Wahid and upbraided him with his treachery. 'If you desire my life,' he is reported to have said, laying his hand upon his dagger, 'here let us try the contest.' But Azim Oshan was no warrior and refused, taking refuge under his viceregal dignity. Then, proceeding to the Hall of Audience, Murshid Kuli Khan called Abdul Wahid, and, after inquiring into the alleged arrears of pay, gave him a settlement in full and dismissed him and his troops from the imperial service.

Azim Oshan, a coward at heart, was thrown into great fear by the failure of this attempt, knowing that his relationship to Aurungzebe would not spare him from that potentate's wrath. Murshid Kuli Khan, returning home, drew up an account of the morning's proceedings and despatched it to Aurungzebe. Then, deeming that he was no longer safe in Dacca, he left the city that same day, accompanied by all his followers and the whole machinery of the Dewani. He departed without paying his respects to the Viceroy. Azim Oshan, from his palace on the river, saw the state barge of his rival pass by with its attendant fleet, and, fearful of the issue of an open contest, made no effort to stop his going. It was well for Murshid Kuli Khan that he had previously disbanded the Viceroy's bodyguard of seven thousand horse.

As the fleet sailed slowly down the Dullasery, carrying with it all the revenue machinery of the province, it tolled the knell of the greatness of Dacca. Murshid Kuli Khan chose Murshidabad as his residence, and it was there and at Rajmahal that the closing scenes of the Mussulman Empire in Bengal were finally enacted. Shortly afterwards there arrived in Dacca the Emperor's orders in response to the protest Murshid Kuli Khan had sent to him. His near relationship to the Emperor did not save Azim Oshan, and Aurungzebe's anger fell upon him in full force. He was ordered to leave Dacca forthwith, and to proceed immediately to Behar. Though he left his son Farrukh Siyar behind him to act as his deputy, it was only for a brief period, and the appointment was apparently never ratified. With Azim Oshan's departure the end had come. Though leaving in disgrace he was still Viceroy, and his love of display led him to depart with all the splendour due to his position. From the landing-stage near his palace, the Pooshtah, taking with him eight crores of rupees as the spoils of his term of office, he embarked, to the sound of cannon and the roll of drums, in the state barge that had been built years before by the ill-fated Sultan Shuja, himself so great a lover of display. With him departed all the public officers—the immense following that gathers round an Eastern Court—and all signs of authority, embarked in a great fleet that covered the river for many miles. Slowly the long procession passed from sight, and Dacca was left strangely quiet and deserted, with its interests dwindled suddenly and become purely local, no more to be the city to which all eyes turned, and from which all orders issued for the whole Province of Bengal. The hundred years of its greatness had passed. The next Viceroy who should tread its streets was destined to be one of that race which, ignorant of future empire, was still struggling manfully against great odds, and suffering many indignities at the hands of Moghul emperors and princes, in its endeavour to gain for itself a trading footing at the head of the Bay. So strange are the turns of the wheel of fate!

CHAPTER VII

THE DECLINE OF THE MOGHUL POWER

The great Aurungzebe lay dying. Before the walls of the city of Ahmednugger, whence twenty years before he had set forth with all the pomp of war to the conquest of the south, the end had come. Worn out with his long campaigns, the old Emperor realised at last that his days were numbered. It was a pathetic scene. Death faced him, and the enemy went as yet unconquered. At the age of ninety-one he looked back upon his life's work still undone and his highest aspirations unfulfilled. The iron had entered deep into the soul of this last great Emperor of Hindustan, and as at length he recognised that his last fight was fought there took possession of him a vast remorse. Alone he faced death; and as he waited the coming of the great conqueror the memories of many years rose up before him and accused him. The faces of those whom he had ruthlessly swept aside to push his way to empire seemed to hover threateningly about his bedside. Fifty years of stern, just rule counted as nothing in his distorted mind against such crimes as these. In his efforts to prevent his sons wading their way through each other's blood to empire as he had done, he had sent them far from him. Brave and an emperor till the end, he would face death alone. Heart-broken, he wrote burning words to his sons, eloquent with pathos and appeal. 'Many stood around me when I came into the world. Alone I go hence. What am I, or for what good purpose came I into the world? I cannot tell. I bewail the moments that I have spent forgetful of God's worship. I have not done well by my country or my people. My years have gone by profitless. God has been in my heart, yet my darkened eyes have not seen his glorious light. The army is confounded and without heart or help, even as I am apart from God, with no rest for my heart. Nothing brought I into this world, but I carry away with me the burden of my sins. Though my trust is in the mercy and goodness of God, yet I fear to think of what I have done. Yet, come what may, I have launched my barque upon the waters. Farewell, farewell, farewell!' He had often expressed the wish that he might die on a Friday, and this small desire of his was granted. He died on Friday, March 4, 1707, and his simple yet dignified burial was carried out according to his last wishes.

'Carry this creature of dust to the nearest spot, and there commit him to the earth with no useless coffin.'

With Aurungzebe died the greatness of the Moghul Empire. Rapidly, during the years that followed, it sank into a decline from which there was no awakening. Over Bengal, its fairest province, it had already relaxed its hold. Within the next sixty years it was doomed to see it slip completely from its grasp.

The century that had dawned so inauspiciously for the English Company in Bengal with worthless promises and fruitless negotiations, and in the midst of alarms from the anger of Aurungzebe and his Viceroys, was destined to see a wonderful transformation before its close. The eighteenth century was the critical period in the history of the English in India. It saw the gradual abandonment of their first timorous attitude as merely a Company for trade, and the gradual forced adoption of a new position of political supremacy. The small company of Englishmen who, beset with danger, gathered on the banks of the Hooghly and in the out-stations of Dacca, Patna, and Cossimbazaar at the beginning of the century, had acquired before its close, thanks to the victories of Clive and the leadership of Warren Hastings, the supreme control of the vast territories of Bengal, Behar, and

Orissa, while the Moghul princes who had so often threatened their extermination survived only as effete puppets living on their bounty.

But there were sixty years of disorder and unrest to come in Eastern Bengal before the beginning of the peace and order that slowly began to descend upon it under British rule. With the departure of Farrukh Siyar on his way to ascend the imperial throne, Dacca fell finally from its high estate. Handed over to a Deputy or Naib Nazim, who governed under the control of the Viceroy at Murshidabad or Rajmahal, it was no longer a city of the first importance. Yet its governorship was still one of the prizes of the imperial service. A huge province stretching from the Garo Hills on the north to the Bay of Bengal on the south, from Tipperah and Chittagong on the east to Orissa on the west, it comprised an area of more than fifteen thousand square miles. It was considered the first and most lucrative appointment under the Nizamut, the jurisdiction being the largest and the province the richest. Such a post Murshid Kuli Khan, now Viceroy of Bengal, was not likely to allow to pass out of his own family, and he bestowed it upon Mirza Lutfullah, who had married his granddaughter. All power during the long rule of this prince centred in the hands of Mir Hubbeeb, a native of Shiraz, in Persia, one of the many keen-

THE EMPEROR FARRUKH SIYAR.

witted adventurers who had come east in search of fortune and found it. It is reported of him that he could neither read nor write, yet that he possessed great activity of mind and expertness in business. It was he to whom fell the honour of adding new conquests to the Moghul Empire in its declining days. Tipperah, which had hitherto lain outside the sphere of Moghul influence, was now first definitely incorporated with Bengal. It was a wild country, with huge stretches of jungle, the home of elephants, where Buktyar Khiliji and Mir Jumla and many other Mussulman generals had penetrated and returned with the spoils of war, but leaving behind them no permanent sign of conquest. It was a quarrel in the Raja of Tipperah's own family which gave the Moghul Naib Nazim at Dacca his opportunity. The nephew of the Raja, having displeased his uncle, fled the country and took refuge with a Mussulman zemindar, Aka Sadik, who, being a friend of Mir Hubbeeb, brought his guest's case to the minister's notice. Mir Hubbeeb was not slow to see the advantage that might be gained. Obtaining a *perwana* from Mirza Lutfullah, he set out with all the troops available in Dacca and, crossing the Megna, marched straight upon the capital of the country, guided by the Raja's nephew. Surprised at the suddenness of the attack, the Raja fled to the mountains, and his nephew, with various conditions that made him completely subordinate to the Moghul power at Dacca, was seated on the *gadi*. Mussulman troops were left in the country, and the name of Tipperah was changed by the Naib Nazim to Roshenabad, the Land of Light, being the most easterly portion of the Moghul Empire on which the sun first shone in its daily course.

Shuja Addin Khan, who had married Zynet-un-Nissa the daughter of Murshid Kuli Khan, now ruled at Murshidabad as Viceroy, and after the success of his deputy in Tipperah he determined to send him to Orissa, another province on the outskirts of the empire where the strong hand was still more necessary. In his place he appointed his own son, Serferaz Khan, Naib Nazim of Eastern Bengal. But Zynet-un-Nissa, the imperious lady who, as the heiress of Murshid Kuli Khan, regarded herself as his successor in political influence, refused to part with her only son, and he remained at Murshidabad, two deputies being sent to Dacca in the persons of Juswunt Roy, who was to be Dewan and to have the active direction of affairs, and Syed Ghalib Ali Khan, who was associated in the government with him. Juswunt Roy, who had been one of the ministers of Murshid Kuli Khan, was a wise ruler and an eminent financier. Abolishing the monopolies imposed by Mir Hubbeeb,

THE WIFE OF THE EMPEROR FARRUKH SIYAR.

he did everything in his power to foster trade. Under the joint rule of these two deputies, Dacca enjoyed again a brief spell of peace and prosperity such as it had not known since the days of Shaista Khan. It was during this time that rice again fell to 320 seers to the rupee, and the western gate of the city, which Shaista Khan had closed on his departure forty-six years before, was once more opened with much ceremony and great rejoicing.

But the spell of prosperity was brief. Again Serferaz Khan, away at Murshidabad, allowed a woman to influence him. His sister Nuffessa Begum, imperious and self-willed, true daughter of Zynet-un-Nissa and granddaughter of Murshid Kuli Khan, persuaded him to recall Ghalib Ali Khan from Dacca and appoint his own son-in-law, Murad Ali, to succeed him. Murad Ali brought with him to Dacca, as his right-hand man, one Rajbullub, and together they commenced a rule of oppression and injustice that quickly reduced the city from its former prosperous condition to a state of poverty and distress. Juswunt Roy, the Dewan, powerless to prevent this ruin of his labours, resigned, and all power fell into the hands of Murad Ali and his satellite.

These were the days of the invasion of the Persian usurper, Nadir Shah, and the central authority at Delhi was tottering to its fall. Its hold over this province of the furthest East had already become practically non-existent, and Serferaz Khan, who seized the viceroyalty on his father's death in 1739, appears never to have been confirmed in office by the Emperor. Bengal, left entirely to itself, quickly became a prey to rival factions. The battle was to the strong, and Serferaz Khan, completely under feminine influence, was not the man for the moment. His rule was brief, and in the following year he fell slain in battle near Murshidabad, and his rival, Ali Verdi Khan, governor of Behar, seized the viceroyalty. He immediately despatched his nephew and son-in-law, Shamut Jung Nowarish Mahomed, to be his Deputy at Dacca, and with strange clemency in the days when even fratricide in the case of newly succeeded monarchs was scarce accounted a crime, sent under his charge the widow and two sons of his rival Serferaz Khan to reside in honourable confinement in the eastern capital. For many years they lived peaceful lives, untouched by the stirring politics of the day, in the Zanjira palace, a beautiful building raised by Ibrahim Khan on the right bank of the Buriganga. Thither the haughty Nuffessa Begum, sister of Serferaz Khan, was also permitted to retire. So devoted was she to her late brother's family that the story goes that she offered to undertake 'the office of superintendent of Nowarish Mahomed's seraglio' if she was allowed to adopt as her heir a posthumous son of her brother named Aga Baba. It was an extraordinary position for the haughty Nuffessa Begum; but she excused the degradation on the ground of her devotion to her brother's family. Yet her pride was not dead, and it is related that so scrupulous was she in her conduct that she was never seen by Nowarish, who used to converse with her on business through a curtain. The infant for whom she sacrificed so much was destined in after-years to rouse an equal devotion in another—one Rahim Allah Khan of the Punjaub, reputed 'the best archer and the stoutest man' throughout the whole army, who for devotion to the cause of Aga Baba suffered imprisonment at the hands of Mir Kassim Khan.

But, like Serferaz Khan, Nowarish Mahomed resided for the most part at Murshidabad, and the glimpses of the Eastern Capital during his long rule by deputy are few and brief. Two years before his death, however, yet another of those dramatic scenes that so constantly recur in Oriental history took place in Dacca, and another act of treachery was added to the long list that fills the city's annals. Ali Verdi Khan, the old Nawab of Bengal, exhausted with his struggle against the Mahrattas, was spending his last days in his beautiful palace at Murshidabad. Infatuated with the evil youth, his grandson Surajudowlah, and regardless of the welfare of the province, he had nominated him his successor as Viceroy of the three Subahs of Bengal, Behar, and Orissa. But Nowarish Mahomed, married to Ghesetti Begum, Ali Verdi's own daughter, was a formidable rival whom Surajudowlah eyed askance. The air was thick with intrigues that spread and ramified as Ali Verdi Khan approached his eightieth year and grew daily more infirm. In the midst of them chance suddenly threw in Surajudowlah's way an opportunity to injure his rival that he was not slow to take. Nowarish had appointed Hossain Kuli Khan his minister at Murshidabad, and the latter's nephew, Hossain Addin Khan, as his deputy at Dacca. With the latter, one Aga Sadoc, the son of a zemindar in the Backergunj district, had come into violent collision. Enraged at a decision of the deputy's, Aga Sadoc had journeyed to Murshidabad to appeal to Nowarish Khan himself. But there he met with scant success, and was thrown into prison by the all-powerful minister, the uncle of Hossain Addin Khan. Enraged still further at this treatment, he eagerly threw himself into the hands of Surajudowlah, who promised to make him Naib in place of Hossain Addin Khan when the latter had been satisfactorily disposed of. Effecting his escape with the help of Surajudowlah, he returned to Dacca, and with his father, Mahomed Bakhar, conspired against Hossain Addin Khan. At the dead of night, with an armed band, they broke secretly into the palace by the riverside and murdered Hossain Addin as he slept, ignorant of the danger that threatened. But Aga Sadoc had reckoned without the people of Dacca. Hossain Addin Khan had ruled them with justice and impartiality, and vague rumours of the excesses and oppressions of Surajudowlah had already reached them. When morning came and they heard of the murder of their chief, they rose in a body and surrounded the palace, where Aga Sadoc and his father, who intended to assume the governorship of the city, had remained. When asked by the people to produce his sunnud of appointment as deputy governor of the city, he pointed significantly to the sword that was still stained with the blood of Hossain Addin. But the populace surged angrily round the palace, and with shouts and cries rushed up the steps and, seizing Mahomed Bakhar, killed him on the spot, while Aga Sadoc, his son, barely succeeded in escaping with his life. So failed, owing to the loyalty of the populace to their dead chief, one of the last attempts in Mussulman annals to seize the government of Dacca by force.

This brutal murder of Hossain Addin Khan together with that of his uncle, Hossain Kuli Khan, which occurred shortly afterwards, seems to have stood out in Surajudowlah's mind, and to have been impressed upon his conscience, beyond all his other misdeeds. It was little more than a year later that, fleeing from the battle-ground of Plassey, and betrayed by a fakir and brought back a prisoner to Murshidabad, he was murdered in his own palace by order of Mir Meerun, his own general's son. When his murderer came into the room in which he was confined it is reported that Surajudowlah cried out 'I must die to atone for the murder of Hossain Kuli Khan!' Then the murderer slew him in cold blood with his sabre, and the wretched youth of scarce twenty years fell exclaiming 'Hossain Kuli is at last avenged!'

Rajbullub, who had been in charge of the Fleet Department, was appointed by Nowarish Mahomed to administer the government, and he at once took the opportunity of confiscating all the property of the conspirators, appropriating to himself the big zemindari of Rajnaghur. Rajbullub was not the man to let opportunities slip, and during the short time he was in command he is said to have amassed two crores of rupees. But his patron died in January 1756, and three months later the death of the old Viceroy Ali Verdi Khan put supreme control into the irresponsible hands of Surajudowlah, who was no friend to Rajbullub, his rival's nominee. He at once demanded from him a large sum of money as the price of his remaining deputy governor of Dacca. Rajbullub, frightened for the safety of his hoarded wealth, conveyed it out of the town secretly under charge of his son, who set out ostensibly for the temple of Juggernath, but with the intention of seeking an asylum for his wealth within the ramparts of Fort William at Calcutta. It is significant of the strong part the English had already come to play in the politics of Bengal that Rajbullub should have chosen them as the guardians of his wealth. It was partly because the English in Fort William refused to deliver up the son of Rajbullub and his wealth that Surajudowlah set out on the expedition against them which ended in the Black Hole, and finally led to his own undoing and their triumphant ascendency in Bengal.

Those were exciting days for the little company of Englishmen in Dacca, during the hot weather and rains of 1756. They were absolutely at the mercy of the local Mussulman authorities. A mere handful of men, the Nawab Jusserat Khan could have overwhelmed them by sheer force of numbers and disposed of them as he pleased. Calcutta itself was far from safe, as events were shortly to prove, and how great was the risk run by the Company's agents in an out-station like Dacca, eleven days' journey distant, may be easily judged. Courage and tact of no mean order were necessary to meet the dangers that beset them. If it came to a question of actual force they were helpless and there was little to protect them but the prestige which attached to the European name. Yet so potent was that prestige that even Surajudowlah, in the hour of his triumph, forbore to take the extreme measures which, at least for the moment, would have freed him completely from the rivalry of the English in Bengal. In Dacca, the Company's staff seems extraordinarily small considering the immense trade interests it possessed there. Mr. Richard Becher was the chief of the factory, and under him were Mr. William Sumner, second in Council, who was absent at this time in Calcutta. Messrs. Luke Scrafton, Thomas Hyndman, Samuel Waller, Mr. John Cartier, a factor of one year's standing and Mr. John Johnstone, an assistant 'just commencing.' Lieutenant John Cudmore was in charge of the garrison and Mr. Nathaniel Wilson was the Company's surgeon. In addition, there were at least three English ladies living in Dacca at the time—Mrs. Becher, wife of the chief of the factory, with her child, a Mrs. Warwick and a Miss Harding. The factory itself, 'little better than a common house, surrounded with a thin brick wall, one half of it not above nine foot high,' offered but poor protection, while the garrison under Lieutenant Cudmore consisted of only 'four sergeants, three corporals, and nineteen European soldiers, beside thirty-four black Christians and sixty *Buxerries*,' the last named probably being Portuguese half-castes.

There could be no question of resistance, and on June 9 advices were received from the Council in Calcutta warning its agents in Dacca to collect the Company's goods and be prepared to seek safety in flight if the danger increased. Anxiously the Englishmen in the far-off out-station awaited further news of the fate of Calcutta, on which so largely depended their own safety and the very existence of all the English factories in Bengal. At length on June 27, news, confirming their worst fears, came in the form of a message from the Nawab Jusserat Khan, announcing the fall of Calcutta and the flight of Governor Drake. Intimation was also sent at the same time of the order of Surajudowlah that the English factory in Dacca should be seized and all the Company's servants thrown into prison.

Astounded at such ill news, the Dacca Council refused for the moment to believe in it, suspicious that it was only a trick on the part of the local authorities to induce their submission. Mr. Scrafton, third in Council, was at once directed to write to M. Courtin, chief of the French factory in Dacca, asking if he had received any confirmation of the news. Letters had already been received from Chandernagore, and these M. Courtin sent across to the English factory for its information. There could be no longer any doubt that the news was true, and, hopeless of assistance from without now that Calcutta had fallen, there was no choice but submission. The French, however, for the time being, were in favour with Surajudowlah, and the English Council in Dacca determined to appeal to M. Courtin to obtain the best terms possible for the Company from the local governor, Jusserat Khan. The French proved true friends in the hour of need. 'Their conduct everywhere to us on this melancholy occasion,' wrote the English Council in putting on record its sense of indebtedness, 'has been such as to merit the grateful acknowledgment of our nation.' Not only did M. Courtin induce the Nawab to forgo any active measures against them, but he even obtained permission for them all to take refuge in the French factory, he himself standing surety for them that they should there peacefully await the orders of Surajudowlah concerning them. All the Company's property, however, to the value, it is said, of 1,400,000 rupees, was at once seized, and so careful was Jusserat Khan that nothing of value should escape his clutches that he refused to allow them to take with them into the French factory anything except the clothes they were actually wearing. Thus for all the necessaries of life they were entirely dependent upon the French, who treated them with the greatest generosity and consideration. Little did the latter foresee that within less than a year the destitute English Company which they were so gallantly befriending would have seized their factory and driven them out of Dacca. It was one of those crises in the affairs of nations when events move with startling rapidity.

For over two months the French extended their hospitality to their English guests, and it was only then—very largely owing to their intercession through M. Law, chief of the French factory at Cossimbazaar—that an order permitting them to join their ships was obtained from Surajudowlah. How great their danger had been may be judged from M. Law's memoir, in which he left on record the story of these eventful days. Writing of the difficulty he experienced in obtaining the order from the Nawab, he adds significantly: 'Surajudowlah, being informed that there were two or three very charming English ladies there, was strongly tempted to adorn his harem with them.' But though the English in Dacca escaped the worst that might have befallen them, all their personal property had been confiscated, and nothing was restored to them. They were still entirely dependent on M. Courtin, and it was to him they owed the means of joining their fellow-countrymen at Fulta, where they arrived in a French sloop on August 26.

It must have been a dispirited remnant of the members of the Calcutta factory that Mr. Becher and his companions found encamped at Fulta. But brighter days were near at hand, and with the coming of Colonel Clive and Admiral Watson from Madras hope again revived for the English in Bengal. On January 2, 1757, just over six months since it had fallen, the English flag once more floated over the ramparts of Fort William, and the English Company, though doubtful and hesitating still, had finally made good its footing in the province. Measures for the recovery of the Dacca factory were promptly undertaken. 'The expedition to Dacca is in great forwardness, which is to be carried on by four hundred sailors in boats under the command of Captain Speke,' wrote Clive on January 28 to the Select Committee at Madras. 'The surprise of this place may be of great consequence to the Company's affairs.' Less than six weeks later the expedition—on March 8—

arrived in Dacca, and retook possession of the English factory. It was not, however, without some opposition that Messrs. Sumner and Waller, who returned to take over charge, resumed the Company's trade. On March 23 they wrote to Calcutta that the Nawab Jusserat Khan refused to accede to their demands to restore the factory cannon or to allow their trade without a new *perwana* from Surajudowlah. So engrossed was the Council in taking measures for its own security, and so uncertain as to the turn affairs would take, that it could offer little immediate help; and although the new *perwana* was obtained, it wrote to its agents in Dacca warning them to look to their own safety in case of need. All the assistance it could render was to send an armed sloop to Luckipore to cover their retreat in the event of its again becoming necessary to quit Dacca. Messrs. Sumner and Waller, fearing the worst, at once hurried down the river all the valuable goods then in the factory and placed them in safety on the sloop. They themselves, anxiously awaiting further news, prepared to follow if need arose. Outwardly, however, they maintained a bold front, carrying on their trade with unabated vigour, and as the days passed and no ill news came confidence was gradually restored. Finally the news of Clive's victory at Plassey on June 23, which quickly reached Dacca, assured them that the danger they had so long feared was safely past for all time.

Meanwhile the French factory had fallen on evil days. The declaration of war between England and France had become known in India early in the year, and it was on March 13 that Clive sent his famous summons to the Governor of Chandernagore to surrender in the King's name. Ten days later the fort had fallen into the hands of the English, and orders had been received by the Company's agents in Dacca to pursue a similar course with regard to the French possessions there. This was an embarrassing duty for the newly returned English agents, whose predecessors had so recently sought shelter in the French factory and received so much kindness at M. Courtin's hands. For a considerable time they apparently took no action beyond communicating to the French the orders they had received, and it was not until June 22 that M. Courtin and his followers finally left Dacca. The English agents were not unmindful of past services, and extended every courtesy to their rivals in their day of distress. They even offered to secure to M. Courtin all his private effects on condition that he made over to them the French factory and all that belonged to the Company, and himself departed for Pondicherry within a given time. Even though he rejected this offer as inconsistent with his personal honour, he was apparently allowed to leave Dacca unmolested, taking with him what he would.

The departure of the French was not the least interesting and momentous of the many scenes that the Eastern Capital had witnessed. Their factory was on the river bank, and from there they set sail in a fleet of thirty-five boats on June 22, 1757. On board, besides M. Courtin, were MM. Chevalier, Brayer, Gourlade, the surgeon, an Augustine Father, chaplain of the factory, eight European soldiers, seventeen gunners, four or five servants, and some twenty or thirty peons. Their object was to join M. Law, the chief of their factory at Cossimbazaar; but a few days after setting sail from Dacca news reached them of the battle of Plassey, and for the next eight months they were wanderers in Northern Bengal, building Fort Bourgogne, contending against hostility and treachery on the part of local zemindars, and waiting with diminishing hope for the long-expected help from Pondicherry, which was destined never to reach them. It was not until March 1758 that they finally gave up the struggle and threw themselves upon the mercy of the English at Murshidabad. One is glad to learn that M. Courtin was treated by the English there as honourably and courteously as he had treated their fellow-countrymen in Dacca two years before. He was not even detained as a prisoner of war, and Clive, in writing to him on July 15, 1758, granting him permission to retire to Pondicherry, concludes by paying him this tribute: 'I am at this moment sending an order to the captain-commandant of our troops to restore to you your two guns. I am charmed at this opportunity of showing you my appreciation of the way in which you have always behaved to the English, and my own regard for your merit.'

One last tragic scene was enacted in Dacca under native rule before the firm hand of the English began to make itself felt. To the Zanjira palace, where, through the clemency of Ali Verdi Khan, had long lived the wife and children of Serferaz Khan, there came after the battle of Plassey, less honoured and well dowered, the household of Surajudowlah—the proud daughters of Ali Verdi Khan himself. Both Ghesetti Begum and Amina Begum, in the days of their father's rule, had played important parts and seen strange and chequered times. Ghesetti Begum the elder, wife of Nowarish Mahomed, who for sixteen years had ruled as deputy governor of Dacca, had lived in luxury in Murshidabad, and after her husband's death had retired with her great wealth and her lover

Mir Nuzur Ali to her splendid palace the Moti Jhil, the Pearl Lake, near Murshidabad, a stately pile, ornamented with pillars of black marble brought from the ruins of the ancient capital of Gaur. But she had spent scarcely four months in this luxurious retreat when her father died, and her nephew Surajudowlah assumed the viceroyalty. Now Ghesetti Begum during her husband's lifetime had done her best to prevent her nephew's accession, and one of the first acts of his reign was to send to his aunt a demand for the wealth of her late husband. But Ghesetti Begum was a woman of spirit, and she attempted to defend her palace of the Pearl Lake against her enemies. It was not until deserted by the last of her attendants in the hour of need, even by her lover Mir Nuzur Ali, who fled with fifteen lacs' worth of jewels to Benares, that she submitted to the troops sent against her. Breaking into the Moti Jhil, they carried off vast quantities of treasure, and rudely drove her from the palace. Treated with little dignity, she was sent off with her women 'huddled together into some bad boats,' with none of the state which was due to her rank, on the long and tedious journey down the river to Dacca. There, 'in the most disgraceful and shameless neglect,' she joined the relatives of Serferaz Khan in the Zanjira palace.

It was but a few months later that Ghesetti Begum was followed into exile by her younger sister Amina Begum, from whom she had been so long estranged, and against whose son she bore so deep a grudge. Amina Begum had experienced vicissitudes amazing even in those stirring times. Cradled in luxury as a viceroy's daughter, she had married her cousin Syud Ahmed, and spent prosperous days with him in Patna when he ruled as governor of Behar. She had seen the uprising of rebellion and the quartered body of Mustapha Khan hung on the four gates of Patna as evidence of her husband's prowess. Then, the enemies of her house defeated, she set out to witness the marriages of her sons, celebrated with all the pomp and splendour that her soul loved in her father's palace at Murshidabad. It was a scene of true Oriental luxury and magnificence. Illuminations that seemed 'to have set both heaven and earth in a blaze,' and the 'splendid pageants and gorgeous processions of the bridegrooms' were spoken of throughout Bengal for years to come with wonder and delight. But it was the luxury that precedes the fall of empires, and it must have been a strange memory to Amina Begum amidst the grief and poverty that befell her later years. Dazzled by the attractions of the viceregal court she plotted with her husband to secure the throne, but treachery met with treachery, and the Afghan chiefs they had called in to their help fell upon Syud Ahmed and, brutally murdering him, carried off Amina Begum as a prisoner to their camp. For seventeen days she was forced to listen to the cries of her father-in-law, tortured by every horrible device known to Oriental cruelty, to reveal the place where his treasure lay hid. Then for well nigh a year she spent anxious days a prisoner in the enemy's camp, waiting for the approach of her father's army that tarried long upon the way. Rescued at last, she returned with Ali Verdi Khan to Murshidabad, and there for seven years set all her hopes upon her son Surajudowlah, scheming to secure for him the kingdom on her father's death. Then, the victory won and Surajudowlah Viceroy of Bengal, she enjoyed her last brief days of splendour. Within a few months the end had come. From her palace windows she had looked down upon her son's dead body carried with scant respect through the streets of Murshidabad, and, forgetful in her grief of all custom and tradition, she had fled out into the public gaze, and thrown herself upon his body in the midst of the crowd, only to be torn aside by the rude hands of the soldiery, denied even the consolation of her dead son's corpse. Stricken with grief, she too was soon pursuing the long and tedious journey to Dacca, there to reside unhonoured and dispossessed of all her former wealth and luxury.

It was thus a strange company that gathered within the walls of the Zanjira palace and looked out at the great city of Dacca across the Buriganga. The family of Serferaz Khan still inhabited the best apartments, living in luxury, though still prisoners, the youths growing up in idleness with all the indolence of the East. It must have been with something of revengeful joy that they watched the approach first of Ghesetti Begum, the elder daughter of their proud enemy Ali Verdi Khan, who had dispossessed them and theirs of their own, and then the younger daughter mourning the extinction of her dignity, with her widowed daughter-in-law by her side, a mere child, yet with a child of her own at her breast. The banks of the river, it is said, were crowded to see them arrive, the wife and mother and child of the man whose name had become a by-word throughout Bengal for cruelty, debauchery, and oppression. In the Zanjira palace they could have met with little welcome even from their own near relative Ghesetti Begum.

But even this refuge was not to be theirs for long. There is one last tragic scene. Mir Jaffir, who was married to the sister of Ali Verdi Khan and who had been placed upon the *musnud* by the

English after Surajudowlah's death, had grown old, and left the management of affairs in the hands of his son Mir Meerun, whose enormities soon caused to be well nigh forgotten even those of Surajudowlah himself. This monster, it is said, had already slain two of his own officers and cut off the heads of two women of his seraglio with his own hand for some trifling offence. On setting out for the defence of Patna, he entered in a note-book the names of three hundred persons who had offended him and whom he determined to put to death on his return. But before starting he sent orders to Jusserat Khan, the governor of Dacca, to put to death the mother, aunt, widow, and daughter of Surajudowlah. It was a cruel order, unprovoked, and with little object. Robbed of all their wealth, these ladies, shut up in the Zanjira palace, could have given but little cause for alarm to Mir Meerun. The governor of Dacca, to his credit, refused to carry out the order. When the news of his refusal reached Meerun, the latter was so enraged that he added the governor's name to the list of persons he had entered in his note-book to be put to death on his return from Patna. Determined that the relatives of Surajudowlah should not escape, he sent one of his own servants with orders to put them on board a vessel, with the pretence of taking them to Murshidabad, and to sink the boat on the way. So on an evening in the hot weather of 1760 the relatives of Surajudowlah embarked from the Zanjira palace on the Buriganga, unsuspicious of their fate. But they were scarcely out of sight of Dacca on the broader waters of the Dullasery, when their escort withdrew the plugs which had been carefully placed in the bottom of the boat, and, putting off in another craft, left the helpless women to their fate. The once haughty Ghesetti Begum, broken and cowed, took fright and shed tears, but Amina Begum cried out against her fate. 'O God Almighty,' she is reported to have cried, 'we are indeed all sinners and culprits, but we have committed no sin against Meerun; nay, rather to us he owes all that he has.' Then their cries rang out across the stillness of the waters far into the night, but no help came, and they perished miserably as the boat slowly sank. So ended the once proud family of Ali Verdi Khan. But vengeance soon overtook their murderer, for from his campaign against the Emperor he never returned. In the neighbourhood of Patna, Mir Meerun was struck dead by lightning as he lay in his tent in the midst of his camp on July 2, 1760, only a few days after the relatives of Surajudowlah had perished by his command.

CHAPTER VIII

DACCA UNDER BRITISH RULE

A NEW day was dawning for the city that had seen so many vicissitudes. The old scenes of lawlessness and disorder, of treachery and intrigue, of murder, rapine, and licence, that had stained her annals, were things of the past. The old typical Eastern unrestraint, and the unchecked play of passions, slowly began to give way to a strange unwonted spirit of law and order which the city even in its best days had never before known.

It was unavoidable that much of the romance should pass with the old rule. The men who were henceforth rulers of Dacca, men for the most part of strict honesty and impartiality, busy with the administration of justice, the punishment of wrongdoing, and the collection of the revenue, and content with the reality, cared little for the show of power. Their factories and offices, their court-houses and jails, rose up scornful of architectural pretensions, hideous and unsightly, built by a company of traders solely for use, with a fine disregard for appearances. Plain, blunt Englishmen, with a touch of Puritanism in their blood, Oriental splendour and magnificence made to them but little appeal. With their advent, the picturesqueness of the old court life at Dacca rapidly disappeared. Jusserat Khan still ruled nominally as Naib Nazim until his death in 1781, but from the year 1765, when Lieutenant Swinton, long remembered among the people as Sooltin Saheb, came to Dacca to take over charge of the revenue after the famous treaty of 1765 had given the English the Dewani of Bengal, Behar, and Orissa, all power gradually passed into the hands of the Company. Jusserat Khan vacated the palace in the Fort, which had been a residence of the rulers of Dacca since Ibrahim Khan built it a hundred and fifty years before, and withdrew to the Bara Katra temporarily, until the Nimtoli Kothi, the new residence which was being prepared for him, was completed. At the Nimtoli Kothi, Jusserat Khan and his descendants lived for three-quarters of a century, holding their mock court, shorn alike of its state and its authority. It was a pathetic lingering of the old *régime*, a mockery of the splendour that was past, paper and tinsel where once there had been vellum and gold. Opposite the eastern gateway, half guard, half escort, was quartered a detachment of the Company's Sepoys—

a constant reminder, if such were needed, that the power of the Moghuls was a thing of the past. Of this last of the palaces of the Naib Nazims nothing now remains save portions of the western gateway and the Baradari, the large hall where they held their diminished court and jealously preserved the few outward symbols of authority that still remained. Close by, in the Hossaini Delan, lie buried the last four Naib Nazims of Dacca: Nusrut Jung and Shams-ud-dowlah, grandsons of Jusserat Khan, Kumr-ud-dowlah, and Ghaziuddin, on whose death, childless, in 1843, the Company at last took full and complete possession.

Innumerable difficulties faced the English when first they assumed control in Dacca. Every department of the State showed unmistakable signs of the corruption and decay that had overtaken the Moghul Empire in the eighteenth century. The famous Mahomed Reza Khan was in charge of the office of Dewan at the time, and an inspection of his accounts revealed the fact that the revenues of Eastern Bengal had fallen to twenty lacs of rupees as compared with thirty-eight lacs in 1722. The lands originally allotted for the maintenance of the Nawara—the fleet—had amounted to over seven lacs, but of this only half a lac was found to be recoverable. The abuses that sprang from the absolute power of the Naib Nazims as to life and death shocked beyond measure the inherent sense of justice of the law-abiding servants of the Company. The Dak, or posting department, is described as being 'involved in a labyrinth of obscurity, without check or system,' and the delays and peculation beyond belief. Of the hundred and ten prisoners in the Dacca jail, it is recorded that ninety-five were employed at work upon the roads in irons, 'whose guilt had never been established,' and many of whom 'had been so circumstanced for nine years.' Encouraged by the weakness of the local government, dacoits infested the rivers, waylaying travellers and seizing valuable merchandise, well nigh totally disorganising trade and commerce. Raiding the villages on the river-banks, they laid waste whole tracts of country, robbing and murdering the unfortunate cultivators without mercy. So bold did they become that they even set upon and murdered a Government officer, one Captain Holland, while on his way from Dacca to Calcutta. Crime of every kind was rife, and no man went secure in life or property.

These must have been busy days for the first English administrators. Their powers ill-defined, and an infinity of difficulties awaiting their solution, it was no easy task that they had to face.

With wise caution they proceeded slowly, tentatively trying method after method of dealing with the colossal work that lay before them until they found the instrument most suited to their need. Step by step, with due order and precision, they gathered up the threads from the tangled skein that little by little fell within their grasp. There was nothing that savoured of revolution. Quietly the servants of the Company stepped into the place of the Moghul administrator and made use at the outset of the much-abused forms of government they found to hand. In 1769 Mr. Kelsall was appointed the first Supervisor of the Revenue, and the great work began in earnest. Everywhere the revenues had fallen, eaten away by wanton extravagance and peculation, and one of the first cares that demanded the attention of the new Supervisor was the reduction of expenditure. The Nawara, the famous fleet, which had been for so long the pride and glory and safety of Dacca as it rode at anchor in the Buriganga, had seen its day, and in the new *régime* it had no place. It was summarily abolished and the ships sold, the lands that were still recoverable of those that had been granted for its maintenance being taken over by the Company. To check the abuses of the Naib Nazim's Courts, prompt measures were adopted. Every sentence of death passed by the Naib Nazim needed confirmation by a representative of the Company before it could be carried into effect, while a European officer was deputed to attend the Adaulat Courts to see that justice was properly administered. But Mr. Kelsall had only four English Assistants at the outset, and it was impossible for a little band of five Englishmen, unversed in the methods of Oriental cunning and intrigue, to make great headway against the mass of corruption and confusion that confronted them. The great wonder is that they were able to do what they did. They make a striking picture, those five Englishmen set in the midst of a vast and alien province, struggling through heat, discomfort, and intrigue to bring order out of chaos, and to lay the foundations of an administration of honesty and integrity that should confer untold benefits upon a harassed and exhausted people, and upon many generations yet to come. Average level-headed Englishmen, in no wise distinguished above their fellows, their very names long since forgotten, they yet played their part in the foundation of a great empire, unostentatious to the end, writing their epitaphs in deeds, not words. In the midst of a newly conquered people whose great traditions had not yet become a memory, they had little but their own prestige, then only in its first youth, to place against overwhelming numbers. The force at their disposal was absurdly small, a mere handful of men in the midst of the teeming population of the great capital which but a few years before had sent out its orders to exterminate them root and branch. Mr. Grewber, appointed to be Supervisor with the new title of Collector in 1772, found only two companies of Sepoys, ill-trained, unproved men from a corps at Chittagong, as the sole defence of English authority in Dacca. It was a strange turn in the wheel of fate that the proud city which had seen great armies contending for its possession should settle down, striking no single blow for independence, under so small a force, led by a little company of Englishmen. The peaceful acquisition of the Eastern Province is one of the most remarkable features in the English annals in Bengal.

It was to face no organised resistance that the Collector was forced in 1773 to ask for an augmentation of the military forces at his command. They were inadequate even for the duties of police. Dacoities and murders were still of everyday occurrence. So weak had become the local Moghul authority in its last days that whole companies of banditti roamed the countryside or infested the great rivers, bent on plunder and rapine. It is said that as many as ten thousand *sunyassees* were collected in one part of the district alone, compelling the wretched inhabitants to pay tribute and driving them in terror from their homes. A detachment of Sepoys sent out against them, completely outnumbered and overwhelmed, met with a severe defeat, and the English officer falling into their hands was brutally murdered. In the following year a regiment of Militia was raised to augment the force, consisting of six companies, each one hundred strong, commanded by an English Captain and a Subaltern, with a native adjutant and a full complement of native officers. The troops thus raised played in those first days many parts. They guarded the Katcheries and the Treasury, they acted as excise officers to prevent the smuggling of salt, they escorted treasure on long and dangerous journeys by land and river, they executed decrees of the Provincial Courts, and they made their way into remote and unknown corners of the district to seize and bring in refractory zemindars who refused to pay their rent or otherwise disobeyed the orders of the Courts. Ten years later the Militia was disbanded and a Provincial Corps raised in its stead.

Reforms in the local administration quickly followed. In 1772 the Company assumed charge of the office of Dewan in place of Mahomed Reza Khan, and a Court of Dewani Adaulat was instituted under the Collector as President, who, with the assistance of a native Dewan, tried all civil suits. Two years later the Provincial Council was established, with the famous Mr. Barwell as chief, but, an experiment in local government, it was abolished in 1781, and Mr. Day was appointed first Magistrate and Collector, while a Court of Judicature was established, of which Mr. Duncanson was first Judge.

It is during these early years of British supremacy that two famous names figure for a brief space in the annals of Dacca. William Makepeace Thackeray, sixteenth child of Dr. Thackeray, Headmaster of Harrow and grandfather of the future novelist, had arrived in India as a Writer in the Company's service in June 1766, at the age of seventeen. For the first five years he was employed in Calcutta, for some time as secretary to Mr. Cartier, who became Governor of Bengal in 1769, and it was during this period that he was joined by two of his sisters, Jane and Henrietta, who were doubtless glad to escape from the overcrowded household at home to the wider outlook that India afforded. Both these ladies, as well as their brother, were soon destined to become intimately connected with Dacca. It was there that Mr. Cartier had spent a large portion of his earlier service, and he had good cause to remember how great were the advantages it offered to a young civilian in the way of private trade and emoluments. Desirous of doing his best for his *protégé* before leaving India, he appointed him factor and fourth in Council at Dacca, and there Thackeray, accompanied by his sisters, arrived in 1771. It was still the time when large fortunes were to be made by the Company's servants in Bengal, and though great changes were impending from the following year when Warren Hastings assumed office as Governor-General, Thackeray in the years that followed found unlimited opportunities, which were regarded as perfectly legitimate, and of which he made good use, of amassing considerable private wealth. He remained only a year in Dacca, being appointed, under Warren Hastings's new system of administration, the first Collector of the neighbouring frontier province of Sylhet in 1772. As virtual ruler of this wild, unexplored country, new opportunities opened out before him, and although he only held the Collectorship for two short years, he associated himself so closely with the district that he has become known for all time as 'Sylhet' Thackeray.

It must have been a fascinating life for a young man of only twenty-three. Though nominally under the control of the Council at Dacca, he was practically in supreme authority over a vast district, untouched as yet by British influence, and waiting to receive the impress of the strong rule that should evolve law and order out of chaos. A free hand and a wide scope gave full play to the young Collector's individuality. The infinite variety of his work is astonishing. First and foremost he was the Collector of the revenue, and so long as the full tale of it in cowries, the local currency, reached the Treasury at Dacca the Council there evinced but little further interest in the Province. Those were the days before the writing of voluminous reports, the laborious making of petitions and appeals, and constant references to higher authorities; and Thackeray was left unhampered in the control of his district, save only in so far as he did not touch the revenue interests of the Company. The summary administration of justice, the making of roads and bridges, the trapping of wild elephants, the building of jails, the control of the Treasury, the organisation of famine relief, the control of the police, the establishment of schools and dispensaries, and the introduction of experiments in agriculture, these were but a few of the subjects with which the young Collector of the district was called upon to deal.

In 1774 Thackeray was back again in Dacca as third in Council, but so profitable had proved his two years' tenure of office in Sylhet that he was already able to turn his thoughts towards retirement. On January 31, 1776, he married Amelia Richmond-Webb, a reigning beauty of the day in Calcutta, and shortly afterwards sailed for home. During just over nine years' service, the most important and lucrative half of which had been spent in Dacca and Sylhet, he had amassed a fortune, which, though not comparing with those of many of the 'nabobs' among his contemporaries, was by no means inconsiderable. William Makepeace Thackeray and his bride—a young man of twenty-six and a girl of eighteen—returning from India with a competence large enough to maintain them in comfort for the rest of their lives, present a sufficiently striking contrast with the changed conditions of modern days.

Meanwhile, both the Thackeray sisters had played important *rôles* in Dacca. Henrietta, the younger of the two and the beauty of the family, had created a great impression on her arrival in the up-country station where ladies were few, and in the following year she had married her brother's chief, Mr. James Harris, head of the Council in Dacca and of the Company's affairs in Eastern Bengal. Reaching India in 1758, Mr. Harris had put in the whole of his district service in Dacca and to such good effect that already in

1772, at the time of his marriage, he was contemplating retirement. The Eastern Capital, with its many opportunities of private trade, had always been one of the prizes of the service. Even in the days of the 'Pirate' Pitt, it had been a coveted post. Writing to a friend in May 1701, the latter says: 'I hope you may go to Dacca, which I take to be as advantageous a post as most in the Company's service,' and it had not lost its reputation during the sixty years that had intervened. Mr. James Harris had exploited its possibilities to the full, and, retiring with a large fortune early in 1773, he settled down in England, living for many years in the typical nabob-like style of the retired Anglo-Indian of the eighteenth century.

Jane Thackeray, the elder sister, spent a considerably longer time in Dacca, and through her famous husband became much more intimately associated with it. In 1772 she was married to Major James Rennell, the distinguished scientist and geographer, whose name occupies so honoured a place among the worthies of the Eastern Capital. His is an interesting figure, that of a man of science and devoted to the arts of peace utterly untouched by the petty rivalries and ambitions of the society in which his lot was cast, yet forced by the exigencies of the times to play his part in the stirring events that accompanied the consolidation of British rule. Early engaged in scientific research, he was appointed Surveyor of the Company's dominions in Bengal on his arrival in India as an ensign in 1764, at the age of twenty-two; and under his personal superintendence the thorough exploration of the Eastern Province was for the first time taken in hand. The services rendered by him to the Company, in penetrating into hitherto unknown regions and adding to its knowledge of the country over which it had just been called to rule, were incalculable. Extraordinary ignorance prevailed in the early days among the Company's agents as to the geography of Bengal outside certain well-known limits, and James Rennell, by clearly defining the extent and characteristics of the Province by means of his maps and surveys, immensely facilitated the work of government.

The story of his labours gives a vivid glimpse of Eastern Bengal in those first days of British suzerainty. It was a wild, turbulent country, lawless and unsettled, on the eve of the final break-up of Mussulman authority while as yet the new authority had not had time to make its power felt. The natural difficulties alone with which Rennell had to contend were appalling. Roads there were none, while dense jungle covered the land wherein tigers and herds of wild elephants roamed at will, a constant source of danger at every camping-place. Most of the travelling was done by river, but even here dangers were to be encountered. The rivers themselves, with their swift undercurrents, were treacherous, and sudden storms drew annually a heavy toll in human life. Still more dreaded were the gangs of marauders which infested all the large rivers, rendering life and property unsafe within their reach. James Rennell himself suffered much from their attacks, and again and again he was able to pursue his labours only at the point of the sword. On one occasion, in 1766, he was set upon by a band of river pirates, some eight hundred strong, and though they were driven off at the first encounter, thanks to the loyalty and discipline of his native escort, they lay in wait for him on the following day and literally cut him and his little troop to pieces. So seriously wounded was he that his life was despaired of. His right shoulder blade was cut through, 'laying him open for nearly a foot down the back, cutting through or wounding several of the ribs.' His left arm was also slashed, and a blow on the hand carried off a finger. More than three hundred miles away from the nearest surgeon, his condition was pitiable, and it was due solely to the devotion of his native servants that he survived the terrible journey by boat down the river to Dacca. For months after reaching the station his life hung in the balance, but, recovering, he was promoted to be Captain of Engineers and Surveyor-General of Bengal, and once more resumed his difficult task. On another occasion, five years later, he was again called upon to disperse a company of marauders who were oppressing the people and interfering with his own survey operations. It was a difficult journey of three hundred and twenty miles from Dacca, but, in spite of the heat, he accomplished it in fifteen days and freed the neighbourhood of the dacoits once and for all. But tasks such as these, in a climate which, he himself wrote, 'proved so prejudicial to European constitutions that scarce one out of seventy ever returned to his native country,' seriously affected his health; and his thoughts, too, turned towards what, in his case at least, was well-earned retirement. He sailed from India in 1777, to continue at home his scientific researches, to reap every possible scientific distinction, and to be laid to rest at last, at the age of eighty-seven, among the dead whom England honours in Westminster Abbey.

But in spite of the energy with which such men as these entered upon the task of reform, abuses and customs sanctioned by long usage died hard. The zemindars in the remoter parts of the district still lived much as they had done before, petty despots on their own estates and a terror to the countryside. Many of them did not disdain to share their spoils with bands of dacoits who were in reality armed retainers in their pay. Slavery still existed, and even seventy years after the English had taken possession, slaves were still bought and sold in Dacca—a male slave for 150 rupees and a female for 100 rupees. Refractory ryots were confined in irons, and the most loathsome forms of torture practised to force from them their rent to the uttermost farthing. It was impossible that the first little company of administrators in Dacca, with the limited means at their disposal, could at once enforce their principles of law and justice in far-off districts where no white man had yet been. Everywhere there was the meeting of the old and the new—the old spirit of lawlessness, tyranny and disorder gradually giving way and disappearing under the strenuous new rule of justice and integrity. The mock court of the Naib Nazims representing centuries of tradition, and all that was past, still existed side by side with the Katcheries of the Magistrate and Collector, typical products of a modern *régime* and symbolic of the new era that was dawning for India and the Indian people.

At the very outset of their rule the English,

inexperienced and beset with difficulties, were called upon to deal with one of those great natural calamities with which, unfortunately, they have become but too familiar in after years elsewhere. Eastern Bengal, a land of rice-fields, fertile and well watered, has known little of the horrors of famine in recent times. But when the land was still unsettled and whole tracts had been laid waste by dacoity, tyranny, and oppression, the unfortunate inhabitants were constantly reduced to the very margin of subsistence, and a partial failure of the crops meant disaster. Three of the worst famines that have ever been visited upon Eastern Bengal occurred in the early years of British rule. Scarcely had Mr. Kelsall been appointed the first Supervisor in Dacca when he was called upon to deal with the terrible famine of 1769–70. Sudden and prolonged inundation destroyed a large proportion of the crops, and a period of great heat and drought following, robbed the unfortunate cultivators of their harvest. Though the distress here was small compared with what it was elsewhere, many of the poorest classes were reduced to great straits.

The famine of 1784 was even more disastrous to Eastern Bengal. A sudden rise in the rivers destroyed whole villages, the mighty force of the swollen currents sweeping away all within their path, houses, people, cattle, and trees, a ghastly wreckage tossed on their whirling eddies. So great was the scarcity that rice, though lately selling for 160 seers to the rupee, fell as low as 16 seers. 'The distress of the inhabitants,' writes Mr. Day, the Collector, 'exceeds all description. The country is in a great measure deserted, and scarcely a cultivated spot is to be seen.' It grew worse as the month of October drew to an end, and it became evident that the winter crop must also fail. The poorer people in Dacca and its neighbourhood, goaded by hunger, grew riotous, and the Collector found it necessary to employ the Sepoys to protect the bazaars from the starving crowds that surrounded them clamouring for food.

But it was left for the third of these terrible visitations to surpass anything that had gone before in horror and severity. In 1787 the rains began unusually early in March and continued without intermission until, in July, the rivers had risen to a height unrecorded in the annals of Dacca before or since. Though the streets of the city stand ordinarily well above high-water mark, they were so completely inundated that boats sailed over them—in fact, it was necessary to go by boat from house to house. All round the city in the low-lying districts the people had to desert their houses, and either erect *machans* or live in floating huts hastily constructed on rafts. The early crops completely failed, and, mindful of the former years of famine, those who possessed a stock of grain hoarded it against the coming season of distress. Prices rose 300 to 400 per cent., and rice fell to four seers to the rupee, and even at that excessive rate but little could be obtained. In July, 1787, the famine began, and continued far into the following year. The poor, homeless and penniless, crowded into Dacca, and though ten thousand of them were fed daily by subscription, these formed but a fraction of those who stood in need. Hundreds died of starvation in the streets of the city, until Dacca became a scene of horror unparalleled even among all its many vicissitudes. To increase the misfortunes of the stricken people, a fire broke out in the city, and no less than seven thousand houses were burned to the ground. Large quantities of grain, for want of which the people died, caught fire before their eyes, and a hundred people perished in the flames, many of them burned in the mad rush to save the grain that to them meant life itself. Mr. Day, the Collector, did what he could to arrest the famine, but in those days, when the means of communication were still imperfect and organisation was not yet complete, the difficulties were great. He applied to Government to ask Collectors in Behar to send down rice to the starving districts in Eastern Bengal, but it was not until August, 1788, that the first consignment came. Even then it only amounted to 7,250 maunds, and that was little when divided among the tens of thousands upon whom famine had fallen. Even when the floods at last subsided the people were in dire distress. Their houses washed away and their cattle drowned, they had nothing wherewith to start life afresh, and it was many years before Dacca and the neighbouring districts returned again to their former prosperity.

But the result of the famine of 1787–88 went much further than mere temporary distress. It left its permanent mark in the acceleration of a great change that had already begun to make itself felt in Eastern Bengal, forming one of the most striking features of the early years of British rule. It was by a strange irony of fate that the coming of a trading company should have coincided with the rapid decline of manufactures and a sudden movement in favour of agriculture and the extension of cultivation. Until the middle of the eighteenth century spinning and weaving had been the main sources of the prosperity of Dacca. The chief interest had centred in the city itself. Ever since its foundation it had drawn the people from the countryside, who had crowded into its many streets and bazaars where highly paid labour was always to be obtained. So great had been the influx that the town of Dacca is said in the days of its greatest prosperity to have extended fourteen miles inland from the bank of the river, while its population numbered nine hundred thousand souls. Outside, in the district near by, vast tracts of land still lay uncultivated, much that had been cultivated in the days of the kingdom of Sonargaon having fallen back again into waste and jungle. The same tendency to desert rural occupations for town life observable in England in the latter half of the nineteenth century had been exhibited in Dacca two centuries before. Even Capassia and Sonargaon, famous of old for their manufacture of muslins and fine cloths, sent their best workmen to swell the population of the overcrowded city. Agriculture, conducted on the crudest principles, was at the best anxious and unprofitable labour, and in the unsettled condition of the time, when dacoity was rife and zemindars oppressed at will, there was no certainty that he who sowed would ever know the joy of harvest.

A succession of events, however, in the last decades of the eighteenth century wrought a sudden change. The famine of 1787–88 left the land desolate, having swept whole villages and homesteads, and in many instances the cultivators themselves, out of existence. There was an urgent demand for labour in the years that followed. Landholders found themselves in possession of large estates with none to cultivate them, and they were driven to offer every inducement to draw the labourer back to the land. The abolition of the export duties on corn and the introduction of indigo came to their assistance, while the Permanent Settlement, whatever its merits or demerits, gave for the time being a feeling of security among the agricultural classes hitherto unknown. Rapidly a return back to the land set in. Under the new government, which every day made its influence more firmly felt in the greater security of life and property, the cultivator began to see that he might carry on his labour with every hope in due time of reaping its reward. The country districts speedily revived, and cultivation extended far beyond its former limits, converting swamps and jungle, in the years that followed, into the fertile rice-fields of Eastern Bengal. To such an extent did the agrarian revolution affect the distribution of population, that Dacca, which had once boasted well nigh a million inhabitants, could only muster some fifty thousand in the early part of the eighteenth century.

But the greatest impetus to the agrarian revolution was undoubtedly to be found in the marked decay of commercial and industrial prosperity. Even in a land of rapid changes this sudden decline is startling. A number of events seemed to have combined to ruin the great industry for which the city had been so long famous. In 1781 the weaving of muslins was introduced into England, and on the expiry of Arkwright's patent and the introduction of mule twist in 1785, the manufacture of cotton goods increased by leaps and bounds. From two millions in 1781 their value sprang to seven and a half millions in 1787, no less than five hundred thousand pieces of muslin being manufactured in one year. They were not muslins of the quality and texture for which Dacca was so well known, but they were of a kind that met with a ready demand. The Moghul Imperial and Provincial Courts, which had entirely monopolised the finest and most costly of the muslins that Dacca had produced, were no longer in a position to make large purchases, and the high prices of the best muslins were prohibitive to any but the richest classes. The old days of luxury and splendour were over, and the change told heavily on the Dacca weaver. Robbed of the demand for their most expensive muslins, they found themselves at the same time called upon to meet the influx of English machine-made cloth, which, owing to its cheapness and durability, at once found a ready market. All classes of the inhabitants were further affected by the introduction of

English-made thread, which quickly superseded that locally prepared. The rapid decline of manufactures was the inevitable result.

In 1787 muslins to the value of thirty lacs of rupees were exported to England. But the flourishing state of the English cotton trade during the last twenty years of the eighteenth century, fostered as it was by the prohibitive duty of 75 per cent. and aided by mechanical device and invention of every kind, was the death-blow of the industry in Dacca. In 1807 only eight and a half lacs' worth found a market in Great Britain, and the total fell again in 1813 to three and a half lacs, while so low had it fallen in 1817 that the Company abolished its commercial Residency in Dacca altogether. An apparently trifling order of the Sultan of Turkey is given as the cause of the death-blow that yet another industry in Dacca received later in the third decade of the nineteenth century. In 1835 *kashida* cloths embroidered in Dacca were sold in Calcutta to the value of four lacs of rupees. In the following year the sales only amounted to two and a half lacs, in 1837 to one and a half lacs, and in 1838 to one lac only. It is said that the majority of these embroidered cloths had been exported to Turkey, where they were used as turbans for the Sultan's troops. But the Sultan issuing an order changing the uniform of his army, the demand from that quarter for the *kashida* cloth altogether ceased, with disastrous results to the industry in Dacca.

In almost every other direction, however, Dacca benefited greatly during the years that followed the assumption of authority by the Company. The condition of the city itself during Moghul times is almost unimaginable from a sanitary point of view to an Englishman of the nineteenth century. Undrained and unswept, the lanes and alleys of the great city of nearly a million inhabitants were foul and pestilent beyond description, and it is small wonder that sickness was prevalent and mortality extraordinarily heavy. In the earlier days large portions of the bazaar, lightly constructed with a view to that end, were burned down every year, a drastic measure of sanitation rendered necessary by months of neglect. Accidental fires, too, were of such common occurrence that people kept their valuables buried under the ground, or placed in boxes on wheels, ready at a moment's notice to be drawn away. Some attempt was made under Moghul rule to care for the poor and sick, a grant from the crown lands for the purposes of a Langar Khana, or refectory for the poor, being set aside for the purpose, but it was too small to have been able to deal at all adequately with the amount of poverty and sickness that must have existed. 'Hospital charges and black doctor with medicines to attend the poor sickly people, 1,578 rupees 10 annas,' 'allowance to lame and blind, 3,600 rupees,' together with a few other items, amounting in all to something under nine thousand rupees, were apparently all that was found existing in the way of official charity in 1769. The Emperor Jehangir's orders for the construction of hospitals and refectories appear to have become a dead letter in Eastern Bengal, like so many other imperial rescripts in the last days of Moghul rule. A hospital was soon started by the Company, and a bequest, at a later date, by Mr. Mitford, once Collector and afterwards judge of the Provincial Court of Appeal in Dacca, to the extent of some eight lacs of rupees for charitable, beneficial, and public works, gave to the city the fine hospital now known by its donor's name.

But it was in the peace and quietness and settled order that the establishment of its rule gave to a distracted province that the English Company's chief claim to gratitude lay. The nineteenth century was the most peaceful that Dacca and Eastern Bengal had ever known. Undisturbed by wars and rumours of wars, and secure in the possession of their own, the people have led for the most part peaceful lives, engaged in agriculture and the growing of indigo and jute, gradually bringing vast tracts of hitherto untouched soil under cultivation. Crime, it is true, was rife in the earlier years, but isolated cases of robbery and dacoity were small evils compared with the ravages of pirates and roving banditti of earlier days, who plundered and murdered and laid waste whole villages unchecked. Excessively prone to litigation, and much given to local disputes among themselves, the people of Eastern Bengal but seldom showed concern in wider interests and the political questions of the day. It was under the English Company as under Hindu and Mussulman rule. The bulk of the population, accepting the fact of a ruling race, cared little who their overlords might be. The spirit of fatalism, inherent among the majority of the people of Eastern Bengal, precluded all thought of rebellion against authority. It had been ordained that they should be governed. It therefore mattered little who their governors might be. If good, so much the better; if evil and tyrannical and oppressive, they must needs submit and wait until the tyranny was overpast. Only very occasionally, as in 1810, when a measure was passed that touched them too closely, have they shown any attempt at resistance. In that year a house-tax was imposed upon the city of Dacca, and the inhabitants rose in a body and presented a petition at the government katchery, which

DINNER-TIME IN THE DACCA JAIL.

PRISONERS AT WORK IN THE DACCA JAIL.

stood in the old Fort, on the site where the jail now stands. The Collector refused to receive the petition from so turbulent a mob. It contained, however, the signatures of nine thousand of the most respectable householders in Dacca, and, apart from the angry crowd that presented it, could not be altogether overlooked. It petitioned not only for the repeal of the house-tax, but also for the abolition of the stamp duty. On the Collector's refusal to receive the petition there was danger of the mob looting the katchery, but a company of Sepoys being called out it speedily dispersed, and the petition was quietly presented on the following day by delegates appointed by the signatories.

An interesting glimpse of Dacca in the first quarter of the nineteenth century has been left on record by the pen of a contemporary writer. Reginald Heber, one of the most famous names on the roll of Calcutta Bishops, visited Eastern Bengal in the course of one of his episcopal visitations in 1824. Setting out from Calcutta on June 15 in 'a fine sixteen-oared pinnace,' accompanied by his domestic chaplain, Mr. Stowe, he reached Dacca by leisurely stages on July 3. 'As we drew nearer,' he writes, 'I was surprised at the extent of the place and the stateliness of the ruins, of which, indeed, the city seemed chiefly to consist.' He was the guest of Mr. Master, the judge of the district, and of his eighteen days' stay he has left a full account. 'Dacca is merely the wreck of its ancient grandeur,' he writes, acknowledging Mr. Master as his informant. 'Its trade is reduced to the sixtieth part of what it was, and all its splendid buildings, the castle of its founder Shahjehanguire, the noble mosque he built, and palaces of the ancient Nawabs, the factories and churches of the Dutch, French, and Portuguese nations, are all sunk into ruin and overgrown with jungle. Mr. Master has himself been present at a tyger-hunt in the court of the old palace, during which the elephant of one of his friends fell into a well overgrown with weeds and bushes. The cotton produced in this district is mostly sent to England raw, and the manufactures of England are preferred by the people of Dacca themselves for their cheapness.'

Bishop Heber was struck by the smallness of the English community in this important outpost of the Company. 'Of English there are none,' he writes, 'except a few indigo planters in the neighbourhood and those in the civil or military service.' There were, however, no less than ten companies of infantry stationed in Dacca at the time; and a small flotilla of gunboats, said to be on its way to guard the Burmese frontier, was also there temporarily. The Hindu and Mussulman population, though less than in the prosperous days of Shaista Khan, was still considerably more than in the present day. Mr. Master estimated it at three hundred thousand, while in the last census returns the population is given as less than one-third of that figure. 'The climate of Dacca Mr. Master reckons one of the mildest in India,' writes the Bishop, 'the heat being always tempered by the vast rivers flowing near it,' and it is curious at the present day to read that 'the neighbourhood affords only one short ride at this season, and not many even when the ground is dry, being much intersected by small rivers and some large and impenetrable jungles coming pretty close to the north-east of the town.'

Of the Nawab Shams-ud-Dowlah, Bishop Heber gives an interesting account. It is with something of surprise that one reads of him as 'fancying himself a critic in Shakespeare.' The grandson of Jusserat Khan, it was only two years before that he had succeeded his brother, Nusrut Jung, as Nawab. Previous to that he had spent several years in Calcutta, where he had been kept in honourable confinement for the part he had played in a conspiracy against the Company. But in 1822 he was considered so harmless that he was allowed to succeed to most of his brother's empty honours. Though denied the State palanquin, the sign of authority, he was granted an allowance of ten thousand rupees a month, with the title of Highness, and was permitted to maintain a Court with a company of guards of his own. His is a pathetic figure. Shorn of all power, life from the outset had little to offer him. From beginning to end it was nothing but a puppet-show. All that he could hope for was to succeed to the empty honours that his brother held. It is small wonder that in his youth he was led into joining a conspiracy that offered him a chance of breaking the bonds and playing a man's part in life. Inheriting much of his grandfather's astuteness and ability, he had no chance to show his worth. In his younger days he is described as a man of 'vigorous and curious mind, who, had his talents enjoyed a proper bent, might have distinguished himself.' But, incentive being lacking, it is not to be wondered at that, when in after days Bishop Heber met him, he had become 'infirm and indolent, more and more addicted to the listless indulgences of the Asiatic prince: pomp so far as he can afford it, dancing girls and opium, having in fact scarce any society but that of his inferiors, and being divested of any of the usual motives by which even Asiatic princes are occasionally roused to exertion.'

Dacca, in 1824, must have been a curious meeting-place of the old order and the new. In

Bishop Heber's account of his visit of ceremony to the Nawab they seem strangely to mingle. 'In the afternoon,' he wrote on July 8, 'I accompanied Mr. Master to pay a visit to the Nawab, according to appointment. We drove a considerable way through the city, then along a shabby avenue of trees intermingled with huts, then through an old brick gateway into a sort of wild-looking close, with a large tree and some bushes in the centre, and ruinous buildings all round. There was a company of Sepoys drawn up to receive us, very neatly dressed and drilled, being in fact a detachment of the Company's local regiment, and assigned to the Nawab as a guard of honour. In front was another really handsome gateway, with an open gallery, where the "nobut," or evening martial music, is performed, a mark of sovereign dignity to which the Nawab never had a just claim, but in which Government continues to indulge him. Here were the Nawab's own guard, in their absurd coats and caps, and a crowd of folk with silver sticks, as well as two *tonjons* and *chahtahs*, to convey us across the inner court. This was a little larger than the small quadrangle at All Souls, surrounded with low and irregular but not inelegant buildings, kept neatly and all whitewashed. On the right hand was a flight of steps leading to a very handsome hall, an octagon, supported by Gothic arches, with a verandah round it, and with high Gothic windows well venetianed. The octagon was fitted up with a large round table covered with red cloth, mahogany drawing-room chairs, two large and handsome convex mirrors, which showed the room and furniture to considerable advantage, two common pier-glasses, some prints of the King, the Emperor Alexander, Lords Wellesley and Hastings and the Duke of Wellington, and two very good portraits by Chinnery of the Nawab himself and the late Nawab, his brother. Nothing was gawdy, but all extremely respectable and noblemanly. The Nawab, his son, his English secretary and the Greek priest whom he had mentioned to me, received us at the door, and he led me by the hand to the upper end of the table. We sate some time, during which conversation was kept up better than I expected: and I left the palace a good deal impressed with the good sense, information, and pleasing manners of our host.' It is the last glimpse of the old *régime*. Within less than twenty years even the very name and symbol of Mussulman authority in Dacca had passed away.

The mutiny of 1857 touched the mass of the people not at all. They watched the short drama that was played out in the Lalbagh as something apart—an interesting spectacle, in which they had no share save as spectators. But for the English in Dacca those few anxious months in 1857 were the most exciting moments of its history throughout the nineteenth century. There were only two companies of the 73rd Native Infantry, numbering no more than two hundred and sixty, with the artillery, stationed in the city at the time. Upon the arrival of news of the outbreak of the mutiny at Meerut a spirit of unrest took possession of the Sepoys, alarming their officers for the safety of the small European community, which lay practically at their mercy. Upon advices being sent to Calcutta, a company of a hundred men of the Indian navy was at once ordered up. It was a small force, but it was the most that could be spared at that critical time, and the station put itself in what state of defence it could by enrolling all the European and Eurasian residents as volunteers. They numbered some sixty, all told. Mr. Davidson was Commissioner of Dacca at the time, Mr. Abercrombie, Judge, and Mr. Carnac, Magistrate and Collector.

All through the rains the Sepoys continued in a state of disquiet, eagerly waiting for the news that filtered down, diluted with many exaggerations, from up country. At last, on November 21, boatmen coming up the river brought the news that the Sepoys at Chittagong had mutinied. Wild stories were soon afloat in the bazaar. It was confidently asserted that the treasuries there had been looted, and three lacs of rupees carried off in triumph by the mutineers. The head officials of the station held a hurried consultation with the officers of the two companies of Sepoys, and it was resolved that the troops should be disarmed if possible by surprise early on the following morning. At five o'clock on Sunday morning, November 22, 1857, in the cold, misty half-light of a winter dawn, thirty European volunteers and the hundred marines formed up in the open space in front of what is now the Victoria Park. From there a small company marched to the treasury, which stood on the site at present occupied by the Central Jail. There they found about thirty of the Sepoys, some on guard, some off duty, and all were disarmed without difficulty. The Sepoys quietly laid down their arms, protesting that they had not merited this disgrace, and that they had had no intention of mutinying.

The treasury secured, the sailors were at once marched to the Lalbagh, where the main body of the Sepoys were quartered. But here news of the disarming of the treasury guard had been before them, and the Sepoys were prepared to resist. As the sailors entered the Lalbagh enclosure through the broken wall near the southern gateway the sentry fired into their midst, and one man fell. The Sepoys, committed to resistance, fired a volley, and the guns which had been placed in front of Peri Bibi's tomb were turned upon the sailors as they advanced. Most of the Sepoys had gathered on the ramparts to the left, and it was soon evident that, deprived of their officers, disorder and confusion reigned among them. Led by Lieutenant Laws, the sailors and volunteers charged the ramparts and drove the Sepoys before them towards their quarters, where they were driven from house to house till at last they reached the turret in the angle of the wall, where they made a stubborn resistance, many of them being driven over the edge of the parapet and falling to the ground, fifty feet below, on the other side. Mr. Mays, a midshipman, at the head of eight men, had meanwhile pluckily charged down upon the guns, which were taken and spiked—a deed which won for him the Victoria Cross. The Sepoys were utterly routed, and the majority of them fled, leaving forty of their number dead upon the field. Among the sailors and volunteers the casualties were few. One man had been killed by the sentry's bullet at their entrance into the fort, and nine were severely injured, of whom four subsequently died. Dr. Green, the civil surgeon, while attending to one of the injured men, was himself wounded in the thigh, and Mr. Bainbridge, the Assistant Magistrate, fell from the ramparts and sustained severe injuries. But these were small calamities in comparison with the dangers that had threatened. Dacca had been entirely at the mercy of the mutineers, and it was largely due to the prompt action taken by the officials that all danger was averted.

The diary of Mr. Brennand, who was Principal of the Government College at the time, throws some interesting sidelights on the Dacca of 1857. Though the danger was real, and there was an undercurrent of excitement and alarm throughout the station, outwardly the daily social round went on much as in more peaceful times. In fact, from an English point of view, Dacca was probably gayer than it had ever been before. The arrival of fresh troops considerably augmented station society and in spite of the anxiety and danger social amenities were not neglected. On October 12, we learn from Mr. Brennand's diary, the Cavalry Volunteers gave a ball to the Infantry, and on November 9 the Infantry Volunteers gave a dinner to the station. It came off in Mr. Brennand's own house, and was one of the largest parties that had ever been given in Dacca. No less than seventy were invited and over fifty sat down to dinner. This was only twelve days before the eventful 22nd when the Sepoys were disarmed and the fight took place in the Lalbagh Fort. Exciting as this event was, however, so little did it affect the official life of Dacca that on the following day Mr. Brennand records that 'everything was quiet again and we were going on with our work as if nothing had happened.' The social life of Dacca was at its height in the months that followed. Even the hot weather and rains seem to have failed to damp its energy. 'The station is very gay' is the entry in Mr. Brennand's diary of the 12th of July. 'A ball at Gunny Meah's, a station ball at Carnegie's, and a bachelor ball after that.' And again on the 15th of August: 'The station is very gay. Three balls in succession.' Six balls in Dacca in a little over a month during the rains! One can only marvel at the energy of a past generation of Anglo-Indians and the transformation that has taken place in the social life of Dacca during the past fifty years.

Great changes were impending in the city which had already seen so many vicissitudes. The marvellous progress in almost every branch of life, that seemed to keep pace with the advancing years of the nineteenth century, was about to rouse even this far-off city of the long sleep. As yet it knew nothing of railways and telegraphs: and it still stood as isolated in the midst of its network of rivers as it had done in the earliest Mussulman days. But in 1858, that year of momentous change in India, the long days of Dacca's isolation were ended and the city was brought into close and immediate touch with the headquarters of the British power in the East. On the 18th of October, we read in Mr. Brennand's diary, telegraphic communication between Dacca and Calcutta was completed, and how great an advance that implied in the slow-moving Eastern city it is difficult to realise in these days of still more wonderful inventions. Owing to the difficulties presented by the many rivers that surround Dacca the question of a railway was less easy of solution, and the line of rail between Calcutta and Dacca is still to-day broken by a six hours' journey by boat.

The last and most important entry in Mr. Brennand's diary was made on the 5th of November 1858. 'The Proclamation of the transfer of the Government of India to the Queen,' it runs, 'was read in English and Bengali on Monday last, in the space in front of the College. The military were drawn up in line and the European residents were upon a platform erected for the purpose. Between two and three thousand people present. Some of the houses were lighted up in the evening in honour of the occasion, and there was a dinner given by the civilians and the military to the station.'

So with its great traditions and wonderful memories the old East India Company ceased to be, and a new Empire rose on the foundations it had laid with so much labour, courage, and persistence.

CHAPTER IX

THE DACCA OF TO-DAY

To-day Dacca stands at the parting of the ways. Behind it lies the past, with its three centuries of memories that crowd close around its crumbling mosques and palaces. Before it, at the beginning of the twentieth century, there has suddenly dawned a new future, fraught with great possibilities to the capital of a newly created province under British rule. Raised suddenly to eminence by Islam Khan, it held for almost a century its proud position as capital of all Bengal. Then, suffering eclipse as suddenly as it had risen to fame, for two centuries it lay apart from the stress and hurry of great events, its splendid traditions neglected and forgotten. In later years, under British rule, it has occupied but a humble place as the headquarters of one of the many districts of Eastern Bengal. Now, after its long sleep, there has come a re-awakening, and once more the name of Dacca figures among the capitals of the East.

The city which has suffered so many vicissitudes bears unmistakable traces to-day of the transition through which it is passing. It is like an old garment with a patch of new cloth flung carelessly here and there upon its dim and fraying texture. The city of many mosques and ruined palaces, of moss-grown walls and crumbling turrets, of tortuous alleys and narrow winding byways, of secluded sunless courts and crowded tenements, still survives, wrapped in its impenetrable cloak of mystery, its countless secrets buried deep in its inmost heart and jealously safeguarded against prying eyes through all the years to come. But in the midst of it, startling in its newness, brick-red against the time-worn grey, a modern city has begun to rise. As yet it is but in its inception, and its first beginnings give but a faint forecast of what it will one day be. Yet already, in a marvellously short space of time, a temporary Government House has sprung into existence, the centre and symbol of the new life that has dawned for the old-time city. The permanent Government House is to rise later, a stately building befitting the new capital, overlooking the racecourse close by the ancient mosque and tomb of Haji Khaja Shahbaz, the merchant prince of Dacca in the days of Shaista Khan. Other buildings, designed to house the army of officials which follows in the wake of governments, are rapidly giving a modern aspect to the time-worn city, the twentieth-century 'purple palaces of the Public Works' contrasting strangely with the graceful domes and minarets of the mosques and palaces of a bygone age.

Yet even to-day there are times when the city assumes an aspect that is wholly reminiscent of the past. Most of the great festivals, though still celebrated, have lost much of their one-time splendour and magnificence, but there is one that still retains all the vigour of its earlier days. It is the special festival of the Dacca weavers, known as the Jamastami, and held in honour of Krishna's birth on the twenty-third day of the lunar month of Sraban (August). Then, for a time, the quiet, sleepy city is transformed. Vast crowds, in all their Oriental picturesqueness, gather from far and near, thronging the main streets from end to end. It is like a scene from the middle ages as the time for the great procession draws near. This might, indeed, be the very city of Shaista Khan. All that is modern seems to have disappeared, hidden by the gaily dressed crowd that fills the roadway and swarms at every vantage-point. From window, balcony, and housetop, group beyond group looks down, alive with colour and expectancy. A company of elephants, ponderous and magnificent, stands drawn in line, waiting to take its place in the long procession as it passes. The blazing sun

THE LINE OF ELEPHANTS AT THE JAMASTAMI FESTIVAL IN DACCA.

beats down, and scarce a breath of wind stirs in the air. Yet, hour after hour, the intense interest holds, undaunted by the heat of the day. And then at last it comes. Slowly, amidst a scene of indescribable excitement the great procession heaves in sight. Merged in the crowd, a veritable sea of heads, it sways from side to side, ever moving like some restless tide that rolls onward almost imperceptibly yet steadily draws near. Huge effigies, representations of gods and goddesses, or grotesque figures of beasts and men in all the glory of tinsel and paint, are borne aloft, the wonder and admiration of the crowd. Some of the erections, lightly constructed of bamboo, stand fifty feet high, depicting whole stories in the glittering scenes and figures that adorn them. The subjects chosen for representation exhibit the widest catholicity of taste. The Fall of Port Arthur, a strangely modern and foreign incident to figure in this old-world festival, is shown in tier on tier of one of the most magnificent structures, the designer's idea of war and of Russian and Japanese being quaint in the extreme. Behind, more in keeping with the celebration of the great god's birth, follows a huge car with an immense representation of Krishna, ablaze with colour and the flash of jewels. And so, with its wonderful Eastern fascination, the great procession winds slowly on, and for a few brief hours the quiet, slow-moving Dacca of to-day is stirred by a passing memory of the life and pageantry of the viceregal capital of the olden times.

But deep down in the heart of the city, close by the river-bank, something of the old aspect it must once have worn in days gone by still remains. Time and climate, and the vandal hand of man, have done their worst, crumbling even the massive walls that the Mussulman architects loved to build, and putting to base uses once proud and noble buildings. Yet much of their dignity and beauty survives even in decay. It is pre-eminently a Mussulman city—a city of mosques built by the Faithful, strong in the belief that for him 'who builds a mosque on earth God will build seventy palaces in Paradise.' Of pre-Mussulman days, before Islam Khan sailed down the river in search of his new capital, there is little to be told. Whether it was already a city with a history of its own, or whether its existence began with the coming of Islam Khan, is still open to dispute, so vague are the traditions that linger round the beginnings of things in Dacca. The Dhakeswari Temple, from which, one tradition has it, the city takes its name, is the most celebrated Hindu building in the district, but its origin is shrouded in mystery that none may penetrate. First built, it is said, by Ballal Sen, on the site where he found the image of the goddess hidden in the jungle, it was restored by Man Singh during his brief stay in the city, the famous Rajput general rejoicing to find this symbol of his creed among the many mosques of another faith. But all signs of these older buildings, if such existed, have disappeared. The present temple is only some two hundred years old, and is said to have been built by a Hindu agent in the employ of the East India Company. Beyond its vague traditions, and the veneration in which it is held by the Hindus for many miles around, there is little of interest in the Temple of Dhakeswari of to-day.

There are few other buildings whose memories carry them back into the remote past beyond the days of Islam Khan. Binat Bibi's mosque is probably the oldest building now standing in the city. It was built in 1456 A.D. in the days when Nasiruddin Mahmud Shah was King of Bengal, with his capital away at Gaur, over a hundred and fifty years before Islam Khan set out to found his new capital in the East. Small and solidly built, with no architectural pretensions, its only interest lies in its antiquity, and in the fact that its existence proves that there were Mussulmans settled where Dacca now stands long before the days of Islam Khan. Who Binat Bibi was, or what memory of her the mosque perpetuates, has long since been forgotten.

In the centre of the town, near by the place where the old fort once stood, survive the remains of another mosque, built, according to the inscription, only two years later than Binat Bibi's. Struck by lightning and shaken by the earthquake of 1897, it has at last, after more than four centuries, succumbed to the ravages of time, and only the walls remain. It was built while Nasiruddin was still King of Bengal, and the inscription, which has survived intact, states that it was finished on 28 Shaban 1458 A.D. The walls, some four feet thick, stand firm as if invulnerable against the onslaught of storm and time.

But it was not until the hundred years of Dacca's viceroyalty that there grew up the numberless mosques and palaces that still dominate the city to-day. Of Islam Khan, the founder of the city, but few memories survive in brick and stone. In Islampore, a quarter of the city which still preserves his name, stands the most important building which tradition ascribes to Dacca's first Viceroy. It is a plain, unpretentious mosque, designed for utility and permanence rather than for architectural effect, and to such good purpose that for three hundred years it has survived the vicissitudes of the city, and to-day the voice of prayer is still heard within its walls as in the days of Islam Khan.

Of the old fort, built by Ibrahim Khan, the third Moghul Viceroy at Dacca, nothing now remains. Containing the Palace, the Courts of Justice, and the Mint, it stood on the site at present occupied by the lunatic asylum and the central jail. It was in the palace in the fort that the Naib Nazim was living when Lieutenant Swinton, the English Agent, came in 1765 to take over the Dewani on behalf of the East India Company. Another residence was found for him and his successors, and the buildings in the fort were used for many years as the headquarters of the newly established British rule in Dacca.

Next to the viceroyalty of Shaista Khan, it is that of Shah Shuja, the pleasure-loving son of Shah Jehan, who was doomed to so tragic an end, which has left its impress most deeply marked on Dacca. Some of the finest buildings in the city bear witness to his taste in architecture and his love of magnificence and display. The son of the builder of the Taj at Agra, it was small wonder that he set himself to beautify the capital in the East over which he had been called to rule. The Bara Katra, the beautiful building that faces the river half a mile down stream from the Lalbagh fort, probably was originally intended as a palace for Shah Shuja. It is effectively designed, stately and imposing as it towers up, turning its solid front to face the river. Its central gateway is of magnificent proportions, lofty, with dome-shaped roof, flanked by smaller entrances and crowned by two octagonal towers. Within is a veritable network of rooms and corridors and terraces, grass-grown now and long since disused, open to all the winds of heaven, a home for bats and owls and every creeping thing. Built by Mir Abul Kasim, the Dewan, in 1644, so great was its beauty when it reached completion that the inscription declares that it puts High Heaven to shame, and is itself a foretaste of the Paradise to come. But Shah Shuja, for some reason unexplained, appears never to have used it as a residence. He established it as a caravanserai, a public halting-place where travellers and the poor might find rest and shelter. 'Sultan Shah Shuja was famed for deeds of charity,' ran the inscription which once stood over the city gate of the Katra. 'Wherefore, being hopeful of the mercy of God, the sacred edifice was endowed with twenty-two shops attached to it, on the rightful and lawful condition that the officials in charge of the endowments should expend the income derived from them upon the repairs of the buildings and upon the poor, and that they should not take any rent

THE SATGUMBAZ MOSQUE.

THE BARA KATRA.

from any deserving person alighting therein. So that the pious act may reflect upon the monarch in this world, and that they should not act contrariwise, or else they would be called to account on the day of retribution.' Shorn now of much of its glory, with its walls broken and decayed, robbed of its northern gateway, and with new buildings crowding it close, it bears upon its face the impress of 'Ichabod' writ large. Yet, so long as the walls remain, nothing can destroy its charm, and it is to be hoped that the new Government will not fail to preserve what is left of one of the most beautiful buildings of the Dacca of a former time.

Another memorial of Sultan Shuja's viceroyalty is the Hossaini Delan. The tradition runs that Mir Murad, Superintendent of the Nawara, dreamed a dream in which the Imam Husain appeared to him and desired him to build a house of mourning in memory of his martyrdom. The very next morning Mir Murad started to build the Hossaini Delan. Here, from that day to this, the great festival of the Mohurrum has been celebrated with all its traditional pomp and circumstance. Lit with a thousand lights on the tenth day of the festival, its courts filled with a throng of eager worshippers, it still retains something of the life and interest of other days. Within a mausoleum close beside it lie buried the last four Naib Nazims of Dacca—Nawab Nusrut Jung, who died in 1822; Shams-ud-Dowlah, 1831; Kumr-ud-Dowlah, 1834; and Ghaziuddin, with whom the line ended in 1843.

A curious tradition lingers round the Churihatta mosque, which is yet another survival of Sultan Shuja's time. It is said that it was originally built as a Hindu temple, a tradition which its vaulted roof and general appearance tend to confirm. The story is told that a Hindu officer of the Moghul Government was ordered to build a mosque, but that, taking advantage of the absence of the viceroy and the chief officers of Government from Dacca during the interval when the city had ceased for a time to be the capital of all Bengal, he built a temple instead, and it was not until it was finished and the idols were placed within it that the fact came to the knowledge of the viceroy. Thereupon orders were issued to cast out the idols and consecrate the building as a mosque of the true faith. In seeming corroboration of this story there was found in the compound some years ago a stone image of the Hindu deity Basudev, which may have been one of those ignominiously cast out of the temple by order of Sultan Shuja. But if this story is true the case was an exceptional one, since the Mahomedan conquerors in Eastern Bengal interfered but little with the worship and religious beliefs of the Hindus, whose temples everywhere remained unmolested in close proximity to the mosques of the Faithful. Religious persecution on any extended scale is one of the evils which Eastern Bengal has escaped through all the many vicissitudes of its long and chequered history.

More than a mile beyond the limits of the present city stands all that remains of the Idgah, the once beautiful building where, in the old days, the Faithful of the city came to offer up their prayers at the great Id festival. Only a single line of wall survives, exquisitely pierced and traced, though sadly broken and fast crumbling to decay. Once the great city of Dacca lay close all round, extending for miles on either hand. The Idgah was in the very centre of the busy life of court, and mart, and camp, and many a stirring sight it must have witnessed as the crowd of white-robed worshippers thronged from every quarter of the vast city to celebrate the welcome festival that closes the long fast of the Ramazan. Now the portion of the city that once lay close around the Idgah has utterly vanished, leaving it solitary and neglected, stranded alone in a wide waste, as if mourning for the days of its glories that have for ever passed.

Beyond the Idgah, further away from the city,

lay another centre of interest, the memories of which have long since grown vague and dim. Out in the waste, half hidden in bramble growth, a well and a broken arch are the only visible signs of the Sikh monastery that once flourished here. The well is known as Guru Nanak's Well, after Guru Nanak, the founder of the Sikh religion. There is a local tradition that the great teacher once visited Dacca and drank from this well, to the waters of which miraculous properties have ever since been attributed. Another and more possible story is that it was Guru Tegh Bahadur, the ninth Guru, who came to Dacca in the time of Aurungzebe and gathered about him a large following, which has never quite died out in the city. Close by the racecourse there is a Sikh temple where the Sikhs still meet and worship.

Much had been done, during this first period of Dacca's prosperity as capital of Bengal, to beautify the city and make it worthy of the honoured position it had so suddenly acquired, but it was not until the long viceroyalty of Shaista Khan that Dacca became famed as the city of mosques and palaces. Himself a great builder, he gave to the architecture of the day in his own capital so distinctive a style that it soon came to be known as *Shaistakhani*. It must have been almost immediately on his arrival in Dacca that he com-

GURU NANAK, THE FOUNDER OF THE SIKH RELIGION.

menced his first work, the Chhota Katra. Overlooking the Buriganga, only a hundred yards away upstream from the Bara Katra, it is a beautiful building, well proportioned, with massive walls that have stoutly withstood the ravages of time. But later years have treated it with scant respect and put it to base uses, making of it a storehouse for coal and lime. Within the courtyard a small circular mausoleum once covered the grave of Bibi Champa who gives her name to this quarter of the city—Champatoli. Of the lady herself nothing is known with certainty, but it is probable that she was one of the daughters of Shaista Khan. Over the door of the mausoleum, it is said, there was once a tablet bearing an inscription, but if such existed, it has long since disappeared, and nothing now remains to tell the story of Bibi Champa. As so often in Dacca, only the name survives. All else is dead.

Close to the Chhota Katra is the Chauk, the market square, its centre filled with a jumble of tiny booths, closely packed on market days with a bantering, gossiping crowd of humanity. Right in the centre, half hidden by the booths, stands a huge cannon, a curious survival in the midst of the busy mart. There is no authentic record of its history, but tradition says that it was one of two such that Islam Khan brought with him when he came to found here his capital. The other one is said to have been lost in the river, and even to-day the superstitious native attributes to this lost gun the curious sounds, as of the distant booming of a cannon, which are occasionally heard in the vicinity, and to account for which no satisfactory explanation is forthcoming. Known locally as the Barisal guns, the deep, vibrating sounds can be distinctly heard in Dacca, and it is small wonder, no other explanation being to hand, that the native superstition attributes them to the gun that lies deep down beneath the river. The gun that still remains in the market-place has become in consequence an object of great veneration, and those who come to buy and sell, place their votive offerings round it before the business of the day begins, with a muttered prayer that their enterprise may prove successful.

Overlooking the Chauk from the west is a handsome three-domed mosque, built in the *Shaista-khani* style of architecture. Raised on a hollow platform some ten feet high, it towers up, a solid mass of masonry, overlooking the flat low-roofed booths of the bazaar. Here the Naib Nazims in the old days came in state to repeat the time-honoured prayers at the great festivals, and though much of the pomp and state have disappeared, the feet of the Faithful still throng the courts of the

Chauk Mosque, and, illuminated at the time of the Id or the Bakrid, it still retains something of its old life and colour.

But the most beautiful of all the buildings erected by Shaista Khan is the mausoleum he caused to be raised over the tomb of his favourite daughter, Peri Bibi. She was the wife of Prince Mahomed Azim, third son of the Emperor Aurungzebe, and he it was who acted as Viceroy of Bengal during Shaista Khan's two years' absence from Dacca in 1678 and 1679. During that time he commenced building a fort which was to be worthy of the capital of a great province, and which he named, after his august father, Fort Aurungabad. It has, however, always been generally known as the Lalbagh Fort, and it is perhaps around it that memories gather closest in Dacca. Planned on a generous scale, it was destined, like many another Mussulman building in Eastern Bengal, never to reach completion. In the second year of his viceroyalty Prince Mahomed Azim was recalled to assist Aurungzebe in his lifelong struggle with the Mahrattas, and Shaista Khan returned, after this brief interval, to take up again the reins of government in his much-loved capital. But the Lalbagh Fort, though far advanced, was little likely to find favour in the eyes of Shaista Khan. It was no child of his, and but few Mussulman governors were content to carry out the designs of their predecessors and complete the buildings that they had begun. And in this case there was another reason that brought the Lalbagh Fort into disfavour with Shaista Khan. It was while her husband had been busy in the building of it that his favourite daughter, Peri Bibi—the 'Lady Fairy,' as she was affectionately called—had died suddenly. To a superstitious Court that alone was sufficient to stamp the enterprise as unlucky, and Shaista Khan added but one thing to his predecessor's work, leaving the rest unfinished. Within the walls of the Fort Peri Bibi lies buried, and over her grave rises the stately mausoleum that the great Viceroy raised to her memory. It is reputed the finest building in all Eastern Bengal. In the inner apartment, built of marble and chunar stone, with doors of sandalwood, lies the tomb itself, and over it a graceful dome exquisitely proportioned. Round the inner sanctuary runs a cloister divided into compartments, once embellished with fine mosaics, which time and many vandal coats of whitewash have done much to obliterate and destroy. But though long neglected and fallen upon evil days, it still remains an abiding monument of Peri Bibi and of Shaista Khan.

Of the Fort itself only the battlements facing the river, with terraces and turrets and two imposing gateways, still remain. Grass-grown and falling to decay, the old red walls, with the thin, flat Mussulman bricks here and there destroyed and broken, have but grown the more picturesque with age, the high-arched gateway, rising tier on tier, looking out like a watchtower over river and land. The river that once flowed beneath its walls has now receded, as if it, too, deserted it in its decay.

Within the Fort, facing Peri Bibi's tomb, stands the Hummam, a two-storied building with stone pillars and turreted roof, now repaired and modernised without, until it looks strangely out of place in its old-world setting. Within, on the lower floor, was the Hummam, the bath from which the building took its name, while the upper floor was used by Prince Mahomed Azim as his Hall of Audience. In later times, it too has fallen on less prosperous days, being recently used by the Bengal Police, whose brand-new quarters, hideously incongruous, now crown the ramparts a few hundred yards away. Further off, beyond the mausoleum of Peri Bibi, against the western wall of the Fort is Prince Mahomed Azim's mosque, built and finished by him during his brief viceroyalty. To-day it bears deep upon it the impress of desolation. The goats and cattle wander unmolested through its once sacred courts and precincts, and the voice of prayer is no longer heard within its gates.

The last stirring events enacted within the walls of the Lalbagh Fort were in the dark days of 1857. Since then the uneventful years have passed and left no record of their passing, save in an added touch of decay and desolation. It is still owned by the descendants of the proud Amir-ul-Umara Shaista Khan, to whom it was given as a favour by the Emperor Aurungzebe. In 1844 it was permanently leased from his heirs by the Government of Bengal at an annual rent of sixty rupees, which is still drawn by the direct descendant of the former Viceroy. Close beside the Bara Katra lives this twentieth-century representative of the once proud family and traditions of Shaista Khan. He is a pathetic figure in the midst of the decay and desolation, a reminder of a day long dead. As he moves through the silent, deserted rooms of the Bara Katra, or walks with humble tread over the historical ground of the Lalbagh Fort, the thoughts go back irresistibly to the great Viceroy, the Amir-ul-Umara Shaista Khan, Lord of the Nobles, and the contrast between his magnificence and the fallen fortunes of his latter-day descendants is a living sermon on the vanity of human greatness. Sadly fallen from the high estate his family once held, and bereft of its once great possessions, the pathetic figure of the heir of Shaista Khan moves like a shadow amidst the scenes and memories of the past.

Some two miles north of the present city there is yet another memorial of Shaista Khan, almost rivalling in elegance and beauty the famous mausoleum of Peri Bibi. The Satgumbaz mosque, so called from its seven domes, stood in the beginning right on the edge of the northern bank of the Buriganga, but the river, fickle in its course like all the rivers of the East, has now receded, leaving a mile or more of low-lying rice land between it and the walls of the mosque by which it once flowed. It is a picturesque building, standing alone on the bank and framed against the low marshland, its seven exquisitely proportioned domes outlined against the sky. In the centre are the three large domes, flanked at the four corners of the mosque by the four smaller ones, each crowning an octagonal tower. Towering above, a slender willowy palm looks down upon them all, adding the last touch of Eastern colour to the scene. The inscription that once stood over the entrance has disappeared, but otherwise the mosque is in a good state of repair, and, though lonely and deserted now that the city and the river have withdrawn, the voice of prayer still ascends from it to heaven as in the days of Shaista Khan.

Though the Amir-ul-Umara has left behind

him so many evidences of his viceroyalty in brick and stone, little remains of the residences where he kept his Court and spent the long years of his stay in Dacca. It is probable that when visited by Tavernier in 1666, which was some twelve years before the Lalbagh Fort was commenced, Shaista Khan was living in the palace known as the Katra Pakartali, which once stood to the north-east of the mosque in Babu Bazaar, on the site of the Modern Medical School and Zenana Hospital. Of the palace itself, of no great pretensions even in its heyday one would gather from Tavernier, no trace survives to-day. But the Babu Bazaar Ghat, close by, still exists, with the foundations of the Naubut Khana still visible, and the mosque, a small, plain building, must be much as it was in the days of Shaista Khan, but little changed by time. The inscription upon it, unique in this respect among all the inscriptions in the city, is in Persian prose, composed apparently by the Viceroy himself. It is said to have been built during the first period of Shaista Khan's governorship, but the inscription has been so much damaged by fire that the date is no longer visible. To the north of the mosque stood the mausoleum of another of the Viceroy's daughters, Shahzadi Khanam, known as Lado Bibi; but this too has been swept away by the modern builder to make room for modern improvements, and the plain, utilitarian structure of the Zenana Hospital now occupies its site.

With the departure of Shaista Khan at the close of his long viceroyalty, the period of Dacca's greatest prosperity came to an end. Since that date few buildings of interest have risen to beautify the city, which for so many years was left forgotten to sleep its long sleep. Khan Mirdha's mosque was one of the last buildings of note erected while Dacca was yet the capital of all Bengal. During the viceroyalty of Murshid Kuli Khan it was built by the order of the chief Qazi of the city, the Defender of the Law, as he is described in the inscription. The mosque has fallen now on evil days, the lower floor being used as stalls for the municipal bullocks, and furnishing a barely sufficient income to pay for the *muezzin* and to light the mosque at sundown. In a better state of repair is the Lalbagh mosque, a large, solid building, just beyond the southern wall of the Fort, with space sufficient for some fifteen hundred worshippers, but with few of the architectural pretensions that mark all the buildings connected with the name of Shaista Khan. It was built on the eve of the final desertion of Dacca by the viceroys of Bengal in the days of Farrukh Siyar, who was destined so shortly afterwards to set out from his eastern capital to ascend the imperial throne at Delhi.

It was in the Nimtoli Kothi that the last scenes of Mussulman Dacca were enacted. Turned out of their palace in the old fort in 1765 when the East India Company took over charge of the Dewani, Nawab Jusserat Khan moved, after a brief stay at the Bara Katra, into the Nimtoli Kothi, which was to be his home and that of his successors until 1843, when the last Naib Nazim died childless, and the Company gathered up into its own hands the last remnants of the sovereignty which it had in reality so long held. The Nimtoli Kothi, which for nearly three-quarters of a century had housed the fading glories of the Naib Nazims, was then put up to auction, and many of the buildings were pulled down. The Baradari, however, a large hall of fine proportions, still survives. It was here that the last of the Naib Nazims held their court, and in imagination one can conjure up again the scene—the great pretensions, the effort at display, the pomp and ceremonial, the pathetic adherence to custom and tradition, and hovering over all, unmistakable but indefinable, the spirit of a departed glory and a lost cause.

In the Dacca of to-day the Nawab Khaja Salimullah Bahadur plays a large part. In no way connected with the old Nawabs of Dacca, whose line expired in 1843, the present title was at first bestowed by the British Government in 1875 as a purely personal distinction upon Khaja Abdul Ghani Mia, grandfather of Nawab Salimullah. The rise of the family to wealth and influence reads almost like a romance of the days of Shaista Khan. Born in Kashmir, Khaja Abdul Hakim, the founder of the family, set out early in life, like many another of his countrymen, to seek fortune at the Imperial Court. There his promising career was cut short only by the final overthrow of the Moghuls, and, doubtless attracted by the rumours of the wealth of the Eastern Province which had always been looked upon in olden days as the treasure-house of the Court of Delhi, he set out to pursue his fortunes on the outskirts of the Empire. Establishing himself as a trader in Sylhet, such success attended his efforts that he was soon able to send for his father and brothers from Kashmir, severing all connection with his old home and settling down with the determination to secure a position for himself in Eastern Bengal. In the next generation the family removed to Dacca, and gradually acquired large landed property in that district and in Barisal, Tipperah, and Mymensingh. It was left, however, for the Nawab Abdul Ghani to reach the highest dignities and honours. The wealthiest and most influential Zemindar in Eastern Bengal at the time of the Mutiny, he loyally placed all his resources at the disposal of the British Government, and himself did much to allay the unrest among the native population. Liberal and enlightened, he was foremost in the relief of distress and in all works of charity, many of his gifts being on a princely scale. To him Dacca owes its splendid water supply, upon which he spent some two and a half lacs of rupees. The foundation-stone of the waterworks was laid in August 1874 by Lord Northbrook, the first Viceroy to visit Dacca since Azim Oshan, Aurungzebe's grandson, had shaken the dust of the city off his feet over a hundred and sixty years before. Created Nawab in 1875, a distinction which was made hereditary in 1877, and K.C.S.I. in 1886, Abdul Ghani died full of years and honours in 1896. His son, Khaja Ahsanulla, who had long been in charge of his father's vast estates, succeeded, and for seven years worthily carried on the great traditions of loyalty and generosity which had been bequeathed to him. It is to him that Dacca owes the installation of the electric light which has done so much to improve the city. Created Nawab in 1875, Nawab Bahadur in 1892, and K.C.I.E. in 1897, he only survived his father seven years, and his son the present Nawab Khaja Salimullah Bahadur now reigns in his stead. The British Government has already shown its appreciation of the loyal assistance he has given to the making of the new Province of Eastern Bengal and Assam by conferring upon him the distinction of the C.S.I. at the commencement of the present year. The leader of the Mussulman community in Eastern Bengal, he holds a position of unrivalled influence and dignity in the new Province of to-day.

Of the various European factories that were established in Dacca during the period when the city was the capital of Bengal all trace, save in one instance, has disappeared. The English factory, the first insignificant outpost in Eastern Bengal of the race destined in the end to found an empire of which Shaista Khan himself could never have dreamed, was started during the early years of the great Viceroy's long reign, in 1668. It stood on the site now occupied by the Dacca College, and for a hundred years it formed the centre of English interests in Eastern Bengal. The French factory, founded within a few years of it, stood where a portion of the palace of the present Nawab now stands, close by the river. For over a hundred years it maintained its struggle for existence, in constant rivalry with the other factories, until it was taken by the English in 1757 during the war with France. The Mitford Hospital now covers the site of the Dutch factory, which survived until 1781, when it, too, was swept out of existence after its long struggle. All that remains to-day of the various factories is a portion of the house which the Portuguese once made their headquarters. It must have been in those days a fine, commodious building; but, like everything else in this city of the long sleep, it is sadly fallen and decayed, retaining but a memory of its better days.

The English cemetery, picturesquely situated a little apart from the noise and stir of the great city, is full of many memories. So utterly unlike the ordered graveyards of the West, there is something strikingly alien and pathetic about this 'God's-acre' of the East. The quaint Moorish gateway, the avenue of sad whispering casuarina trees, the luxuriant vegetation, the moss-grown pyramids and obelisks, seem to accentuate the sense of exile and decay. As one moves along the narrow paths among the graves, some surmounted by pretentious mausoleums, some beneath modest headstones, some with only a mound of earth to mark their site, one is irresistibly carried back in thought to those early days of the English pioneers when death lurked near, and few families escaped homewards leaving no toll behind them in the graveyards of the East. It was among the children, the young Englishmen fresh from home, and the young Englishwomen who had braved the dangers of the unknown to share a brother's or a husband's lot, that death was busiest. How many hopes and ambitions have been laid to rest beneath those silent stones! Here lies the infant child of James Rennell and Jane Thackeray, a model of whose grave in silver, taken by the heart-broken mother to her English home, is still among the possessions of the family. Here, beneath the oldest inscription of all, lie the remains of the Rev. Joseph Paget, Chaplain of Bengal, who died while visiting Dacca, aged only twenty-six, on March 26, 1724, just two years less one day since his arrival in India, his sudden death leaving Bengal without a chaplain for two years and five months. Not far off stand the monuments of Thomas Teake, October 1750, and Nicholas Clerembault, November 1755, chiefs of the Dacca factory, the former aged only thirty-two. Here, side by side, beneath a curious double tomb, lie Robert Crawfurd, factor of the Company, and his wife, the latter dying in June 1776, aged twenty-three, and the former surviving her less than two months. Reading strangely beside these English names is the inscription to one Wonsi Quan, erected by his friend Wona Chow in 1796, both Chinese converts to Christianity. Still more strange is the most imposing monument of all, which bears no inscription to tell who rests beneath. A high octagonal Gothic tower with eight windows, the whole surmounted by a cupola in the same style, it stands nameless, dominating the whole cemetery and jealously keeping watch over the three graves that lie within. Only the vague tradition survives that it is the tomb of 'Columbo Saheb, a Servant of the Company,' but a search among all available sources fails to bring to light any such name in the Company's annals. Even so long ago as 1824, Bishop Heber, who consecrated the cemetery on July 10 of that year, could obtain no further information about it from the officials of the day. Silent and impressive, the towering mausoleum keeps well the secret that it holds.

CHAPTER X

THE EIGHTH DAY OF THE MOON IN CHAIT.

'Whosoever bathes in the water of the Brahmaputra on the eighth day of the moon in the month of Chait finds shelter and forgiveness beneath the omnipotent feet of Brahma the Divine.'

In one long continuous stream, ceaseless, unending, like the river that flows beside the sacred ghats, the pilgrims come, wending their way towards the holy place, as the appointed hour draws nigh. All day long on the seventh day of the moon they have hurried onward, winding along the narrow paths between the fields like busy ants that turn aside neither to the right hand nor to the left, but press straight onward to their goal. This is to them the greatest of all the yearly round of many festivals. 'Know this, O thou that seekest after truth. The virtues of all the holy places in the world meet in the Brahmaputra on the eighth day of the moon in Chait.' The day is full of hope and expectation for the morrow. 'At the very touch of the water of the river all are absolved from sin, and by him who bathes in its sacred waters everlasting salvation is attained.' The stream of pilgrims, moved by one common impulse, presses onward, eager to obtain the beneficent promises of the gods.

It is a wonderful crowd. Many a weary mile has been tramped ere the sacred river is reached, and often the pilgrims bear upon them plainly marked the burden and heat of the way. From Dacca and Naraingunj near at hand, from Mymensingh, Comilla and Barisal further afield, from every corner of Eastern Bengal, they have come in their tens of thousands, by train, by boat, and on foot, to this great festival of the washing away of sins. Strangely intent, strangely earnest, this is to them no mere occasion of merrymaking, tinged only with the scant performance of some perfunctory rite, almost forgotten amidst the cries of them that buy and sell even in the very precincts of the most holy place. Buying and selling and all the accompaniments of a *mela* there must necessarily be where half a million people of the East gather, but the one main object of the festival, the washing away of sins, is marked clearly in the eager faces of the pilgrims as they hurry onward with bent heads. Unmindful, oblivious of the way and all its incidents, they pass on, silent for the most part as if in meditation on the greatness of the gods and the wonder of the promise that on the morrow shall meet with its fulfilment. Only occasionally, as they near the holy place and the tide of enthusiasm surges high, they give vent to one long continuous cry, weird and plaintive, rising higher and higher like the appeal of some mysterious denizen of the jungle throwing its note of mystery and wonder out upon the silent awe-some world.

They have banded themselves together in groups of a dozen or twenty for safety by the way. Quaintly a line of women marches, single file, one man only with them, tramping steadily ahead in charge. Each group represents some far-off village, all the women of which have started on this journey of such promise, leaving their men-folk behind, and taking with them but one of the village elders to protect them by the way. The women outnumber the men by five to one. It is a striking fact among this people in whose midst the women play so small a part. As the endless stream of pilgrims passes by, one's wonder grows. The element of youth seems almost wanting. Old, feeble, wrinkled beyond belief, bent with age and weary with the way, they pass on, each with the roll of bedding, and bundle containing the few necessities of life, which are all the comforts they will know throughout the great Snan Festival.

Timorous and weak, scarce ever moving from the tiny plot of ground that they call home, this journey is to them a thing of great adventure. None knows just where and how the vast crowd of pilgrims will spend the coming night. Booths there are to be had, rough roofs of matting lightly held on bamboo posts, but these are only for the more fortunate among the pilgrims, for those endowed with the wherewithal to pay, and these are few. For, next to the fact that they are old, one sees that they are poor. This is no festival of the rich. The zemindar, the opulent money-lender, the well-to-do babu, these are all there, but lost to sight among the hundreds of thousands of the poor and needy. Ill clad in a single garment of white, the pilgrims look almost as if they had adopted some sombre uniform for this great festival. Only here and there, a woman, younger than the rest, has given her love of colour rein in a light red-bordered sari that adds a welcome touch of brilliance to the white-robed throng. But for most of them the joys and vanities of life are past. With youth gone—fled with all the rapidity of youth in the East—perchance widowed, ousted from place and power in the home by the springing up of younger generations, their thoughts linger on the promises of the gods and the blessedness of that nirvana which for them may be so

THE WASHING AWAY OF SINS IN THE BRAHMAPUTRA DURING THE NANGALBANDH MELA

soon attained. So each with her joys and sorrows, her hopes and fears, each with her own life-story hidden in her great reserve in the innermost recesses of the heart, the seekers after the great washing away of sins pass on to await the hour when the waters shall be stirred to such sublime and wonderful effect.

Suddenly, with all the variableness of the East, a storm sweeps over the pilgrims' way. The white-robed figures disappear as if by magic, like ferrets seeking cover underground. The paths so lately thronged lie silent and deserted. The rain pours down as if the floodgates of heaven had been unloosed. Huge puddles fill the paddy-fields. The roads that the pilgrims so lately trod dryshod are damp and slippery, soon, under the passing of many feet, to become a veritable sea of mud. It is an extraordinary sight, this sudden cessation of all life. Only the heavy, pitiless rain beats down upon a world that waits its passing. Then, no less wonderful, there comes the re-awakening. The storm of wind and rain dies down. As swiftly as it came it passes. And even as it ceases the whole world within one's ken awakens. The white-robed figures creep out like rabbits from a warren. From mysterious and unsuspected hiding-places, where they had sheltered from the storm, they rise and shake their rain-soaked garments, flying them wide to dry in the breeze beneath the returning sun. Then the endless stream of pilgrims sets in again, until at last the sun wanes, and the brief Indian twilight hovers in a wondrous haze of purple and gold, ere it sinks, reluctant, into the grey-clad arms of night. And even then, in the light of the moon and the stars, the ceaseless tide of pilgrims still moves on.

All night in the vast encampment on the river-bank there is a stir of expectation. The hoarse babel of tens of thousands of voices goes out into the night, dull, monotonous, ebbing and flowing, yet continuous, like the roar of some distant sea upon the beach. A myriad lights twinkle out in the blackness of the night, tiny *chiraghs*, nothing but rough-cut wicks in earthen saucers of oil. The boats along the bank lie close packed, wedged in, each filled with its full tale of humanity. The outlines of the country-boats, of every shape and size, rise black and weird in the ruddy glow. Faces, old and young, peer out of the darkness, distorted into phantom elflike shapes by the flickering light. The noise of the tomtoms throbs out, but the stirring cries of the day have ceased. The faintest breath of air stirs the dead stillness of the night. It is the herald of the dawn, and one by one the lamps flicker and die out as if they feared to meet the coming day. The Brahmaputra, the Great, the

Divine, flows by unceasingly, waiting for the dawn that shall bring to it its few brief hours of healing and omnipotence.

The origin of the Nangalbandh festival is as shrouded in mystery as most other things in this land of fleeting memories. One asks in vain of the worshippers who throng with eager feet the way to this most holy place. They only know that it is holy. This they cling to as the unquestioned belief of centuries. Into the why and wherefore they make no search, blissfully content, as is the nature of the Oriental, to accept what is and let things be. Only here and there from some venerable patriarch, in whose memory the stories of his childhood's days still vaguely linger, can be gleaned strange rambling tales of gods and men. Once in the distant past, no man knows where, there lived a great and holy sage, one Jamadagni. His wife was Renuka, a princess of royal blood, famed for her rank and beauty. To them were born five sons, but of them all there was none to be compared with Ram, the youngest. In all manly sports he excelled, and, his favourite weapon being the axe, they gave to him the name of Parasuram. But in spite of the devotion of her five sons and of the holy sage her husband, Renuka sighed for the gaiety of the days she had once known. The sage lived the life of an ascetic in the forest, and his wife's thoughts flew back with regret continually to her life as a princess in her father's court.

Now it chanced one day that there passed before the door of her humble abode a neighbouring king with all his following, and Renuka, seeing them, wept for the pomps and vanities of life that were no longer hers. In this mood there came to her Jamadagni, her husband. Discovering why she wept, he grew enraged that this worldliness should have survived in the woman he had so long since taken to wife, and who had become the mother of his children. Turning to his sons in his anger, he ordered them to take their mother's life. But each in turn refused in horror, until he came to his favourite son, Parasuram, the youngest. Unhesitatingly, at his father's command, Parasuram raised his axe and struck off his mother's head. His punishment was swift and terrible. The axe with which he had committed the awful crime of matricide remained fixed in his hand, and no effort that he could make succeeded in detaching it. Finally he gave up hope, and, overburdened with remorse and grief, spent his days in meditation. To him at last there came a rumour of the sanctity of the waters of the Brahmaputra, a lake that lay far off concealed in the mighty ranges of the Himalayas. Hope reviving, Parasuram set out to search for the sacred waters that might wash away his sin and free him from the curse that had fallen so heavily upon him. For many years he trod the desolate mountain region unrewarded, his penance long protracted by the gods. But at length, one morning, as the mist rose up from the valley below, there lay disclosed a lake of purest crystal in the hollows, on which the rising sun shone till it glittered like a lake of purple and gold. Parasuram, trembling at the glad sight, rose up and falteringly spread his hands in supplication. 'O Thou whose limpid waters the foot of mortal man hath not defiled, let all thy sacred attributes combine to wash away my punishment and my sin.' So saying he cast himself into the sparkling waters, and straightway the axe fell from his hand, and he knew that in that selfsame moment his sin had been washed away. To give this healing water to the world and as a work of penance, Parasuram fashioned the axe that he had so long held into a plough, and ploughed a way through the mountains that the Brahmaputra might flow down to the plains. After many years of toil and labour he brought the river down to the place where Nangalbandh now stands. Here the plough stuck, and Parasuram, considering that his work was done, went on a pilgrimage to proclaim the healing powers of the great river, vowing that he would make it first among all the sacred rivers of the world. But close by, where the Brahmaputra had stopped, flowed Sitalakhiya, most beautiful of rivers, fair and luxuriant in the pride of her youth. The fame of her beauty reached even to the ears of Brahmaputra, mighty in sanctity and strength, and the god greatly desired to see her. Breaking all bounds by the force of its current, the mighty river advanced with a roar of triumph. Sitalakhiya, afraid at the sight of this impetuous and majestic river, swifter and mightier than her own placid stream, hid her beauty, and presented herself to Brahmaputra in the guise of an old woman, the Buriganga. When the great river saw her he was disappointed, and cried out to her 'Where, old woman, is Lakhiya in the bloom of her youth and beauty?' And Lakhiya, veiling her face, replied, 'I am that Lakhiya.' Then Brahmaputra, rushing onwards, tore aside the veil, and found that Lakhiya was indeed beautiful, and mingling his waters with hers they flowed on together. Now upon that very day Parasuram returned from his pilgrimage, and beheld that the river he had blessed and brought to earth had left him and joined the beautiful Sitalakhiya. Thereupon his anger blazed forth, and he cursed them both. But Brahmaputra prayed for forgiveness, reminding Parasuram of the benefits he had once conferred upon him. So Parasuram, remembering, relented, and said 'O thou whom it was my intention to make the most sacred of the rivers of the world, that daily thou mightest confer blessings on those that came to bathe in thee, now only on one day in all the year shalt thou be holy. Only on the eighth day of the moon, in the month of Chait, shall especial virtue be found in thee.'

So, as on the appointed day the first faint stir of dawn appears in the eastern sky, a wonderful thrill of awe and mystery vibrates through the great encampment on the river's bank. In the last watches of the night, the pilgrims, tired out with the long day's march, have slept. Only the few, tense and eager with the excitement of the day to come, have lain wakeful or told one to the other strange tales of the greatness of the gods and the healing waters of the river on this the great day of all the year. But with the approach of dawn there comes a great awakening. Nature and man rise up jubilant to await its coming, which to-day is fraught with so much promise.

Slowly across the sacred river the sun rises. Radiant and triumphant, it would seem to have reserved for this day of days its most glorious and wonderful apparel. Rose-pink and exquisite shades of green merge imperceptibly into flashes of saffron and silver and a broad expanse of blue, bathing the sacred stream in a dazzling glow of colour and light. And as the great sun-god lifts his golden orb above the eastern horizon, the whole vast assemblage of pilgrims stirs responsive to his coming.

The bank above the sacred ghats is alive, black with its dense moving throng of humanity. It is a never to be forgotten sight. For miles the countless multitude of worshippers—some half a million souls—extends along the river's edge, moving continually, ebbing and flowing, restless, like an ever-surging tide. The deep broad steps of the ghats, packed beyond belief, stand hidden from sight by the press of many eager feet. In one great wave of expectation the pilgrims push their way towards the stream whose waters are already stirred to such miraculous effect. Far out into its midst they wade, eager that the cleansing tide should not pass them by unlaved. Many of them bear in their hands their simple offerings to the great river. They are small, unpretentious gifts, a few flowers, a circlet of the strong-smelling *genda* blossoms, a bunch of plantains or merely a pepul leaf, for the pilgrims are poor and the expenses of the way have swallowed up their hard-earned savings. With many a prayer and oft-repeated formula they cast their gifts upon the great

ONE OF THE SACRED GHATS ON THE BRAHMAPUTRA DURING THE NANGALBANDH MELA.

PILGRIMS BATHING IN THE SACRED RIVER DURING THE NANGALBANDH MELA.

river, that with their sins it may carry away some outward tokens of their gratitude and faith. Again and again they plunge beneath the stream that no part of them may go uncleansed. Men of every age and caste, from the venerable Brahmin patriarch to the low-caste Manjhi youth, women old and worn, bareheaded, with grey hair streaming in the breeze, uncared for and unkempt, stand waist-deep with folded hands and moving lips, absorbed in prayer. Regardless of the jostling crowd around them, each intent with her own petitions and her own needs, with eager faces and straining eyes that see only into the future or back into the past, with no thought of external, fleeting, momentary things, they fervently repeat the time-honoured formulas of their religion. 'Om Brahmaputra!' is the salutation on every lip to the great river as each worshipper salaams before the mystic cleansing power that on this great day has stirred its waters.

The murmur of the vast multitudes that swarm the bank is like the roar of a distant sea. Long strings of worshippers, one behind the other, hand in hand, pass through the crowds, making their way with wild, unearthly cries, from ghat to ghat. For each of the ghats must be visited for the full benefits to be attained. It is a marvellous crowd of pilgrims of every age and many castes, fired by an enthusiasm that carries it beyond the thought of trivial passing things. That is one of its chief characteristics—its absolute unselfconsciousness. It has gathered, inspired by one great purpose, which leaves no thought for aught besides. Here in a circle, breast-deep in the stream, is a group that arrests the eye. Four generations strong, a family has come for prayer and the cleansing away of sins. Forgetful of all else, they perform the elaborate rites of their worship, turning aside neither to the right nor to the left to watch the ceaseless panorama that unfolds itself on either hand. Intensely earnest, with clasped hands and moving lips, each claims a special blessing from the gods.

So throughout the morning hours the wonderful bathing festival continues. The great river that at dawn had flowed by, clear and limpid, is churned to a deep mud-brown by the stirring of many feet on its shallow bed. The *genda* blossoms float down, trampled and stained. Yet still the worshippers push their way far out into the stream, eager to immerse themselves beneath the muddy waters which have been so divinely stirred to cleanse away their sins. Not until the sun is high overhead at noonday does the crowd along the bank begin to thin.

Then, the end and object of their pilgrimage

attained, there is time for rest and relaxation ere they take again the homeward way, to begin once more the common round of daily things. Many shrines raised here and there about the vast encampment attract the more devout, gorgeous presentments of the gods in all the glory of tinsel and paint, where offerings of pice and fruit and flowers must needs be made. Beyond, strongly reminiscent of an English village fair, but cruder and less finished, are roundabouts and shooting-galleries and peep-shows which never fail to attract the youthful native mind. Yet, considering the vast crowd of pilgrims that has assembled, these are comparatively but little patronised. The Snan Festival is one of such intense earnestness, so eminently religious, that the ordinary amusements of a festival, the gaieties, the feastings, the buying and selling that the heart of a native loves, play but a secondary part. All the pice that still remain are reserved for the shrines of the gods and goddesses whose special blessings the pilgrims most desire.

Slowly the great day passes. Streams of pilgrims throng the homeward way. Far off in the crimson west the sun sets in a blaze of splendour, leaving the river and eastern sky alight with its reflected glow. Clear again, and flowing swiftly, the great river hurries onwards with its ceaseless murmur, the mighty Brahmaputra, carrying away on its broad bosom, out of sight, out to the great engulfing sea beyond, the sins of the countless throng of pilgrims who have bathed in its waters on this one day in all the year, on the eighth day of the moon in the month of Chait.

CHAPTER XI

A MEETING-PLACE OF EAST AND WEST

WITHIN sight, far as the eye can reach, there is no other symbol of the West. The expanse of broken ground, reclaimed from the jungle in days gone by, stretches beyond, desolate and forgotten, shrub-studded and bramble-grown, unkempt, like a woman in rags. Groups of mud-built, straw-thatched huts dot the landscape, slung together, battered and worn, marked with the angry passing of many a storm of wind and rain. Tiny nut-brown urchins play in the mud, lazy and somnolent, naked and unashamed, in a necklace of coral or a single string with a golden charm. Teams of oxen, four abreast, move slowly with all the languor of the East as they turn the heavy sunbaked soil of the homestead fields. The cry of the elephant-driver and the deep-voiced tinkling of the bell come faintly as the huge beast lumbers away along the grass-grown path. All these are of the East, Eastern. Only the low whitewashed building, round which the monarchs of the forest seem to have grouped themselves in loving and protecting care, bears fearlessly aloft the symbol of the West. Raised heavenwards above the western porch there stands the Cross, triumphant over the storm and stress of centuries, steadfastly looking out at once a challenge and an appeal to the alien faiths that lie within its ken.

Out of the east a great storm gathers. Light masses of film-like cloud race onward, precursors of the dead, dull, bank of grey that moves more slowly in their wake across the sky. The air grows full of the noiseless sound of abundance of rain. The rustle of leaves, the bending boughs, the sough of the wind, make sad music like the voices of mourners mourning for their dead. The world grows dark as if at twilight. Deep gloom reigns in the dim dark shadows of the trees. Athwart the Cross a ray of light still lingers like a living flame from an ashen sky. A mighty rush of wind sweeps over the plain, bending the forest trees with sudden force. It is as if the world, moved by a sudden impulse, bowed down before the Cross that stands alone unmoved by the gathering storm. Firm like a rock in a troubled sea, it rises white against the darkening sky.

The first huge drops of rain strike heavily on the fallen leaves like the patter of feet that flee in terror from the anger of the storm. The doors of the church stand open, thrown back wide, as if in mute offering of sanctuary from the raging elements without.

Buffeted by the wind and rain outside, there is a wonderful calm within. The great empty church, with its silent time-worn walls, is like a sudden haven of rest in the storm-tossed world. Straight from the wild Eastern scene without, one is caught in a strange atmosphere of familiarity and peace. This might be some village church in the far-off West. The stoup of holy water, the Stations of the Cross, the side chapels with their bright figures of the saints, and high above them all, towards the east, the dim brilliance of the altar, far off and mystic, clothed in the surrounding gloom as in a veil—here there is nothing of the East. Outside, save the church itself and the Cross it bears aloft, there is nothing of the West. In all this land of great and vivid contrasts, there could scarcely be one more sudden and complete.

It is with something akin to awe that one pauses on the threshold. This is all that has survived of the once great quarter of the city that stretched for miles on either hand. Here, in days gone by, the English, the French, the Dutch and the Portuguese once had their settlements, while beyond and around, to the river to the south and to Tungi on the north, lay the great city of the Moghuls, the capital of all Bengal. Four miles, silent and deserted, lie between it and the Dacca of to-day. Gone are the palaces of the Viceroys and the garden-houses of the merchants; gone are the busy streets and market-places and the clamouring camps of armies. Of all that stood in the olden days on this once densely populated spot, only the church of our Lady of Rosary survives.

How this outpost of the Faith came there, no man knows. It may be that the Syrian Christians, whom Vertomannus found in the opening days of the sixteenth century in Bengal, first worshipped here, and that the Portuguese, hastening in the van of European nations in the East, but restored and added, making what they found tenantless fit for the service of their Church. But of the story of these early days no record has survived. The builders have left an enduring monument of their piety and faith, and with that they have been content. Their names are forgotten, but their work remains. The faith and the ritual that had been their birthright in their own land in the West they brought through much strife and tribulation, bravely planting it in their new home in the East among a hostile and fanatical people. They came of a magnificent, fearless race—the race of Henry the Navigator, of Cortez and Vasco da Gama—a race of intrepid explorers, of skilled seamen, first in the field in the new world that suddenly opened its gates upon the old in the fifteenth and sixteenth centuries, eager to push the fame of their great little country into untrodden paths. In India they had quickly taken their place in the east and south and west of the great peninsula, founding their factories and building their churches, showing the way to the other nations, who were not slow to follow in their wake. When they reached as far as Dacca in the east one asks in vain. Now almost all visible sign of their presence has passed away. This enduring monument of their faith, four miles north of the city, is one of the few traces that still remain of their one-time power and influence in the land.

Within the church itself there is evidence sufficient of its antiquity. As one treads with reverent feet the time-worn stones in nave and chancel, one passes above the resting-places of many a worthy of a bygone age. The epitaphs commemorative of their virtues still remain, faithfully preserving their memories among succeeding generations that would elsewise have long since forgotten. Scattered here and there in no set order, but casually, as if each sought in death the familiar spot where each in life had worshipped, they lie beneath the stones inscribed in Armenian and old Portuguese, difficult to decipher and worn by the passing of many feet. Here lies the oldest inscription of them all—to one Choy Daviatis, who died on June 7, 1714—a long narrow slab, half in Armenian, half in Portuguese, carrying one back to the days when Mussulman Viceroys still strove to rob the English of their privileges in Bengal, and Farrukh Siyar, setting out from Dacca, had but a little while before made his triumphal march to Delhi and seated himself upon the great Aurungzebe's throne.

The rain has begun to fall with a ceaseless patter on the roof. The great nave of the church grows dim and shadowy as if at nightfall. Over the chancel a veil has fallen. From without there comes the glorious scent of the refreshing rain upon the grateful earth. A sudden gust of wind sweeps in through the open door, swinging the lamps like censers before the altar.

Suddenly, unexpectedly, from overhead there comes the call to prayer. It rings out into the storm, slowly and solemnly, pregnant with warning and appeal. Along the path the quick patter of bare feet comes hurrying out of the rain, and the figure of a girl stands framed in the great stone doorway, her steps arrested, her large dark eyes widening at the unfamiliar sight of a stranger in the familiar place. Her spotless sari, white, neat-bordered, drawn gracefully over her head, clings to her slim body, heavily soaked through with the rain. Great drops fall from it, forming little puddles on the flagstones as she stands. But it is only for a brief moment. Then, the old hereditary instinct surviving even after long centuries of Christianity, she hastily draws the veil across her face and, dipping her finger in the stoup, makes the sign of the Cross and moves noiselessly to her place before the altar of the Virgin. There is no backward glance, no furtive look from behind the veil. Nothing but the momentary startled flash in the eyes showed her knowledge of the unaccustomed. Absorbed in her devotion, she kneels, oblivious of all else.

Then in straggling groups or one by one they come, these simple worshippers in the church of our Lady of Rosary of Tezgaon. Descendants, many of them, of the original builders of the church and bearing their names, there is little now, after the lapse of many generations, to distinguish them from the natives among whom they dwell. Others of pure native strain, they and theirs have so long professed the Christian faith that they have forgotten their own past days and know not whether their forbears once were Mussulmans or Hindus. It is a wonderful sight. Here, on one common ground, East and West seem to have met. All caste distinctions long since forgotten, they have united now for many generations in the *Credo* of the Catholic Faith. As one watches them, each so utterly Indian of the East, yet performing the observances that one associates so entirely with the West—the finger reverently dipped in holy water, the signing of the Cross, the genuflexion towards the altar and the silent passing with hushed feet to the appointed place with no glance to the right hand or to the left—it seems to be given to one to see as in a glass darkly a dim vision of the great miracle of the drawing together of East and West.

An acolyte in spotless white moves silently with lighted taper before the altar. One by one the tiny flames gleam warm and red, out of the surrounding gloom. On blue and white and gold the light falls with marvellous effect. Raised aloft, the massive candlesticks seem to lift heavenward the light they bear. Out of the dim grey shadows they gleam like beacons. Everywhere the familiar symbols of the great Faith of the West stand out pre-eminent.

The fretful cry of a child breaks suddenly upon the stillness. One is back again in the East as one turns towards it. A mother is rocking at her breast a naked, struggling, brown baby, crooning to him softly in hushed whispers. A jingle of bracelet and anklet, as a girl beside her moves from her cramped position on the narrow wooden footstool, makes unaccustomed music. A tiny urchin calmly unwinds his scanty garment, soaked through with the rain, and, spreading it on the ground to dry, stands forth naked, sublimely unselfconscious and sublimely happy. Another lies on the floor, with laughing eyes, and plays with the hem of his mother's robe. The mother, a still smaller infant in her arms, kneels on regardless. The rest of the white-robed throng, noting none of these things, kneel motionless, absorbed and unobservant.

The service has begun. The hushed voice of the priest, speaking the first solemn words of the Mass, breaks the silence. 'Introibo ad altare Dei.' Could there well be anything more of the West, Western? The majestic Latin words ring with strange insistence in this far-off and forgotten outpost of the Faith. 'Dominus vobiscum,' and its quick response, 'Et cum spiritu tuo.' Then the thrice repeated 'Kyrie eleison, Christe eleison, Kyrie eleison,' and again 'Dominus vobiscum' and the unfailing answer 'Et cum spiritu tuo.' Things of the East and things of the West fade out of sight. The 'one Church' of the magnificent confession of faith in the words of the *Credo* is without distinction of race or language, of peoples or nations, of East or West. In a flash one sees the consummation of all that men deem impossible. For a moment the difficulties seem no longer insurmountable, and the differences fade away and vanish.

The great service, which has been repeated such countless times, which has survived such marvellous vicissitudes, which has been the light and life of such unnumbered generations, draws towards its consummation. Out of the shadow round the altar the priest, and the acolyte, swaying the censer, move slowly. Censing the kneeling worshippers, they stand in the fuller light of the chancel steps, and a wonderful silence falls. Absorbed in the service of the West, forgetful of the East, one's eyes fall suddenly on the bare brown feet of the acolyte, and things of the East, with their immeasurable remoteness, crowd back again, and the dim vision that had held one, in spite of oneself, half slips away. The spotless robes are the robes of the West, but all else in the small figure that stands beside the priest is so strikingly of the East. Then, as swiftly as it came, the momentary confusion of thought ceases, checked in the wonder of the deeper hush that has fallen upon the reverent worshippers. The tinkling of the bell proclaims the passing of a mystery. The climax of the great service is reached, and the people wait with bowed heads the solemn moment of the Elevation of the Host. 'Sanctus, Sanctus,

Dominus Deus Sabaoth.' Again all distinctions are swallowed up. One watches, spell-bound, the passing of this magnificent service of the Mass here in the midst of these unexpected surroundings. It is the same wonderful mystery, the same solemn ritual, the same faith that has been as the soul of nations, for which men have fought and died, which has held enthralled the greatest minds that the civilisation of the West has given forth, to which one may deny allegiance, but not admiration and respect. It is the same great act of worship here, in this far-off Indian countryside, as in the magnificent cathedrals and churches of the West. The same reverent hush falls at the tinkling of the bell. The gentle whimpering of the child at its mother's breast, that one only notes at its cessation, is stilled. The jingling of anklet and bracelet ceases. There is not a movement. The silence is oppressive, such a one as makes its presence felt. One is carried back in thought to that great silence that falls upon the vast throng of waiting people in the courtyard of St. Peter's as they hear the momentous words ring out, 'Habemus Papam,' or when the Holy Father from the loggia, turning about to the four quarters of the globe, solemnly bestows his blessing on the world. Surely, if ever, it is here, in the common profession of a great faith, that East and West shall meet.

And then again one's eyes fall upon the kneeling worshippers, and in a flash it seems to be borne in upon one that 'East is East and West is West, and never the twain shall meet.' They are repeating the Rosary, reverently, befittingly. But it is in a tongue unknown in the West—a soft, sibilant tongue, yet strange, uncomprehended, fixed like a barrier between them and the West. Clad in their saris, their veils half drawn across the face, these women of the East have so little in common with their sisters of the West, and those with whom they have come in contact have mostly passed them by. The men, living the simple life of the cultivator and the labourer, knowing nothing beyond the joys and sorrows of the moment, in thought, in speech, in manner of life, lie centuries behind the West. Is there a force in the world that could furnish them a meeting-place ?

A sudden ray of light falls full across the altar. One had almost failed to notice that the rain had ceased. Brilliantly the sunshine falls on white and blue and gold, and upon the Cross that towers above. It illuminates the face of the priest as he turns once more to give the blessing. 'Dominus vobiscum,' and again the answer comes, 'Et cum spiritu tuo.'

There is a stir at last among the congregation.

The solemn service is at an end and the worshippers file slowly out. The tiny urchin gathers up his single garment, and winding it round his waist, with eyes wide fixed upon the stranger, toddles out, holding his mother's robe. The women, still with bent, reverent heads, pass by with gaze averted. Only when outside the sacred precincts do they allow their curiosity full play as they glance back furtively before they hurry out into the warring elements beyond. For the storm has begun again, and the earth is given over to the wind and the rain.

The acolyte hastily puts out the lights upon the altar, and the chancel falls back again into shadow. The outlines of the Cross grow faint and indistinct. The wonderful vision that it was given to one to see of the drawing together of East and West has passed. In the great emptiness and silence of the deserted church it seems but as a dream when one awaketh. Yet as one passes out and leaves the church behind, the last backward glance reveals the uplifted symbol of a faith of world-wide claims and aspirations, crowned in a halo of light, triumphant, insistent, a steadfast beacon of hope through every change and for all time. And one knows that within its shadow the East and the West have met.

CHAPTER XII

ON THE LAKHIYA

It is just before the dawn.

Overhead the stars blink clear on a dead blue sky. The waning moon, low on its back, mirrors its silver light in every dancing wave of the great broad stream that flows on ceaselessly into the night. The banks on either side rise black, studded with twinkling lights that gleam like eyes of fire. Beyond, on river and land, a faint white mist has fallen like a garment of sleep on a sleeping world.

The busy traffic of the river is stayed. The noisy hum of the teeming mart is stilled. Over all there has fallen the great Silence and the great Peace.

Unchecked, untrammelled, the river slips by, laughing as if with joy to be free. Like some refrain sung by a mother to the child at her breast, its ceaseless ripple breaks in upon the silence of the night, lulling a time-worn world to slumber. Gently lapping the banks on either hand, striving ever to rise higher and enfold them in its close embrace, it seems to murmur softly of the vanity of human life and wishes, as if it laughed, in its own great constancy, at the petty passing cares of men. On these same banks for centuries it has watched men come and go. It has seen great principalities and kingdoms rise and fall, the fleeting glories of a fickle world. On its broad bosom it has borne brave fleets and armies to victory and defeat. Now they rise but as ghostly memories out of the past. Their day has waned, and no man is mindful of their passing. Only the great river, through all the changing years, flows onwards, and as it ripples by it murmurs, half mocking, half consoling, its constant message and refrain. 'Vanity, vanity, vanity,' it seems to whisper, and again the oft-repeated 'All is vanity.'

Slowly the waning moon sinks out of sight, hidden behind the masts of the shipping that line the further bank. The clear dark waters throw back the light of a myriad stars that shine the brighter for the passing of the moon. A breathless silence enfolds the earth, as if reluctant to yield it to the coming day. Even the murmur of the river dies down to but the faintest whisper. That wonderful brief hush that comes before the dawn enfolds the world.

Only on the huge river steamers that lie at anchor beside the wharf away up-stream is there any sign of life. Lit with electric light, their great hulls stand out clear-cut against the lesser blackness of the night, illumined by the dazzling glare within. Here night is as the day. Innumerable dark forms passing from out the shadow across the radius of the light, like marionettes, move silently, crouched low beneath huge burdens. The clank of chains, the thud of burdens cast aside, the quick, hoarse cries of orders oft repeated, float ever and anon across the rippling waters, heard only like some faint stirring from another world, apart from the peaceful sleeping world of the river and the land.

Then suddenly, unseen, unheralded, there comes a strange, mysterious stirring in the air. It is as if the world were young again, when the stars of the morning sang together, and all the sons of God shouted for very joy of heart. All to the naked eye is as it was before—asleep. But to the ear attuned there comes the first faint sound of the awakening dawn. It is as if the Great Spirit breathed the breath of life upon the waiting earth, and bade the night awake. So faint it is, so mysterious, so all-enthralling, that as in a dream one knows and feels that which it is not given to the eye of man to see. To that sixth sense that

LANDING JUTE AT NARAINGUNJ.

NARAINGUNJ.

lies deep down in the unprobed depths of man, it makes its own most wonderful appeal.

The first great mystery of the coming dawn is past. The wonder of the unseen passes into the knowledge of things seen. A soft, cool breeze, grateful after the stillness of the night, sweeps over river and land. Every leaf on every tree leaps gladly to its coming, and sings aloud its song of thankfulness. The tall bamboos sway gracefully in its embrace and kiss the water's edge. Roused from their sleep among the branches, a crowd of *minas* start the day with loud-voiced chattering and much ruffling of their dew-drenched plumes. Like evil revellers of the night, caught by the dawn, a company of rooks sweeps low over the face of the waters to their home among the poinsettia trees that overtop the buildings on the further bank.

A siren cry from one of the river steamers breaks the silence like a warning voice. Slowly, like a giant shaking aside his chains, it moves, with clatter, and shout, and groaning, free from its moorings against the bank. A dazzling flash from its search-light throws clear its path before it, bathing the dancing waters of the river, the shipping, and the frowning mass of bank, in its weird, white, ghostly radiance. Defying the night, it makes the darkness light as the day; but, kinder than the day, while making all things clear, it lends to all a strange, mysterious charm. Even the row of boats, hideous by day, with corrugated iron roofs, shine out beautified, bright like silver, in the fantastic, unaccustomed light. Slowly the great steamer, its bulk magnified in the darkness behind the light, moves out into mid-stream, and, girding its strength, passes straight and purposeful out into the coming dawn.

A dead, pale grey light creeps out of the east, outlining the masts of the shipping that ride at anchor up-stream. The huge hulls of the sloops close at hand loom out black and phantom-like in the faint half-light, half-darkness of the dawn. Their masts and spars and rigging rise up clear-cut against the lightening sky. The brilliant lights in the river steamers that still remain beside the landing-stage go suddenly out. The eyes of fire that here and there gleamed red from either bank have disappeared as if by magic. The world is a study in grey.

A blush rose pink creeps into the grey. The white mist that hangs beyond, where river and sky unite, melts ghost-like into the dawn. The stars blink sleepily in the face of the rising sun and one by one go out.

The world is suddenly awake. From under the shelter of the banks, where they have lain all night, tiny skiffs creep out into the stream, paddled by dark brown forms in the bows. Huddled close in their cotton cloths in the damp morning air, the fishermen make ready their nets against the long day's work. Narrow *goyna* boats glide noiselessly down the stream. A dinghy unfurls its nut-brown sail and, catching the morning breeze, skims swiftly out of sight. A brig, heavy and age-worn, looking like some survival out of the past, begins to discharge its cargo of English salt into the iron-roofed warehouse on the wharf. The long-deserted banks swarm once again with the busy hive of men.

The sun arises like a giant refreshed with sleep. The shadows flee noiselessly to join the vanished forces of the night. The silver river dons new robes, reflecting every colour and shade of the coming dawn. Red and orange and gold, purple and yellow and mauve, they break like waves on a boundless sea. Glory of dawn and wonder of night have met and merged in the day. Steadfastly the river flows on unheeding, yet throwing back every passing change as if accentuating its own constancy and the inconstancy of all besides.

The daily round of life has begun. It is the midst of the jute season, and Naraingunj is one of the busiest centres of its trade. Huge go-downs line the banks on either side, tin-roofed, red-bricked, ugly with all modernity, yet adding their note of life and colour to the scene. Tall chimneys tower behind them and huge cranes swing on the landing stages, symbols of the activity and stir of the busy mart. Solid, stone-built bungalows, screened by a wealth of trees from the water's edge, or standing out boldly, set in shady garden or well-trimmed lawns of exquisite green, look out over the broad expanse of the river. Close anchored against the banks are boats innumerable of every size and kind, each intent on landing the burden of jute it has carried down from the low-lying fields up stream.

The river is alive with craft. Tiny black fishing boats that scarcely seem to touch the water, prow and stern high in the air, skim over the shining surface. Dinghies, with circular roof of thatch, skilfully propelled by a single oar-rudder, roughly tied near the bow with a piece of rope, pass on more slowly. A steamer, lithe and buoyant moves out into mid-stream, then steadies itself as it settles down to tow three of the huge iron-roofed flats that have lain like sleeping monsters under the lee of the wharf. A whole fleet of jute boats, mat-thatched, start slowly up the stream, rowed by oarsmen quaintly standing on platforms on the roof.

It is a fascinating scene. Every moment the interest changes as the launch leaves its moorings and picks its way along the crowded stream. The glory of the first morning hours is bathing the world in light. In the first clear brilliance of the day returned, the earth and river seem to palpitate anew with life, grow buoyant and sing with joy. The trim little steamer seems literally to dance upon the sparkling river as it rushes through, lashing it into a froth of foam and leaving its long broadening ripples on its surface like a lingering caress. On either hand it is historic ground. Hidden, forgotten in the noise and stir of the busy mart, memories still cling thick round these lower reaches of the Lakhiya, close by where the great rivers meet. But just below, the Megna, the Ganges, the Brahmaputra, the Dullasery, and the Ishamutti, all unite, and this meeting-place of the giant watercourses is the most historic spot in all Eastern Bengal. The many tides that have ebbed and flowed this way have seen strange scenes. Behind to the left lies the ancient kingdom of Vikrampur, with its memories of the famous Ballal Sen and the ruins of its once great capital of Rampal. Back but a short way to the right stretches the kingdom of Sonargaon, for centuries the centre of all interest in Eastern Bengal, to-day but a peaceful rural countryside, yet studded with the remains of its once great forts and palaces that, grass-grown and crumbling to decay, survive as fading memories of the past. Feringhi Bazaar, just below on the Ishamutti, recalls to mind the days of Portuguese adventure when these same rivers swarmed with seamen roving, in the true spirit of the age, in search of whatever enterprise might chance to hand. In their wake, learning from them new skill in navigation, came the Mughs, plundering, murdering, and laying waste, impudently defying the Moghul power. Close by, on both banks, stand the forts of Kalagachhia, Sonakunda, Tribeni, and Hajigunj, built by Isha Khan and Mir Jumla to drive back their fleets. From Hajigunj it was that Man Singh, Akbar's great Rajput general, set out against them. It must have been a brave sight that the Lakhiya saw that day. A great fleet that covered the river for a mile on either hand had gathered here, huge ships manned by forty rowers with towering hulls, a forest of rigging and great sails, cumbersome, unwieldy, no match for the nimble craft of the Mughs when it came to a hand-to-hand encounter. But they won in the end by their very stolidity and strength, these great fleets of a great empire. Sonakanda, only the barest outline of its fort surviving, teems with memories of Isha Khan, last of the famous Afghan chiefs in Sonargaon, and of Sona Bibi, his heroic wife and comrade in the field. It was here that he, a follower of the

Prophet, brought her, in the heyday of her youth and far-famed beauty, straight from Chandpur across the river, whence he had taken her by force, a Hindu child widow, the daughter of his deadliest foe. It was here in after years that, widowed again, the widow of Isha Khan, she defended her dead lord's fortress against his foes, even though they were of her own kith and kin, making the city at last her funeral pyre rather than that it should fall into the enemy's hands.

Further on up-stream, just as Naraingunj is left behind, stands the Kudam Rasul containing the print of the Prophet's foot, its huge gateway, massive and imposing, half hidden in a wealth of trees. Opposite, close by where the Hajigunj Fort once stood, still survive the mosque and mausoleum that Shaista Khan, the greatest of Viceroys, raised to the memory of his daughter Miriam Bibi, who died on her father's state barge while it lay at anchor in the river. And so, on past the last of the huge jute go-downs, leaving the masts of the shipping and the stir of the busy port behind, one hurries onwards, away up-stream.

Out beyond, the years have wrought less change. So, save for the jute that everywhere meets the eye, might it have seemed to the Portuguese sailors as they looked out from over the prows of their high-pooped ships, scanning the horizon in search of adventure; or fair as it seemed to Miriam Bibi as she peeped from behind the silken curtains that screened the daughter of the Viceroy from the vulgar gaze. Tranquil and smiling, the most beautiful of all the rivers of Eastern Bengal, the Lakhiya stretches northwards straight and wide and rippling silver in the morning sun. The stream sweeps down a mighty current, straining to burst its bounds like a boy at school. It leaps and engulfs the overhanging branches of the trees that fringe the banks. For miles they stretch, a glorious jungle growth, untouched now as when in the days of their youth they first bent down their heads to listen to the song of the river. Banyan and nim and pepul, palas and mango and tamarind, they crowd rank on rank, thick like a wall of green. Here and there a palm towers up above the rest. A group of plantain trees, with their cool pale-green leaves, stands out, the purple sheaves of their buds a brilliant patch against the green. The delicate sprays of the willowy bamboos sway gently in the breeze, a study in exquisite form and grace. White sails belly and bend in the lap of the breeze. Brown sails throw their deep rich touch of colour on the scene. Blue sails flaunt their heads to heaven, putting the bluest of skies to shame.

For every pulse-beat of the plucky little steamer

A FISHING-BOAT ON THE LAKHIYA.

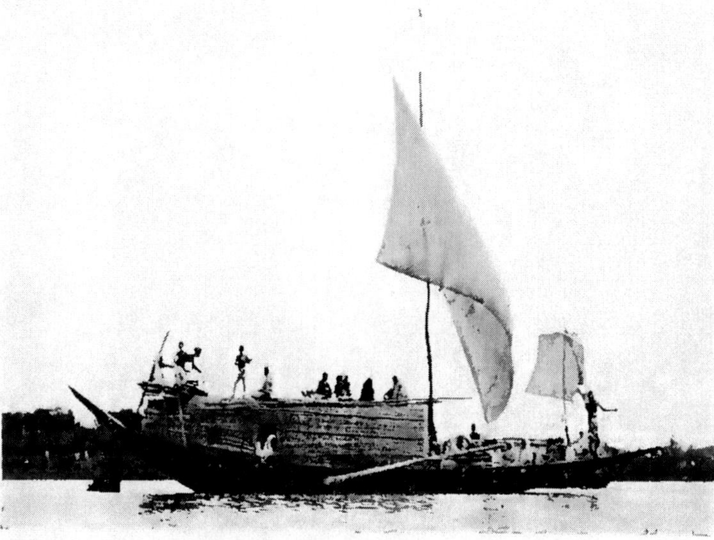

HOMEWARD-BOUND AT EVENING.

as she gallantly ploughs her way up-stream there is some new glimpse. A high wooden bridge, frail but rustic, set in a background of trees, spans a tiny creek that joins the river, and over it a line of women passes slowly single file, balancing their waterpots upon their heads with typical Eastern grace. Nut-brown urchins play among the goats that browse contentedly on the lush green grass upon the banks. A herd of buffaloes squelches in the mud where the land lies low, a crowd of paddy-birds hovering near, fearless and alert to pick up whatever of insect life the cloven feet of the huge great beasts disturb. Well-thatched roofs and neat mat walls peep out among the trees with an air of opulence and comfort. For it is a fertile land, and jute has proved a source of much wealth to many. Living is dear on the banks of the Lakhiya, compared with Western Bengal, but wages are good and the standard of comfort is high. The talukdar, the petty zemindar, and the merchant sleep snug within trim homesteads or more pretentious houses of brick, that add their touch of opulence to the exuberant luxuriance of the tree-clad banks.

Under a huge banyan sits the Panchayet, administering village justice, inquiring into the rights and wrongs of some dispute that is agitating the little community, or discussing a sin against his caste which one of their number has committed. Two brothers, it may be, are quarrelling over their inheritance. The journey to court is long and the expenses many, and for once the brothers are wise. The President of the Panchayet is a just man and impartial. Who should decide better than he, the venerable old man in their midst, who has known them from their youth up and their father before them, and is fully conversant with the custom and rules of succession among them and theirs? What he decides will be right, and they have agreed to abide by his decision. Or it may be that the dispute is as to a boundary between neighbours, or a question of fishing rights in one of the numerous *khals* that branch off from the main river; or a man may have complained that another has forcibly cut and stolen his jute, and the case has been sent by the Court to the President to inquire on the spot where all the villagers know the facts of the case, and where the truth, concealed by many an art and subterfuge, is most likely to be found. A thousand and one things claim the attention of the Panchayet. Nothing is too small for it to be called upon to decide. Under the trees the village elders form a picturesque group, like patriarchs of old, recalling far-off early English days, when the Witenagemot deliberated on affairs of State in like primitive and informal way. The President rises and salaams with courtly grace as the steamer passes close beside the bank, a venerable Mussulman figure with flowing beard and long white robes, the very personification of dignity and repose.

On past Murapara, with its handsome modern house built by a rich zemindar, one races up the stream. Ornamented in red and white, with its trim set trees and shrubs, its broad steps leading to the water's edge, the house stands out a strange thing of modern days, thrust on the peace and old-world beauty of the river. Behind, in sharp contrast, crumbling and lichen-grown, still stand the ruins of the palaces and mosques once peopled by the descendants of the haughty Shaista Khan, when the first days of the greatness of his house had passed and the last evil days were still far distant. Opposite, the Rupgunj Thana peeps out among the trees, mat-walled, tin-roofed, an unimposing outpost of the British Raj. On the open space in front sits row on row of blue-coated, blue-and-white turbaned chowkidars, waiting with pleased anticipation the distribution of their three months' pay. A picturesque group they make as their khaki-coated, red-turbaned duffadars move in and out among them, forming the first link in the mighty chain of British justice. The foundation-stone of our Indian administration, the chowkidar represents in every village the primitive and ever-present source of the greatness and majesty of the law.

A sudden bend of the river, a glimpse of rich red banks that rise up like the ruins of some old fortress crowned by a wealth of foliage, and again the ever-varying scene is changed. The brilliant sun, a ball of blazing fire, creeps high overhead. Giant betel-nut palms tower up against the sapphire blue of the sky, tall and stately, their tapering stems ending in a crown of spear-like leaves. For a space the banks are higher, and the river races by, baffled and kept in bounds, chafing to expand and embrace the fields that lie behind.

Round the bend in the river the breeze freshens. A huge *bepari* boat, heavy laden with jute, lies low down in the stream, stolid and slow-moving. The rowers on the platforms on the mat-thatched roof cease toiling and lay aside the oars at the grateful touch of the wind. With noise and clatter and shouts, as if they made ready a man-of-war with the enemy already in sight, they unfurl the enormous sails that flap and stagger, then, catching the swell of the wind, fly taut, and the heavy lumbering boat, suddenly awake, leaps forward on its way. Every craft on the river follows suit, and, with sails spread full in the breeze, pulsates with life renewed. It is the last little note of beauty and grace, as when the painter skilfully plies his brush for the finishing touch ere he casts his palette aside. White sails, brown sails, sails patched and torn yet picturesque still in their last days as in their first, they crowd the river, each one straining at the ropes held taut in the grip of the breeze. The river is a pathway of hurrying life. Heavy boats, jute-laden, that have crept along in the lee of the bank, slowly and with much toil, now sail out lightly in midstream to catch the swell of the wind, and speed on, stately and majestic, over the rippling stream. Tiny dinghies and *jalkar* boats, top-heavy with hastily rigged sails, sway and dance and skim over the laughing water like great white birds on the wing. Full of the joy of life and in a great content the river slips by, murmuring still that the great and wonderful present—the hour of life and duty—is slipping by, and that all besides is vanity.

So on past Denga, with its busy market-place in full view from the river, where many of them that buy and sell gather from all the countryside. It is market day, and beneath the rough mat sheds one catches a glimpse of wares exposed, and the noise of loud-voiced bargaining floats out across the river. The native loves to haggle, and parts with his pice only after due deliberation and with much grudging. So the buyers and sellers make long talk though the sun beats high overhead.

It is almost noon. The sun strikes full on the river, making it flash in a blaze of dazzling light. Slowly the breeze dies down as if it grew weary in the all-pervading languor of the heat of the day. The tall cocoanut palms stand stiff and straight, their dignity unruffled by the faintest puff of wind. The sails on the boats flap lazily, and one by one fall limp. The heavier craft put in to the bank to await the return of the breeze or to let the heat of the day pass by before the rowers toil again at the oars. The trees on the banks stand motionless as if cut in stone. Not a leaf stirs, not a blade of paddy in the fields moves. The cattle lie in the shade, only their tails alive as they ceaselessly flick off the crowd of flies that worry them eternally. So for a time again life sleeps. Only the river flows onward, as steadfast and purposeful in the languor and heat of the day as in the silent watches of the night.

This is the broadest stretch of the stream away past Kaligunj, with its rows of jute go-downs and boats of many kinds waiting for their burdens, all asleep now in the blazing light. Beyond, the banks lie low, and the river has long since burst its bounds and engulfed the fields on either hand. Save for the trees and the crops, it is hard to see where the river ends and the banks begin. A clump of bamboos stands out in the stream, a group of betel-nut palms rise up straight out of the river, mirroring their long light stems to greater height in the water at their feet. Patches of jute submerged look as if they floated on the flood. The paddy in the hidden fields throws up its fresh young shoots, struggling to raise itself above the water's level.

Everywhere now there is evidence that jute is the predominating interest of the river and of those that dwell upon its banks. Here, where the land lies low, buried beneath the flood, one sees the full extent of its cultivation. Field after field of it stretches away, towering ten feet high in flourishing patches of rich dark green. The brief spell of rest in the heat of the day is over, and the river is alive with busy workers, standing knee-deep in the water as they cut the long shoots and bind them up in bundles. These, laid side by side, are left to steep in the shallows where the stream runs clear. There for days they lie, till the river has washed them through and through. Men and boys stand waist-deep out in the water, fixing them firm with bamboo sticks, that the stream may not carry them away. Huge straw-plaited hats on their heads, at once a protection from the sun and rain, the workers work with a will, their nut-brown bodies, bare save for a cloth about the waist, gleaming with heat in the sun.

Further on they are beating out the jute that

has been sufficiently steeped. Peeling off the long white strips of fibre from the stalks, they wash it in the water, beating it, as a *dhobi* washes clothes, then hanging it up on a bamboo rail to dry in the sun. All along the river-banks there are groups at work. The sharp, rhythmical thud of the coils of jute as they hit the water sounds like an accompaniment all the way up the stream.

Out of the west a mass of fleecy cloud has crept up unperceived, scarce dimming the joyousness of the day till it draws near the face of the sun. Soft white feathery clouds race over the sky, chasing one another like children at play. Grey clouds, slower and more sombre, follow in their wake, and a grateful shadow falls on river and land. The glaring heat of the sun is stayed. A sudden gust of tempestuous wind blows straight from east to west across the river. Raindrops beat down heavily, till they make the face of the water splash in a thousand jets. The river breaks like a sea, and leaps in a thousand waves. The racing clouds roll on, and the sun escapes again like a giant released from the toils. Nothing remains of the April storm save a glorious freshness in the air. Sails leap up again to catch the fickle breeze. The water laughs and leaps on its way as if refreshed, and revels again in the sparkling light of the sun.

Slowly it draws to evening. A kingfisher flashes out across the stream, a glorious lithe vision of black and white, swoops suddenly and, with flutter of wing, splashes the smooth mirror-like surface of the river, and is away again poised lightly on the air. A single sail, chasing the setting sun, glides on till it loses itself in the golden west. Slowly the cattle come down to the water's edge to drink in the shadows under the trees. A tiny urchin leads them, with the air of a man and a staff just twice his length, demanding and obtaining unquestioning obedience. A herd of buffaloes wades far out into the shallows to revel full length in the cool of the stream. Only their great long plaintive heads rise up above the water's level. The urchin, leaving the cattle, wades out and belabours their leader with his staff and, clambering fearlessly astride as the huge beast gets ponderously to its feet in the mud, he leads them slowly home.

Across the water, soft and low, there comes the call to prayer from the mosque beyond the trees. The cry of the muezzin rings out suddenly, like a challenge on the evening air, "There is but one God." Throughout the East, the wonderful, mystic East, throbbing with the hopes and fears of its countless people, from a thousand mosques and villages the same call to prayer goes forth. At eventide, as the sun dies down and night begins to fall, the oft-repeated name of God floats out to reassure the Faithful. Long, weird, rising and falling in thrilling cadences, the cry vibrates upon the evening air and lingeringly dies away. On the bank close by a little company of villagers, hurrying home from the *hât*, laden with their purchases, hastily place their burdens on the ground and, looking towards Mecca, kneel reverently in prayer. Absorbed and forgetful for the moment of all else, with many genuflections, bending their foreheads to the ground, they repeat the magnificent confession and supplications of their faith. The oarsmen on the passing boats cease from their labours and, laying by their oars, kneel on the mat platform above the roof, their faces turned towards the west. A hush seems to have fallen over all the river. The earth lies still as if content to listen. Everywhere the voice of prayer and praise fills the world. All things cry aloud that there is but the one God of a great Faith, and that the work of His hands is good.

The sun sinks low. Focussed until now in one great ball of fire, it breaks suddenly, spread left and right in a blaze of colour over the west. Sapphire and topaz and pearl, opal and amethyst and onyx, it blends them all in a glorious blaze of light. Faithfully the river mirrors them back. One moment

ON THE LAKHIYA.

a shimmer of gold, the next a leaping column of fire, it pales at last to orange and mauve and grey. The river itself grows almost still. Placid and calm it seems to rest from its strenuous race. Subduing its murmur as the world prepares for slumber, it grows limpid and clear like a lake revealing itself deep down. The hot impetuous rush of its youth in the dawn has gone. Its mocking note is hushed, lost in the great peace that its scarce-moving stream bears softly on its bosom. Even as it moves, the river seems to sleep. The cares of the day have fallen away down stream. They grow far off, unreal, like things of a dream. The petty strivings and the paltry ambitions of men fade out of sight in the length and breadth and depth of this twilight world. It is needless longer for the river to murmur that all is vanity, for the vanity of the world is already far behind. Its message is all of quietness and peace. Men and nations and empires come and pass, but on the broad bosom of the river there is for all time forgetfulness and rest.

The palm trees cast long shadows out into the stream. Tiny fishing-boats shoot out like long black lines against the paling river, the naked black figures propelling them clear cut like an etching. Dark, silent, with a fascinating air of mystery, they glide by into the night. Across the river there comes the first short, sharp cry of a jackal. A dog in the village close by barks at the coming night. Fires, one by one, gleam out on either bank. The sky is filled with a thousand stars that watch the world asleep. Slowly a great peace falls over all, and river and land grow still. And so at last there comes a little folding of the hands to slumber, a little pillowing of weary heads to sweet forgetfulness, ere the long Indian day of toil begins anew.

LIST OF SOME OF THE MORE IMPORTANT AUTHORITIES.

Sir William Hunter's 'History of British India.'
Stewart's 'History of Bengal.'
Bernier's 'Travels in Hindustan.'
Seir Mutaqherin.
Bishop Heber's 'Journal.'
Ralph Fitch's 'Travels.'
'Statistical Account of Bengal,' Vol. V.
'Riyyus-Salatin.'
Hill's 'Three Frenchmen in Bengal.'
Tavernier's 'Travels in India.'
Sir William Hunter's 'Thackerays in India.'
Ain-i-Akbari, Lucknow edition.
Sir Charles D'Oyley's 'Ruins of Dacca.'
Dr. Taylor's 'Topography of Dacca.'
Sayid Aulad Hasan's 'Antiquities of Dacca.'
Marshman's 'History.'
Tarikh-i-Firuz Shahi.
'History and Statistics, Dacca Division, 1868.'
Blackman's 'Geography and History of Bengal.'
Long's 'Selections from Unpublished Records.'
'Subarnagramer Itihas.'
Hill's 'Indian Record Series.'
Wheeler's 'History of India.'
Wilson's 'Early Annals of the English in Bengal.'
Numerous Articles in the 'Journal of the Asiatic Society of Bengal,' the 'Calcutta Review' and elsewhere, chiefly those by Dr. Wise, one time Civil Surgeon of Dacca.

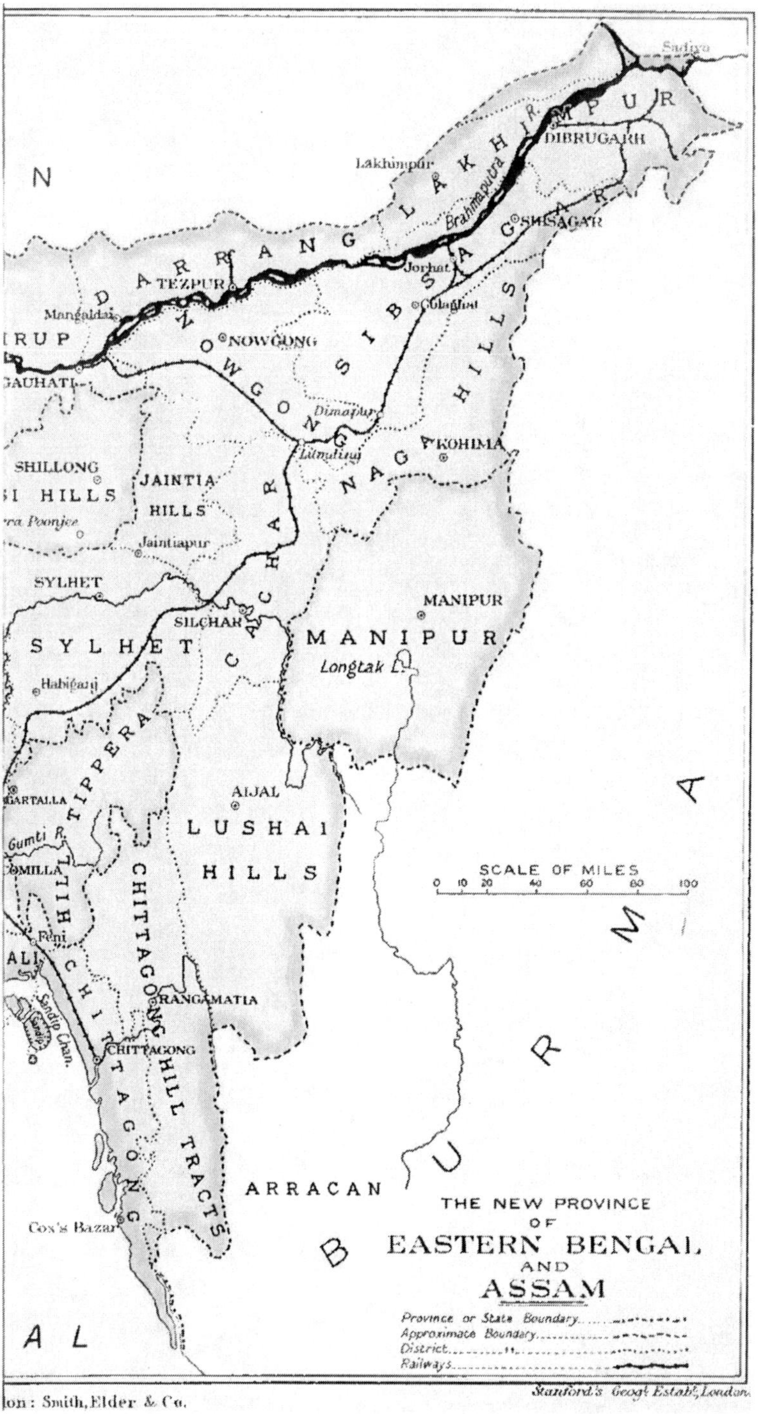
THE NEW PROVINCE
OF
EASTERN BENGAL
AND
ASSAM
SCALE OF MILES
0 10 20 40 60 80 100
Province or State Boundary
Approximate Boundary
District
Railways
DARRANG
LAKHIMPUR
SIBSAGAR
NOWGONG
NAGA HILLS
CACHAR
MANIPUR
SYLHET
JAINTIA HILLS
LUSHAI HILLS
HILL TIPPERA
CHITTAGONG
CHITTAGONG HILL TRACTS
ARRACAN
BURMA
Sadiya
Dibrugarh
Lakhimpur
Brahmaputra
Sibsagar
Jorhat
Golaghat
Tezpur
Mangaldai
Nowgong
Gauhati
Dimapur
Lumding
Kohima
Shillong
Jaintiapur
Sylhet
Silchar
Manipur
Longtak L.
Habiganj
Aijal
Gartalla
Gumti R.
Comilla
Feni
Rangamatia
Sandip Chan.
Chittagong
Cox's Bazar
Smith, Elder & Co.
Stanford's Geog. Estab. London

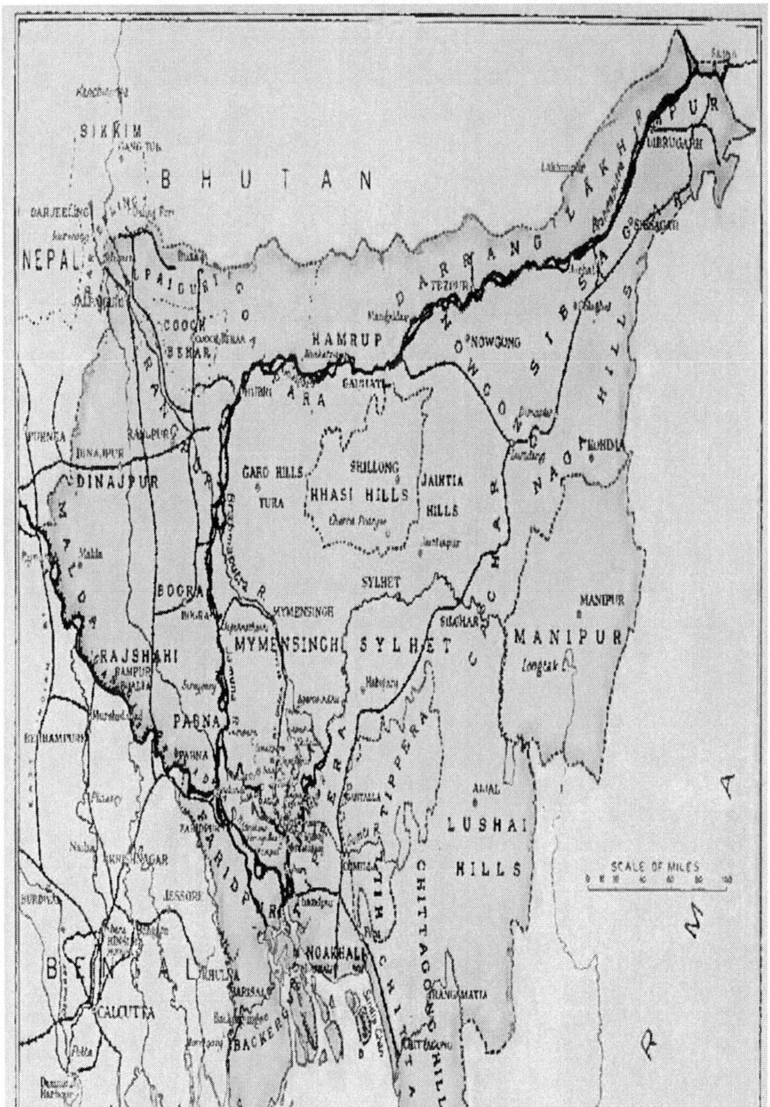

London, Smith, Elder & Co

INDEX

A A

SMITH, ELDER, & CO.'S PUBLICATIONS.

THE ROLL-CALL OF WESTMINSTER ABBEY. By Mrs. A. MURRAY SMITH (E. T. Bradley), Author of 'Annals of Westminster Abbey' &c. FOURTH EDITION. With 25 Full-page Illustrations and 5 Plans. Large crown 8vo. 6*s.*

TIMES.—'It is impossible to read even the first chapter of this highly interesting volume without forthwith realising that we have here a work of a totally different order from the cheap book-making which year by year selects Westminster Abbey for its subject. Such a book as the "Roll-Call" could have been penned only by one who knows and loves every feature in that glorious old pile; who has wandered through its aisles every hour of the day and night; who has watched the wondrous effects produced by the subtlest changes of light and temperature: one, in short, who for upwards of twenty years has drunk deeply of the spirit which haunts Westminster Abbey from end to end. We must therefore offer a hearty welcome to this really excellent work, and we are convinced that the great mass of historical material which it contains will become more and more valuable as time goes on.'

MATTHEW ARNOLD'S NOTE-BOOKS. By the Hon. Mrs. WODEHOUSE. SECOND IMPRESSION. Small crown 8vo. 4*s.* 6*d.*

TIMES.—'No one who is interested in Matthew Arnold can afford to be without this book, which gives us the thoughts he chose as his own to live with, and reveals him intimately without violating a single secret.'

THE NOISY YEARS. By Mrs. PERCY DEARMER, Author of 'Roundabout Rhymes' &c. With Illustrations by EVA ROOS. Crown 8vo. 6*s.*

PALL MALL GAZETTE.—'The "Noisy Years" is really delicious. Indeed, among the books about those small folk who have a "kingdom of their own," we cannot think of any other coming within reasonable distance ot it for tenderness, grace, and charming humour.'

THE ADVENTURES OF DOWNY V. GREEN, RHODES SCHOLAR AT OXFORD. By GEORGE CALDERON. FOURTH IMPRESSION. With 16 Illustrations by the Author. Crown 8vo. 3*s.* 6*d.*

MONTHLY REVIEW.—'Mr. George Calderon has joined in a conspiracy with the Kiplings, the Somervilles, and other persons of ambidextrous gifts to raise the standard of authorship to a height beyond the reach of ordinary genius.'

THE STORY OF THE BOLD PÉCOPIN: a Legend of the Rhine. By VICTOR HUGO. Done into English by ELEANOR and AUGUSTINE BIRRELL. With 8 Illustrations by H. R. MILLAR. Fcp. 4to. 7*s.* 6*d.*

GENTLEWOMAN.—'Too high praise cannot be given to the translators for the manner in which they have rendered the legend into pure and delightful English, whilst preserving the beauty of thought and the romantic picturesqueness of the original.'

WELLINGTON'S LIEUTENANTS. By ALEXANDER INNES SHAND, Author of 'The Life of General Sir Edward Hamley,' 'General John Jacob of Jacobabad,' 'The War in the Peninsula,' &c. With 8 Portraits and a Map. Crown 8vo. 7*s.* 6*d.*

YORKSHIRE POST.—'A series of soldiers' memoirs which, on the whole, make the most fascinating and exciting reading we have encountered for a long time. There is not a dull page in the book; it is everywhere bright and spirited.'

SONGS OF AN ENGLISH ESAU. By CLIVE PHILLIPPS-WOLLEY, Author of 'One of the Broken Brigade,' 'The Chicamon Stone,' &c. Fcp. 8vo. 5*s.*

TIMES.—'These are bracing songs, full of the Imperial spirit, of healthy sentiment and fresh air, and not without a true sense of poetic style.'

OUTLOOK.—'They throb with love of Britain and Empire, and are appropriately virile and straightforward.'

THE LIGHTHOUSE WORK OF SIR JAMES CHANCE, BARONET. By J. F. CHANCE. With a Preface by JAMES KENWARD, C.E., F.S.A. With 2 Portraits. 8vo. 5*s.* net.

SPECTATOR.—'This excellent book will interest ordinary readers as well as the experts, who will enjoy its scientific details and figures.'

COLLOQUIES OF COMMON PEOPLE. By JAMES ANSTIE, K.C. Large post 8vo. 10*s.* 6*d.*

TIMES.—'Mr. Anstie's discussions show a clear apprehension of philosophical arguments and counter-arguments; and the various positions advanced and criticised are aptly and precisely stated. . . . The measure of success achieved is to Mr. Anstie's credit.'

London: SMITH, ELDER, & CO., 15 Waterloo Place, S.W.

NEW AND FORTHCOMING WORKS.

SOCIAL SILHOUETTES. By GEORGE W. E. RUSSELL, Author of 'Collections and Recollections,' &c. Large post 8vo. 7*s*. 6*d*. net.

THE GATE OF DEATH: a Diary. Large post 8vo. 6*s*. net.

THE FRIENDS OF VOLTAIRE. By S. G. TALLENTYRE, Author of 'The Women of the Salons,' 'The Life of Voltaire,' &c. With Portraits. Small demy 8vo. 9*s*. net.

RICHARD III.: his Life and Character reviewed in the Light of Recent Research. By Sir CLEMENTS R. MARKHAM, K.C.B., F.R.S., Author of 'The Life of the Great Lord Fairfax,' 'The Fighting Veres,' &c. With a Portrait of Richard III. and a Map. Small demy 8vo. 10*s*. 6*d*. net.

THE GREAT DAYS OF VERSAILLES: Studies from Court Life in the Later Years of Louis XIV. By G. F. BRADBY, Author of 'The Marquis's Eye,' 'Dick: a Story without a Plot,' &c. With Illustrations. Small demy 8vo. 10*s*. 6*d*. net.

OUR HERITAGE THE SEA. By FRANK T. BULLEN, F.R.G.S., Author of 'The Cruise of the "Cachalot,"' 'The Log of a Sea-Waif,' &c. With a Frontispiece by ARTHUR TWIDLE. Crown 8vo. 6*s*.

LETTERS TO YOUNG AND OLD. By Mrs. C. W. EARLE, Author of 'Pot Pourri from a Surrey Garden,' &c. Large crown 8vo. 7*s*. 6*d*. net.

SKETCHES IN MAFEKING AND SOUTH AFRICA. By Major-General R. S. S. BADEN-POWELL, C.B., F.R.G.S., Author of 'The Matabele Campaign,' 'Sport in War,' &c. With several Coloured Plates and a large number of Half-tone and Line Illustrations. Oblong 4to. 21*s*. net.

THE ROMANCE OF AN EASTERN CAPITAL. By F. B. BRADLEY-BIRT, B.A., F.R.G.S., I.C.S., Author of 'Chota Nagpore: a Little-known Province of the Empire,' 'The Story of an Indian Upland,' &c. With 16 Full-page Illustrations and a Map. Demy 8vo. 12*s*. 6*d*. net.

THE FUTURE OF RUSSIA. Translated from the German of Regierungsrat Rudolf Martin by Miss HULDA FRIEDERICHS. Large post 8vo. 7*s*. 6*d*. net.

THE NEW PHYSICS AND CHEMISTRY: A Series of Popular Essays on Physical and Chemical Subjects. By W. A. SHENSTONE, F.R.S., Senior Science Master in Clifton College, Author of 'The Life and Work of Justus von Liebig,' &c. Large post 8vo. 7*s*. 6*d*. net.

THE LETTERS of a BETROTHED, 1803-1814. By the Baroness EDITH VON CRAMM. Translated by LEONARD HUXLEY. With Portraits. Large post 8vo. 6*s*. net.

THE RISE AND DECLINE of the NETHERLANDS: a Political and Economic History and a Study in Practical Statesmanship. By. J. ELLIS BARKER, Author of 'Modern Germany: her Political and Economic Problems, her Ambitions, and the Causes of her Success.' Small demy 8vo. 10*s*. 6*d*. net.

PROVINCIAL LETTERS, and other Papers. By the Author of 'Pages from a Private Diary.' Crown 8vo. 5*s*. net.

THE TEACHING OF THE LORD CONTAINED IN THE GOSPELS. BROUGHT TOGETHER UNDER ITS PRINCIPAL HEADS. By JOHN BOYD KINNEAR, Author of 'The Foundations of Religion,' &c. Crown 8vo. 2*s*. 6*d*. net.

THE HOUSE OF THE LUCK. By MARY J. H. SKRINE. With 8 Full-page Illustrations by her Daughter, MARGARET S. SKRINE. Pott 4to. 6*s*. net.

THE BOOK OF GILLY: Four Months out of a Life. By the Hon. EMILY LAWLESS, Litt.D., Author of 'Hurrish,' 'With Essex in Ireland,' &c. With Illustrations by L. LESLIE BROOKE. Pott 4to. 7*s*. 6*d*. net.

London: SMITH, ELDER, & CO., 15 Waterloo Place S.W.